REDISCOVERING THE BIBLE

HADDAM HOUSE is an editorial venture in the area of religious literature, which has grown out of the common concerns of The Edward W. Hazen Foundation, the Young Men's Christian Association, and the Young Women's Christian Association. It is interested primarily in the moral and religious questions of students and other young people, although many of its books appeal to a wider audience, including the leaders and teachers of youth.

Through an Editorial Advisory Committee HADDAM HOUSE studies the changing needs for religious literature, plans books, and seeks as authors not only experienced writers but also new voices qualified to give fresh guidance to young men and women in these days. The present membership of the Editorial Advisory Committee includes: Richard T. Baker, *Chairman,* Wayne Cowan, *Secretary,* Graham Baldwin, David Byers, Virginia Corwin, John D. Maguire, John O. Nelson, James Rietmulder, Roger L. Shinn, Jean M. Whittet, Winnifred Wygal.

Haddam House Books

PRIMER FOR PROTESTANTS, *James Hastings Nichols*
YOUTH ASKS ABOUT RELIGION, *Jack Finegan*
THE HUMAN VENTURE IN SEX, LOVE, AND MARRIAGE, *Peter A. Bertocci*
SCIENCE AND CHRISTIAN FAITH, *Edward LeRoy Long, Jr.*
REDISCOVERING THE BIBLE, *Bernhard W. Anderson*
THE UNFOLDING DRAMA OF THE BIBLE, *Bernhard W. Anderson*
THE STUDENT PRAYERBOOK, *John Oliver Nelson and Others, Editors*
COMMUNITY OF FAITH, *T. Ralph Morton*
POLITICS FOR CHRISTIANS, *William Muehl*
THE PARADOXES OF DEMOCRACY, *Kermit Eby and June Greenlief*
THE TRAGIC VISION AND THE CHRISTIAN FAITH, *Nathan A. Scott, Editor*
CONSCIENCE ON CAMPUS, *Waldo Beach*
THE PROPHETIC VOICE IN MODERN FICTION, *William R. Mueller*
THE RENEWAL OF HOPE, *Howard Clark Kee*
CHRISTIANITY AND COMMUNISM TODAY, *John C. Bennett*
THE CHRISTIAN AS A DOCTOR, *James T. Stephens and Edward LeRoy Long, Jr.*
CHRISTIANITY AND THE SCIENTIST, *Ian G. Barbour*
THE ART OF CHRISTIAN DOUBT, *Fred Denbeaux*
THE CHRISTIAN AS A JOURNALIST, *Richard T. Baker*
AS CHRISTIANS FACE RIVAL RELIGIONS, *Gerald B. Cooke*
EXPLORING THE LOGIC OF FAITH, *Kent Bendall and Frederick Ferré*
TAKING THE BIBLE SERIOUSLY, *Leander Keck*
RECOVERY OF LIFE'S MEANING, *W. Paul Jones*

BERNHARD W. ANDERSON
Professor of Old Testament Interpretation
Colgate-Rochester Divinity School

REDISCOVERING THE BIBLE

ASSOCIATION PRESS · NEW YORK

REDISCOVERING THE BIBLE

Association Press, 291 Broadway, New York, N. Y. 10007

Twelfth Printing, 1965

Publisher's title stock number: 1159

PRINTED IN THE UNITED STATES OF AMERICA

Gratefully Dedicated

to my esteemed teacher and friend,

JAMES MUILENBURG

"The grass withereth, the flower fadeth:
But the word of our God shall stand for ever."

—Isaiah 40:8

Preface

THERE COMES A TIME in the life of many a maturing young person when the lines of that humorous song from *Porgy and Bess* suggest a possibility which is not just a laughing matter:

> The things that you're liable
> To read in the Bible
> Ain't necessarily so.

Many of us have been brought up in Christian homes. We have been at least exposed to Sunday School teaching of one kind or another. We have seen the Bible handled with due reverence, have heard ministers preach from it, and have read parts of it or simplified stories from it. Sooner or later, however, our "faith in the Bible" is put to the test.

The transition from the precritical stage of naive acceptance to the critical stage of serious questioning is crucial, for only as we go through the struggle of "honest doubt" can the "faith of our fathers" become *our* faith. As someone has said, the Christian heritage cannot be passed on with the same ease as a son may inherit his father's bank account or the family estate. Each generation must go through the valley of decision. Each one of us must come to terms personally with the high calling of God in Jesus Christ. A second-hand Christianity is not worth much in times of testing when men are asked to live and die for the faith that is in them.

This book is designed primarily for young people who face this issue inescapably. No naive understanding of the Bible can stand up long under the ruthless battering of the modern world. In a book review, one of my students stated the matter well in these words: "The average college student is very confused as to what to believe and what not to believe, especially after a course or two in modern biology, and stands in great need of being shown the relevance of the message of the Good Book. Theologians and biblical scholars alike, even though they unearth vast amounts of material which give valuable insight into the events of the Bible, have a tendency to leave their findings remotely situated on some far-away cloud, or at least out of the reach of the ordinary person." These lines are all too true. We are living in a time when, at least in some circles, the Bible is being rediscovered. The labors of scholars and theologians have opened up frontiers of biblical understanding, the exploration of which is an exciting adventure along strange paths. Moreover, contemporary preoccupation with the meaning of history has led many alert people to a deeper grasp of the urgency and relevance of the biblical message. But for the younger generation, perhaps, much of this is "remotely situated on some far-away cloud." Therefore this book humbly sets about the task of bringing the results of biblical scholarship and theology "down to earth" in order that, in the spirit of the Protestant Reformation, the Bible may be accessible to ordinary people, rather than being the special province of a select group.

This book is addressed to those who have the courage to go beyond a precritical acceptance of the Bible. Throughout we shall assume that one can take the Bible seriously without taking it literally. Our discussion will rest not upon faith in the Bible itself, but commitment to the Christ whom the Bible presents. This will be the basis of our critical approach to Scripture. Just as friends are those who can be most honestly critical of each other, so Christians, trusting in Christ, can be most "objectively" critical of Christian Scripture. It can be put down as an axiom that being a committed Christian does not necessitate the surrender of one's critical faculties.

The reader should understand that this book does not pretend to be a defense of the Christian faith, unless it can be said that the best apologetic is a sincere effort to let the Bible speak in its own terms. It will be evident that the presentation is made from a "confessional" rather than an allegedly neutral standpoint. When dealing with the issue of the ultimate meaning of human life there can be no neutrality. Any questioning or rejection of the biblical faith will be made from another faith-standpoint, not from an impartial consideration of the facts. For the Protestant, faith is reliance upon God's love manifested in Christ; it is personal response—within the Church and guided by the Holy Spirit—to God's Word which is mediated through the Bible. But this faith does not demand a retreat into blind acceptance of the literal statements of the Bible or the dogmas of the Church; nor will the Christian say that this is a flip-of-the-coin decision as to the meaning of life. While faith is primary, such faith provides the light which enables reason to see life in its wholeness and to defend the realism of the Christian interpretation against all rival faiths which appeal for men's allegiance. However, the discussion of apologetic issues lies beyond the purpose of this book.

A word should be said about the scope and method of the book. Assuming with the Christian Church that the Bible—both Old and New Testaments—is a unity, we shall attempt to present the forward-moving drama of God's action in the history of his people, Israel. The Bible presents a historical pageant, the theme of which is the triumphant working out of God's purpose in spite of all attempts to oppose it. With this central theme in view, we shall attempt to describe the dynamic movement of the drama toward that climax which is the "good news" of the New Testament. Moreover, each chapter also will be anchored to a specific problem which young people often discuss: the Bible as "the Word of God" (chapter 1), the "chosen people" (chapter 2), the miracles of the Old Testament (chapter 3), the immoralities of the Old Testament (chapter 4), the "wrath" of God (chapter 5), the problem of suffering (chapter 6), the fulfillment of prophecy (chapter 7), the person of Christ (chapter 8), the Resurrection (chapter 9), and the stories of the beginning and end of history (chapter 10). Thus the chapter-by-chapter discussion interweaves both a problem-centered approach and a consideration of the dramatic unity of Scripture. While this method results in glaring omissions and a certain amount of oversimplification, perhaps this may be pardoned in a book that seeks to awaken the interest of ordinary young people, not to satisfy the needs of the advanced student or the biblical specialist.

This book has been written in close co-operation with students at the University of North Carolina. Not only has the material been used as collateral reading in several courses, and subjected to the book-review criticisms of many students, but every chapter has been thoroughly discussed by a committee of students who met regularly at my home. The committee, kept small for the purpose of discussion, represented a cross section of campus interests and denominational backgrounds (Episcopal, Methodist, Baptist, Presbyterian, Lutheran). Regardless of the quality of the resulting work, this group discussion of the Bible was an exciting venture in which all of us profited immensely. Whatever merit there is in the book, I should like to attribute to my student commentators; for whatever defects appear, I alone am responsible. Since in a real sense these students are the co-authors of this book, they deserve to be mentioned here by name:

David M. Anderson, Jr.
John A. Bridges
Ann Marshall Emmert
Samuel Hays Magill
Michael C. D. McDaniel
Barbara R. McIntyre
Paul Livingston Ritch

I should like to point out, further, that this book first began to take shape, though in unwritten form, during my teaching at Colgate University where I found myself in an atmosphere congenial to understanding the biblical faith in relation to the living issues of our day.

If space permitted, I should like to mention the names of my colleagues and friends who have read the manuscript and generously have made valuable suggestions and criticisms. Especially, I should like to express my gratitude to my wife, whose constant encouragement and help have made this book possible.

Any book about the Bible inevitably will be inadequate, for it is the very nature of the biblical faith that it resists all attempts to imprison its dynamic witness within the confines of any single presentation or within the understanding of any particular generation. However, Haddam House will have been justified in encouraging and sponsoring this project if the book, despite its limitations, helps to open a door into the world of the Bible so that some of the younger generation may hear anew the Word of God in their time.

BERNHARD W. ANDERSON

ACKNOWLEDGMENTS

Grateful acknowledgment is made to the following individuals and publishers who kindly granted permission to reprint from their copyrighted material:

Mr. Virgil Markham for the poem, "Brotherhood," by Edwin Markham.

Mrs. William Herbert Carruth for the first stanza of the poem, "Each in His Own Tongue," by William Herbert Carruth.

The Pilgrim Press for lines from the hymn, "I Sought the Lord," from *The Pilgrim Hymnal.*

The Macmillan Company for quotations from *The Modern Use of the Bible,* by Harry Emerson Fosdick; *Down Peacock's Feathers,* by D. R. Davies; *The Relevance of the Prophets,* by R. B. Y. Scott; *Screwtape Letters,* by C. S. Lewis; and four lines from the poem, *Saint Paul,* by Frederic W. H. Myers.

Charles Scribner's Sons for quotation from *Christianity and History,* by Herbert Butterfield.

Professor W. F. Albright and Pelican Books for quotation from *The Archaeology of Palestine*, by W. F. Albright.

Alfred A. Knopf for permission to quote "Sonnet XI" from *Selected Poems of Robert Nathan.*

Harper and Brothers for quotation from *Christian Apologetics*, by Alan Richardson.

Theology Today for quotation from article in the issue of April, 1950, by Gilbert Baker, "The Christian Church under non-Christian Rulers."

The University of Chicago Press for Old Testament quotations from *The Bible: An American Translation*, by J. M. Powis Smith and Edgar G. Goodspeed.

The Division of Christian Education of the National Council of Churches of Christ in the United States of America (formerly the International Council of Religious Education) for New Testament quotations from the *Revised Standard Version of the New Testament*, published by Thomas Nelson and Sons. Copyright 1946 by the International Council of Religious Education.

The Westminster Press for quotation from *Westminster Study Edition of the Holy Bible.*

The Westminster Press and Hodder and Stoughton (London) for quotation from *Jesus, the Messiah*, by William Manson.

The Westminster Press and the Student Christian Movement Press (London) for quotations from *A Preface to Bible Study*, by Alan Richardson, and *Christ and Time*, by Oscar Cullman.

B.W.A.

Contents

REDISCOVERING THE BIBLE

1

The New World of the Bible

UNLIKE THE PROVERBIAL MONTH of March, the twentieth century came in like a lamb, bringing with it hopes of brotherhood, security, and universal peace. It is difficult for the present generation of youth to understand the high hopes that their fathers and grandfathers cherished in days past. Progress, technology, popular education, science—these were words which heralded the transformation of the earth into a fair paradise. Then came a world war, a world depression, the demonic furies of Hitler, the Spanish prelude to a second global war, atomic explosions in Japan, and—the rest is well known. Even before the twentieth century had reached its halfway mark, it had threatened to go out like a lion.

Reading the Bible as Shipwrecked Men

One result of these devastating experiences is that people have been going back to the Bible with a new seriousness. The phrase "back to the Bible" may seem inaccurate. In one sense, of course, Americans could not get away from the Bible any more than an individual can escape his heredity. The words and teachings of the Bible have been plowed deeply into the soil of our history. Our language, literature, democratic institutions, and public education—to mention only a few things—have been molded in part by biblical influence. To use the metaphor of an Old Testament prophet, the Bible is the rock from which we have been hewn, the quarry from which we have been dug. Even a brief study of early American history will reveal that our nation was cradled in a biblical faith. And since we cannot obliterate these historical memories which are enshrined in our traditions, it is inevitable that men should revere the Bible even when they do not take it seriously, and that they should give it a permanent place at the head of the list of best-sellers even when they no longer read it.

It is one thing, however, to respect the Bible or to adore it as a fetish; it is quite another thing to live by the faith of the Bible. The appalling biblical illiteracy of the present day indicates that we have not been true to the "faith of our fathers." This is not just a failure in religious education. A brief survey of American history discloses that serious concern for a biblical *Weltanschauung*, or world-view, was gradually eclipsed by the adoption of a set of convictions drawn from another source. In the language of the historian, Puritanism was gradually superseded by the faith of the Enlightenment, an intellectual movement of the eighteenth century which represented the flowering of the Renaissance.

The characteristic doctrine of the Enlightenment was the belief in inevitable progress "onward and ever upward." Those who gave expression to this belief little realized how profoundly indebted they were to the interpretation of history given in the Bible. However, the leaders of the Enlightenment defended their confidence in the future by arguments that revealed the increasingly secular spirit of the age. The Christian belief in man as a sinner was replaced by the view that man is rational and morally virtuous; the Christian emphasis upon salvation through God's grace was surrendered in favor of confidence in science; and the Christian belief in divine Providence was superseded by the belief in the operation of "natural law" which guaranteed the progressive movement of history. The Reformation had stressed the glory of God and man's inability to save himself; the Enlightenment, however, gloried in man's ability to achieve the ideals of the French Revolution: liberty, equality, and fraternity. Essentially this was a revolutionary doctrine. It gave bourgeois society the justification for breaking away from the restraints of medieval feudalism and seeking fullness of life in this world, not in heaven beyond.

When Thomas Jefferson drew up the Declaration of Independence in 1776, he could not help giving expression to the new ideology: man is endowed with the "unalienable rights" of life, liberty, and the pursuit of happiness; his chief end in life, therefore, is not to "glorify God and enjoy him forever," as the old Catechism stated, but to find fulfillment in the achievement of a just and happy life. This was a reasonable faith whose truths were "self-evident" to rational man. It was an optimistic faith which enabled revolutionary Americans to break with the past and create a better world. The law of progress, the power of reason, the essential goodness of human nature—these were sufficient guarantees of the validity of the faith. In one sense the Declaration of Independence was man's declaration of his independence from God, for, as Walter Marshal Horton has said, republicanism reacted against a God who bore more resemblance to George III than to George Washington. The years which followed brought additional confirmation of the truth of the new faith: the brilliant achievements of science, the acquisition of tremendous national wealth, the spread of popular education. Edwin Markham was expressing the spirit of the nineteenth and twentieth centuries when he wrote:

> Come, clear the way, then, clear the way:
> Blind creeds and kings have had their day.
> Break the dead branches from the path:
> Our hope is in the aftermath—
> Our hope is in heroic men,
> Star-led to build the world again.
> To this event the ages ran:
> Make way for Brotherhood—make way for Man! [1]

---

[1] Reprinted by permission.

Then the lamb became a lion. There was blood, sweat, and tears; disillusionment, cynicism, and despair. Civilization was shaken to its foundations by a world war, and dazed men wandered about in the rubble of shattered dreams. Long-accepted beliefs proved bankrupt. In Europe, Karl Barth saw the folly of proclaiming the gospel of modern man under the pretense that he was preaching from the Bible. Faced with the minister's weekly problem, the sermon, he began to interpret the Scriptures to his expectant congregation. "As a minister," he later wrote, "I wanted to speak to the *people* in the infinite contradiction of their life, but to speak the no less infinite message of the *Bible* which was as much of a riddle as life." As one of the companions of this Swiss minister said, the Bible was read "with the eyes of shipwrecked people whose everything had gone overboard." The reverberations went far beyond his parish. In Europe, England, America, and elsewhere the biblical message increasingly was proclaimed with new urgency. To some it seemed as though a spiritual movement, comparable to the Protestant Reformation of the sixteenth century, was spreading across the world. That was about thirty years ago, and even today the movement has not yet reached its full tide. Many people who would not call themselves "Barthians" have found what Barth aptly described as "that strange new world of the Bible."

Is this rediscovery of the Bible the result of a "failure of nerve"? Is it explainable as man's attempt to cushion the unpleasant and painful shocks of life and to find happiness in his environment at the expense of an illusion? Or, on the other hand, is the world crisis in some sense the work of God, whose Voice speaks to men above the tumult of the times:

> Be still and know that I am God!
> I will be exalted among the heathen,
> I will be exalted in the earth.
>
> —Psalm 46:10

This question cannot be dismissed lightly. We should recognize, however, that any discrediting of the biblical faith in the sovereignty of God over human history must be done from the standpoint of a different and a rival faith. Faith is inescapable. If life is to be meaningful in any sense, every person must commit himself to a scale of values, a supreme loyalty, a cause in which, by losing himself, he can find himself. In this sense there are no "atheists," for as Martin Luther observed, "Trust and faith of the heart alone make both God and idol. . . . Whatever then thy heart clings to and relies upon, that is properly thy God."[2] Life is a battle of the gods, and unfortunately there is no spectators' grandstand from which we can view this rivalry disinterestedly. We must take a position in the struggle if we are to think, act, or live. We are truly living in a world crisis, for this is a time of decision, as the Greek word *krisis* means. The issue is precisely that which Joshua presented to his fellow Israelites long ago: "Choose ye this day whom ye will serve." In our time we must decide whether we will serve the Lord who speaks to men through the Bible, or whether we will serve the gods of man's making.

The Bible is meant to be read and understood in times like these. The literature of the Old and New Testaments is the deposit of a succession of historical crises in which men were faced with the question of the meaning of their existence. With stark realism the Bible describes events which rocked the very foundation of life, which destroyed nations and displaced populations, which wrought havoc, suffering, and anxiety. This drama of faith was enacted upon a stage where poor people were the victims of the rich, where Palestinian rulers were drawn into the maelstrom of international events, and where one great nation after another sought to create a world empire by the power of the sword. Situated strategically at

---

[2] Quoted by Richard Niebuhr in his excellent article, "The Nature and Existence of God," in *Motive* (Magazine of the Methodist Student Movement), December, 1943.

the crossroads of the ancient world, Palestine was the very storm center of life. The Bible, therefore, does not come from a sheltered valley of Shangri-la; its message was forged out of circumstances in which people felt the maximum of tension and suffering. This book speaks out of the immediate and concrete realities of history, where men doubted and believed, hated and loved, despaired and hoped. Its message comes from the depth of life and speaks to the depth within us. It finds us where we are living. Therefore it is understandable that as modern people wrestle with the issues of destiny in their own contemporary situation, they often find themselves in rapport with the prophets and apostles of the Bible. Perhaps the Bible is most deeply understood only by shipwrecked men.

The Humanity of Scripture

From one point of view the Bible is a very human book. The word "bible," derived from a Greek plural word meaning "booklets," is descriptive of its diverse character. Here is a *library* of sacred writings. Protestants count sixty-six books: thirty-nine in the Old Testament and twenty-seven in the New. In this, Protestants differ from Roman Catholics who include in the Old Testament several additional writings which were admitted at the time when the first Greek translation, known as the Septuagint, was made by Greek-speaking Jews of Alexandria (about 250 B.C. and on). Since these books were never included in the *Hebrew* Bible, Protestants relegate them to the "Apocrypha" and consider them to be outside the limits of sacred scripture.

This library covers a long period of time. In fact, if we begin with Abraham, it includes almost two thousand years of historical remembrance. We would have some idea of the time span covered by the Bible if we could imagine a similar book of writings and traditions produced in the course of Western history from the period of Julius Caesar to the period of Joseph Stalin. The diversity of the Bible, therefore, is the kaleidoscopic diversity of Israelite history in the long and inexorable march of time.

Moreover, the Bible mirrors the experience of a great variety of people who were involved personally in these events. Many who contributed to the biblical epic are unknown to us by name; the Bible, however, bears the imprint of their lives. Prophets and apostles, kings and priests, wise men and scribes, have made their individual contribution. Side by side in this library, and often intermingled in separate books, are poetry and prose, law and prophecy, history and fiction, wisdom literature and devotional hymns, sermons and epistles. Sometimes the language moves in the majestic cadences of stately prose (as in Genesis 1), sometimes in the balanced rhythms of poetry (as in Isaiah 40-55), sometimes in the vivid style of narrative (as in the story of the Exodus, or the Nativity stories), sometimes in symbolic flights of religious imagination (as in Daniel and Revelation). All of the available literary forms and all of the rich variety of human expression enter into the proclamation of the biblical message.

In this library the human situation is presented with the utmost realism. Nothing human is alien to its range of interest. Stories about murder, rape, trickery, war, religious persecution, and church jealousies are mingled with accounts of divine action, heavenly visions, ventures of faith, and hymns of hope. This is especially noticeable in the Old Testament where often the most shocking things are said and done in the name of religion. In fact, there are whole tracts of Scripture in which the sacred element is not readily obvious, as, for instance, in the book of Esther where the name of God is not clearly mentioned even once, or the Song of Songs where sexual passion seems to predominate. Consequently, from the earliest times there have been attempts to present an expurgated edition of the Bible, either by omitting the all too human passages found particularly in the Old Testament, or by toning down the offensive passages with the aid of a symbolic (allegorical) interpretation. In its original form, however, the Bible gives an uncensored description of the human situation. The picture of human life is not "touched up" to make it appear better than it is. Many of the biblical stories verify a central truth of the biblical revelation, namely, that man is a sinner who often attempts to justify himself in his sin by means of his religion. In one sense a more human library has never been written.

Presently we shall look at the other side of the picture: the Bible as the witness to God's revelation. Now, however, it is important to notice that the human aspect of the Bible has enabled scholars to study it with the same critical methodology which is applicable in the study of other literature, like the Hindu Vedas, the Homeric poems, or the plays of Shakespeare. In fact, there is probably no other literature which has been studied more earnestly and intensively than the Bible.

The beginnings of biblical criticism can be traced back to the very dawn of the Christian era, when scholars began to raise questions as to the accuracy of the received text of the Bible and to notice difficulties that the rigid dogmas of the faith could not eliminate. The Renaissance, bringing a new sense of mental freedom and reviving an interest in the documents of the past, gave a fresh impetus to the study. Likewise the Protestant Reformation made its contribution by emphasizing the sole authority of Scripture in the Christian faith and by insisting upon making the Bible accessible to the masses. Finally, the rise of the scientific movement brought to the investigation both a passion for the attainment of truth and a critical methodology, by the use of which men sought to purge Christianity of error and superstition. Here we cannot go into the fascinating story of the many scholars who added their creative labors, often at the price of ostracism or excommunication from the Christian community. Many of the scientific hypotheses proposed were fanciful; many of the interpretations set forth were more expressive of the spirit of the age in which the scholar lived than representative of the biblical faith itself. But today we have the advantage of standing on the shoulders of these men of the past. Thanks to the labors of experts in Hebrew and Greek, it is now possible to present a translation of the Bible which overcomes some of the limitations of the classical King James Version. Archaeologists have excavated many places in the Near East and have thrown new light on the historical period and cultural situation in which the Bible was written. Historians have enabled us to read the writings of the Bible in the approximate chronological order in which they were composed, and have helped us to understand the message of each book in the light of the circumstances of its composition. Because of these critical labors, our knowledge of the human aspect of Scripture is far in advance of that of past theological leaders like Augustine, Aquinas, Luther, or Calvin.

The Bible as the Word of God

The uniqueness of the Bible, however, cannot be understood adequately by treating it merely as a human book. The Bible was never designed to be read as great literature, sober history, naive philosophy, or primitive science. Men remembered stories, treasured traditions, and wrote in various forms of literature because of one inescapable conviction: they had been confronted by God in events which had taken place in their history. Though hidden from mortal sight in light unapproachable, the holy God had revealed himself to mankind. He had taken the initiative to establish a relationship with his people. He had spoken his Word of judgment and of mercy. "In many and various ways God spoke of old to our fathers by the prophets; but in these last days he has spoken to us by a Son." These opening words of the Letter to the Hebrews strike the keynote of the Bible. It is this central conviction which gives the Bible, both Old and New Testaments, the status of sacred scripture in the Christian Church.

This faith is a stumbling block to the modern mind. It

would be more honest, however, to reject the biblical claim outright than to insist that the message of God's revelation is peripheral and that these people actually meant to say something other than they seem to say. The Bible has suffered seriously from readers who, like the legendary highwayman of ancient Greece, have attempted to force its message into the Procrustean bed of modern ways of thinking. As a consequence, some people have dismissed the theology of the Bible as a poetic or mythical embellishment of men's maturing awareness of the distinction between right and wrong. Others have treated it as elementary philosophy, the first efforts of the Hebrews reflectively to understand Reality. These approaches to the meaning of human existence may be adequate outside the Bible. But the men of the Bible say something very different. It is their claim that God himself has spoken with a decisiveness, a once-for-all-ness. They do not tell us about searching for moral values, or attempting to reach a more satisfying philosophy by standing a bit taller on their intellectual tiptoes. Rather, they bear witness to their encounter with God in the midst of crucial events of history, their engagement with him in moments of historical crisis. And, above all, this revelation was not peripheral or incidental to their message; it was the vantage point from which they viewed everything else—politics, social injustice, and war; past, present, and future. They do not argue this faith; they proclaim it with confessional language: "Here I stand, I cannot do otherwise."

The subject matter of the Bible, then, is God's self-revelation to men. Because of this stupendous theme, traditional Christianity has described the Bible as the "Word of God" and has insisted upon the divine authorship of Scripture. Says a New Testament writer: "All Scripture is given by inspiration of God," that is, as the Greek word suggests, it is "God-breathed" or "filled with the breath of God" (II Timothy 3: 16). However seriously one may take the human dimension of Scripture, he cannot easily disregard the central claim of the

Bible itself to be the record and witness of revelatory events in which God has spoken. This is sacred scripture because the Holy Spirit breathes through the ancient words and reveals to men in every age the Word of truth.

The Inspiration of the Bible

What does it mean to say that the Bible is inspired? This is the heart of our problem. It is no easy task to deal with the Bible in such a manner that one does justice both to its humanity and its divine authorship. Much confusion has been brought about by those who would oversimplify the matter, either by emphasizing the human element in Scripture to the point of stultifying its divine authorship, or by emphasizing the divine character of the Bible to the point of ignoring that it is a human book. The major cleavage in the Protestant churches in America is no longer denominational, geographical, or even doctrinal. The line is drawn at the point of the authority of the Bible, and in general Protestants can be divided according to which side they take in the debate over biblical inspiration.

Many Protestants have adopted a position which has been labeled "liberalism." Instead of hiding their heads, ostrich-like, in the barren sands of the past, these Christians sincerely and devoutly have attempted to make the Bible speak relevantly to the modern situation. A Christian cannot believe one set of ideas on Sunday and then live by another set of assumptions the rest of the week. Such religious "schizophrenia" is intolerable, for the Christian faith jealously demands the allegiance of the whole man. Therefore, liberals sought to adjust the inherited faith to the bewildering modern world whose outlook had been defined by the achievements of science. It was their intention to remain loyal to the biblical faith, but to make this faith relevant by translating its truths into the language of the modern age. This point of view was championed brilliantly by Harry Emerson Fosdick, who popularized the phrase, "abiding experiences in changing categories," and insisted that biblical truth could be lifted out of the biblical framework of expression and reinterpreted in the categories of modern thought.[3]

Specifically, this meant reinterpreting the Bible in terms of the concept of evolution, a scientific hypothesis which originally was applied in the field of biology but which soon was transferred to other fields of investigation until it became the dominant philosophical point of view on the American scene. This outlook found theological expression in the toning down or outright rejection of supernaturalism in favor of the idea of divine immanence, that is, God's indwelling in man and nature. For instance, creation by supernatural fiat was reinterpreted to mean God's continuing creation, his immanence in the long evolutionary upthrust. In "Each in His Own Tongue," William Herbert Carruth gave poetic expression to the new interpretation of creation:

A fire-mist and a planet,
  A crystal and a cell,
A jelly-fish and a saurian,
  And caves where the cave-men dwell;
Then a sense of law and beauty
  And a face turned from the clod,—
Some call it Evolution,
  And others call it God.*

Applied to religious knowledge, the evolutionary interpretation found expression in the idea of "progressive revelation." That is to say, God works immanently within the historical process, revealing his timeless truths up to man's ability to understand; on man's side, this progressive illumination yields increasing "discovery" or expanding "insight." The Bible allegedly gives evidence of such progress. The

---

[3] See Fosdick's book, *The Modern Use of the Bible* (Macmillan, 1929), especially chap. 4.

* By William Herbert Carruth. Permission of Mrs. William Herbert Carruth.

religion of Moses is said to be comparatively primitive. But under the influence of the prophetic "genius," crude and barbarous elements were gradually removed, until Jesus finally came as the great discoverer of God and the teacher of the loftiest ethical principles. Since all humanity is involved in the evolutionary process, it is no more surprising that religions outside the biblical tradition should arrive at the same insights than it is that both Russia and America, working independently, should unlock the secret of the atom. According to this view, the greatness of Jesus is that he saw what many others had seen, or could have seen, but by his forceful teaching and sacrificial death he helped men to take truth seriously.

This modern view of the Bible enabled Christians to keep their heads erect in a world where only fools or fanatics would dare to challenge the assured results of science. Of course, liberals were also children of their time, and therefore fell into the temptation of revising the Bible in accordance with their own presuppositions. Nevertheless, liberalism at its best was governed by the spirit of evangelical Christianity.[4] This is noticeable, for example, in one of the characteristic elements of the liberal attitude: devotion to truth. A critical principle lies at the heart of the liberal attitude, the fearless application of which is akin to the spirit of ancient prophets who challenged all human securities. Just as the Protestant Reformation broke upon the world in protest against a Church which had identified itself with God's Kingdom on earth, so liberalism emerged as a prophetic challenge to a decadent Protestantism that had prematurely congealed Christian truth into a static system of belief. According to liberalism, all conclusions must be judged by truth itself. This attitude, when applied to biblical study, has aided in our rediscovery of the Bible by enabling us to read it in the light of the circumstances in which it was written.

---

[4] See H. P. Van Dusen's discussion of liberal theology in *The Vitality of the Christian Tradition*, ed. George Thomas (Harper, 1941), pp. 168-174.

Moreover, Protestant liberalism was a healthy relief from the one-sided emphasis upon the salvation of the individual soul. Liberalism flowered in the "social gospel" movement, as ably represented by men like Walter Rauschenbusch. If the liberal's expectancy of building a Christian society on earth was too much under the influence of the faith of the Enlightenment, it was certainly akin to the this-worldly religion of the Bible according to which all of life must be brought under the sovereignty of God. Finally, liberalism at its best was motivated by a vivid and vital rediscovery of Christian experience. If, as Luther said, "every Christian must do his own believing, just as he must do his own dying," then likewise each age must make its own discovery of Christ and express its faith in its unique way. Liberalism did this for the late nineteenth and early twentieth centuries. Indeed, future historians undoubtedly will appraise liberalism as one of the most dynamic movements in the history of Christianity.

Although liberalism was swept along by a powerful current of evangelical Christianity, the theology of liberalism came too much under the influence of the modern world-view. It is one thing to attempt to translate the biblical faith into categories which modern man can understand; it is quite another thing to adopt modern categories as ruling principles of interpretation. In attempting to bring Christianity up to date, liberals virtually capitulated to the prevailing world-view of the day, so much so that the dividing line between liberal Protestantism and secularism became increasingly dim. Reaction was inevitable.

The reaction came in the form of a movement known as fundamentalism. Beginning during the period 1910-20 on an organized interdenominational basis, it was led by conservative Protestants who felt that "modernists" were "throwing out the baby with the bath" in their streamlining of the Christian faith. The historian will point out precedents for this movement in the sterile orthodoxy which set in shortly after the outburst of the Protestant Reformation, and in the decadent

Calvinism which persisted in America, especially in rural areas, throughout the eighteenth and nineteenth centuries. Fundamentalism as such, however, is a distinctly twentieth century phenomenon, and is properly regarded as essentially a reactionary protest against the excesses of the modernizing of the Bible. Precipitated by the crisis occasioned by the introduction of the theory of evolution, it was aimed at restoring and preserving the fundamentals of the Faith. The movement gained national and even international attention through the "heresy" investigation of Harry Emerson Fosdick in 1923, and the infamous Scopes "monkey" trial at Dayton, Tennessee, in 1925 where the anti-evolution case was championed eloquently by William Jennings Bryan. Even yet, fundamentalism is a powerful force in the American religious scene. Young people become familiar with crusading fundamentalism through the "Youth for Christ" movement or, on the college campus, through the "Inter-Varsity Fellowship."

The key "fundamental" of the faith, according to this group, is the inerrancy of Scripture. In the words of a representative statement, it is "an essential doctrine of the Word of God and our standards that the Holy Spirit did so inspire, guide, and move the writers of the Holy Scripture as to keep them from error." This means that the words of the Bible are the very words of God himself. The writers of the Bible were mere passive secretaries who mechanically transcribed the divine words, these words being the media for conveying the thoughts of the Infinite Intelligence who knows everything past, present, and future. Because God is literally the author of Holy Scripture, the whole Bible "from cover to cover" is held to be absolutely infallible. In popular practice fundamentalists have claimed infallibility for a particular version of the Bible: the King James Version of 1611! Apparent contradictions in Scripture, they say, are not real and are made to vanish by the magic of an interpretative method which weaves together texts from all over the Bible. It is supposedly a matter of faith for the Christian to take the Bible exactly for what it says. If the Bible says that the world was created in six days, that God made a woman out of Adam's rib, that Joshua commanded the sun to stand still, that Balaam's ass talked, or that Jesus turned water into wine, then these matters must be accepted as facts. Many young people have gone away to college burdened with the anxiety that it is a sin to question the literal accuracy of the biblical stories.

Fundamentalists argue that the doctrine of the inerrancy of Scripture is a Christian belief of long standing. It is quite true that both Protestantism and Roman Catholicism have spoken of the Bible in the highest terms. Calvin, for instance, referred to the Bible as the infallible Word of God, and described it by such phrases as "God's own voice," "dictated by the Holy Spirit," and so on. Moreover, a recent Vatican Council declared that the books of the Bible are sacred "not because, having been composed by human industry, they were afterward approved by her [the Church's] authority, nor merely because they contain revelation without error, but because having been written under the inspiration of the Holy Spirit, they have God for their author, and as such were handed down to the Church herself." But in neither case did insistence upon the divine authorship of Scripture carry with it a slavish devotion to the letter of the Scriptures or involve the belief that the Bible is the sole norm for everything under the sun.[5] It is a great mistake to identify fundamentalism with the thinking of men like Luther or Calvin. Unlike classical Christian orthodoxy, fundamentalism is slavishly bound to the literal text of the Bible, and manifests open hostility to anything which goes under the name of biblical criticism. The point bears repetition that fundamentalism is a twentieth-century reactionary movement.

To the credit of fundamentalism it should be said that these

---

[5] For a treatment of "The Reformer's Use of the Bible," see Paul Lehmann, *Theology Today*, October, 1946, pp. 328ff. For a recent Catholic statement giving limited encouragement to biblical criticism, see the encyclical letter of Pope Pius XII, *Divino Afflante Spiritu* (1943).

conservative Christians have been sincere and devout in their attempt to defend the fundamentals of Christianity behind a Maginot line of biblical literalism. As we have observed, liberalism tended to veer away from the main stream of evangelical Christianity and to become a "modernism" carried along by the current of secularism. Thus one may say that fundamentalists, in their dogmatic way, have been making a valid protest against a secularized Christianity which failed to remember Paul's advice: "Be not conformed to this world. . . ." The protest, however, has had little effect on the real frontiers of theological thinking. It is significant that the current theological revival, spoken of earlier, has not been led by fundamentalists but by liberal Protestants whose liberalism was deepened and chastened by involvement in the world crisis.[6]

The real strength of fundamentalism lies in its weaknesses. When the securities of life are threatened, men seek an authority which is visible and absolute. The Bible, therefore, came to be an Ark of salvation in which, like Noah and his family, the faithful could find refuge from the storms of agnosticism and change which were sweeping the world. Fundamentalism is really a form of bibliolatry, that is, it is a faith in the Bible itself, rather than faith in the God who speaks his Word through the Bible. Despite its high regard for the Bible, this movement offers men a false and—paradoxical though this may seem—an *unbiblical* authority.

Moreover, part of the appeal of fundamentalism lies in its reactionary social position. Too often the defense of the Bible has been allied curiously with a reactionary defense of the status quo. It is hardly accidental that frequently the fundamentalist leadership has been recruited from, and the financial support for the movement given by, successful businessmen who have been more concerned about "saving souls" for

---

[6] See the series of articles by Charles Clayton Morrison, "Neo-Orthodoxy's Liberalism," in *The Christian Century*, June 7, 14, and 21, 1950.

eternity than about redeeming society in the name of Jesus Christ. The biblical justification for this escape from social radicalism has been the "premillennial" hope, that is, the belief that Christ must come again before the millennium of justice and peace can be introduced; in the meantime, the evils of society must continue and even become worse.[7] The belief that "Jesus is coming soon"—as one reads on signs along our highways—produces evangelists, but does not inspire a "social gospel." If liberalism has capitulated to secularism, it is equally true that fundamentalism in its own way has made even more dangerous concessions to the status quo.

In summary, fundamentalism and liberalism are both partly right and partly wrong. Fundamentalists are right in insisting that the Bible on its own witness presents men with the Word of God. When liberals equate "progressive revelation" with "increasing discovery," the word revelation is virtually emptied of meaning. The reality has gone, leaving behind only the empty word, like the lingering grin after the disappearance of the Cheshire cat; for that which men can discover potentially—like the secret of the atom—is scarcely the traditional meaning of "revelation." If there is revelation, God must reveal to man what man in his blindness cannot or will not see. He must shed eternal light upon the mystery of life. He must offer a divine solution to an otherwise insoluble human problem. Fundamentalists are keen enough to see this. But unfortunately they make so much of the divine authorship of Scripture that the human element is virtually eliminated, the human secretary being only a mechanical or passive transmitter of God's revelation.

Liberalism, on the other hand, is right in emphasizing the humanity of Scripture—"the warp of human life on the loom of Scripture, across which the shuttle of the Spirit of God so

---

[7] Fundamentalists base this belief on Revelation 20:2–3, which they interpret to mean that Christ must come to inaugurate the "thousand years" of peace.

constantly moved," as H. Wheeler Robinson has put it. Whatever the inspired content of the Bible is, "we have this treasure in a frail earthen vessel." If God speaks his Word, men must hear it and respond within the limitations of concrete historical situations. Since the men of the Bible were men and not God they inevitably used the language of their time to communicate their faith. These things liberalism emphasized and brilliantly verified by means of historical criticism. Unfortunately, however, the human element of Scripture was overemphasized, especially under the influence of the dominant evolutionary philosophy, with the result that "God" became little more than a force at work in the social process, leading men to the formulation of loftier ideas and sounder ethical insights. Thus the uniqueness of the biblical revelation was often discounted and the divine authorship of Scripture reduced to an empty figure of speech. As liberal scholars are now recognizing increasingly, the weakness of the liberalism of the past was not in the use of the method of historical criticism, but rather the fault lay in the dubious presuppositions about the nature of man and history which governed the use of the method.[8]

The Word Behind the Words

In the following chapters we shall attempt to take up the task of interpretation where liberalism left off, or at the point where liberalism went astray because it was too much influenced by the modern world-view. Unlike fundamentalism, we shall not take the Bible literally; like liberalism, we shall take the Bible seriously—more seriously than liberals of the past have been wont to do. In so far as possible the approach to Scripture will be *inductive*. We shall attempt to let the Bible speak for itself rather than force it to uphold any theological

---

[8] See the essay by T. W. Manson, "The Failure of Liberalism to Interpret the Bible as the Word of God," in *The Interpretation of the Bible*, ed. C. W. Dugmore (London: Society for Promoting Christian Knowledge, 1944).

dogma or preferred way of thinking. Our aim will be to view the Bible from the "inside out," rather than from the "outside in." Thus we shall hope to do justice to both the "deity" and the "humanity" of Scripture, that is, to both divine revelation and human response.

What do we mean when we speak of the Bible as the "Word of God"? Let us recognize at the outset that we are using the language of metaphor. When the prophets exclaimed "thus saith the Lord" they were not putting quotation marks around the actual words which had been spoken by God; and when they exhorted their countrymen to "hear the Word of the Lord" they did not refer to a Voice which was carried to them on the sound waves. Speaking and hearing are the ways in which persons become related to one another.[9] If my friend speaks to me and I hear his word, a bridge of communication is thrown out from his life to mine, with the result that a relationship exists between us. Analogously, the Word of God, when heard in a historical crisis, is the medium through which God enters into *relationship* with men. Thus it is proper to speak of God revealing himself by his Word—the word of the prophets of old, and Jesus Christ, "the Word made flesh."

According to the Bible, man encounters God in history. Sometimes we say that we are most aware of God as we behold the beauties of nature. So Wordsworth—that mystic lover of nature—has caught our poetic fancy:

And I have felt
A presence that disturbs me with the joy
Of elevated thoughts; a sense sublime
Of something far more deeply interfused,
Whose dwelling is the light of setting suns,
And the round ocean, and the living air,
And the blue sky, and in the mind of men.

---

[9] C. H. Dodd has discussed this matter nicely in *The Bible Today* (Macmillan, 1947), pp. 104 ff. This book, based on a series of "open lectures" at the University of Cambridge, provides a readable and valuable introduction to the Bible.

The men of the Bible testify that the heavens and earth declare the glory of God, but to them nature was not the *primary* sphere of God's revelation. They first heard God's Word in moments of historical crisis, in events which were experienced with a unique meaning. To be sure, the encounter with God often took place in a setting of nature. Moses heard the divine call in the severe grandeur and serene solitude of the desert of Sinai; Elijah was addressed by God in the silence which followed nature's tumultuous display of earthquake, wind, and fire; and Amos received the divine summons as he was tending his flocks in the rugged wilderness of Tekoa. But in each of these cases there was an acute awareness of the historical crisis in which Israel was involved at the moment. Thus the "Word of God" was essentially the interpretation of a historical crisis in which men were grasped by God's claim upon them. In order to communicate the discerned meaning of events, the writers of the Bible employed words, but words, of course, are only symbols for the conveyance of meaning. Therefore the biblical interpreter must go beyond the letter of Scripture to the meaning. He must seek "the Word behind the words," as someone has put it.

In the strict sense, then, it is inaccurate to speak of the Bible itself as the Word of God. Properly speaking, the Bible *contains* the Word of God. The subject matter of the Bible is God's approach to man in history, in particular the stream of Hebraic-Christian history which begins with the Exodus and culminates in the coming of Jesus Christ. Though this book is characterized by great diversity and variety, both in literary form and religious content, its internal unity is the drama of the working out of God's purpose in the events of Israel's history. As someone has said, this biblical history is His-Story, in which he reveals his judgment upon men's sin and his intention and power to recreate mankind. The plot has God's purpose at the beginning, God's ultimate triumph at the conclusion, and—at the tragic and victorious climax—a Cross, the sign of God's omnipotent love. Because the Bible is both the record of these unique events and the witness to their divine meaning, it may be called the Word of God.

If we are to hear God's Word spoken through the Bible to our situation today, our first task is to put ourselves within the world of the Bible. No casual or superficial reading of Scripture can accomplish this. We must avail ourselves of the results of historical criticism and biblical theology so that we may imaginatively relive the actual historical situation in which an Amos or a Paul heard the high calling of God. We must, as it were, sit where these ancient people sat and learn to look at the human scene from their unique point of view. We must live with the Bible until it becomes part of us, just as the actor identifies himself with the role that he plays. It is then, perhaps, that the Holy Spirit, breathing through the ancient words of the sacred page, will lead us to know that the "Word of the Lord" spoken by the prophets and embodied in Jesus Christ is actually the deepest interpretation of our own life situation and our world crisis in the twentieth century.

2

God's Action in History

In the prologue to his novel, *Joseph the Provider*, Thomas Mann transports his reader imaginatively into heaven, where he hears the gossip of the angels. It seems that angelic noses had been put out of joint because God had decided upon a fantastic experiment: the creation of a man who was a precarious combination of the angel and the brute. Like the angels, he was made in the image of God; but he also was endowed with creative powers which made him different from the angels. So against the better judgment of self-righteous angels, "One [God] entangled One-self in folly and created a being notoriously unstable and embarrassing. And then, precisely because it was such an undeniable miscreation, One set One's heart upon it in magnificent self-will and made such a point of the thing that all heaven was offended." But this was not all. Not only had God's initial failure resulted in the "Fall" of man (and angelic murmurings, "I told you so"), but in his magnificent ambition to win back his lost creation he was planning to "condescend mightily." The holy God was going to stoop to the level of a humiliating "folk-incarnation"—an embodiment in history as the folk-god of a chosen people! This was more than ever a matter for angelic gossip.

God's Search for Man

This prologue by Thomas Mann is an admirable introduction to the theme of the entire Bible. The biblical faith rests upon the stupendous claim that God has "condescended mightily," that his Word has entered history, that he himself has taken the initiative to seek and to save. Here is the perfect contrast to Aristotle's God, the "Unmoved Mover" who, lost in contemplation of his perfection, passively attracts the whole creation to himself. The God of the Bible is the God who acts. For this reason writers of the Bible employed, not abstract concepts to describe his "nature," but verbs and daringly human (anthropomorphic) expressions to declare what he has done, is doing, and will do. According to the Bible, history is the theater in which God, the Aggressor, establishes and secures a beachhead in his struggle against the opposing force of man's sin. For men of faith, therefore, crucial events are under the sign of *Immanuel*—"God with us."

Sometimes it is said that religion is man's search for God, and that the Bible is the record of that human quest. If, however, we are to rely upon the witness of the Bible itself this statement needs modification. True, we often read of devout souls seeking, waiting, and longing for God; but much oftener we read about unsought and unexpected visitations from God. Indeed, from one point of view the Bible is not so much the record of man's quest for God as it is the drama of man's attempt to flee from the "Hound of Heaven" who pursues men down the labyrinthine corridors of the years.[1] When our more theologically minded forefathers spoke of God's "prevenient" action, they were expressing a basic conviction of the Bible: God's search for man precedes man's search for God. Though resting upon man's free decision, faith is really the *response* to the prior intention and activity of God. So we express our faith in the words of the familiar hymn:

> I sought the Lord and *afterward I knew*
> He moved my soul to seek Him, seeking me;
> It was not I that found, O Savior true,
> No, I was found of Thee.*

[1] See further the illuminating book by Paul S. Minear, *Eyes of Faith* (Westminster, 1946), chap. 1.

* From *The Pilgrim Hymnal.* Copyright, The Pilgrim Press. Used by permission.

Thus every genuine moment of worship is a right-about-face and a confronting of the God who ever pursues close at man's heels. Whether we realize it or not, here we are speaking of the paradox of "predestination," a doctrine which too often is caricatured as religious fatalism. Predestination means that man's free decision, as viewed in the retrospect of faith, is really a response to the initiative of God. Thus, for instance, Jeremiah—after the struggles of soul which finally crystallized in his call—could look back over his career and affirm that he was predestined from birth to be a prophet (Jeremiah 1:5). This is the language of faith, not the language of logic.

The Bible, then, is the drama of God's search for man. For most of us this truth is clearest in the New Testament, where it is illustrated in Jesus' parables and where it is made concrete in Jesus' sacrifice. But it is no less basic to the Old Testament where God's action in history takes the form of a "folk-incarnation"—his choice of Israel and his self-revelation within the limitations of Israel's history. God's "incarnation" in the career of the particular people, Israel, is the prelude to his final incarnation in the particular Person, Jesus of Nazareth. Both Testaments describe God's initiative, God's action in history, God's seeking for man.

The Biblical Scandal

If we are to be fair to the biblical witness, two things must be said: first, there is a sense in which God acts in *all* human history, even when men are unaware of his presence and his purpose; second, God's action is *revealed* or exposed in the unique series of events which constitute the biblical drama. Merely to state the matter in this way, however, is to invite a whole host of questions, especially the question about the "chosen people."

One does not have to read very far in the Bible before coming upon the chapter in which the Lord, promising the land of Palestine to Abraham, says: "I will make of thee a great nation, and I will bless thee, and make thy name great; and thou shalt be a blessing. And I will bless them that bless thee, and curse him that curseth thee: and in thee shall all families of the earth be blessed" (Genesis 12:2-3). To many modern people this passage is a "scandal," that is, a stumbling block—as the original Greek *skandalon* means. Those very same words, addressed by Hitler to the German *Herrenvolk,* would have received tremendous applause. Also, some of us have heard advocates of "white supremacy" defend their position by reference to the biblical precedent of a chosen people. On the face of it, this biblical doctrine sounds too much like the perverted racial theories of our time to be readily acceptable. Moreover, at the theological level this "scandal of particularity," as it has been called, raises many problems. Does this imply that other peoples, not fortunate enough to be among God's elect, were left "out in the dark"? Does this mean that God actually sanctioned Israel's snatching Palestine from the native inhabitants? And if God were to select a people for his special revelation, why *this* people rather than some other?

Before dealing with these issues, let us recognize honestly that the idea of the chosen people is native to the Bible, both Old and New Testaments. We cannot bypass the problem by assuming that the doctrine is a museum piece of Scripture held over from a primitive period when every nation had a folk-god from whom special favors were received. True, the doctrine of Israel's election was modified in the course of time as horizons widened and experience deepened; but it was never removed from its old position of centrality even when Israel's faith became more consciously monotheistic. An excellent example is found in a series of poems in Isaiah 40-55. No writing of the Old Testament more exuberantly proclaims God's sovereignty over all peoples and all creation. Yet these poems were intended primarily to remind Israel in an hour of tragedy that God had not forgotten the people who were precious in his sight and dearer than other nations.

Likewise everywhere in the New Testament there is the good news that God's sovereignty has been declared unto all mankind. Nevertheless the emphasis upon God's election of Israel is not surrendered. "Salvation is from the Jews," Jesus is said to have reminded a Samaritan woman almost in the same breath that he insisted that the worship of God cannot be confined to particular places or symbols (John 4:22). Moreover, in the New Testament the Church is described as the "Israel of God," the community elected by God to be the bearer of his revelation to the whole world (Galatians 6:16). Though differing from the Old Israel in that it includes people from all nations and races, the New Israel appropriates the major attributes which previously had been applied to the chosen people (compare I Peter 2:9-10 with Exodus 19:4-6). In spite of the adjective "new," the Church of the New Testament is "the continuing embodiment of the historic 'Israel of God,'" as C. H. Dodd has observed. The conception of the chosen community is the line of unity which runs throughout the Bible.

The "scandal of particularity," then, lies at the very heart of the Bible. Let us notice, however, that this disturbing idea is inseparable from the basic biblical belief that God's revelation is given in historical events. Perhaps we can appreciate this better by first outlining a point of view characteristic of religions and philosophies which do not take history as seriously as does the Bible.

According to most classical philosophies and religions, ultimate reality is disclosed when man, either by rational contemplation or mystic ascent, goes beyond the flow of events which we call "history." The goal is the apprehension of an order of reality unaffected by the fleeting days or by the unpredictable fortunes of mankind. In Hinduism, for instance, the world of sense experience is regarded as *maya*, illusion; the religious man, therefore, seeks release from the wheel of life in order that his individuality may fade out into the World-Soul, Brahma. Or, Greek philosophers looked upon the world as a natural process which, like the rotations of the seasons, always follows the same rational scheme. The philosopher, however, could soar above the recurring cycles of history by fixing his mind upon the unchanging absolutes which belong to the eternal order. Both of these views are vastly different from the biblical claim that God is found within the limitations of the world of change and struggle, and especially that he reveals himself in events which are unique, particular, and unrepeatable. For the Bible, history is neither *maya* nor a circular process of nature; it is the arena of God's purposive activity.

In its very character, history is defined by the concrete realities of time, place, and circumstance. Unique events occur within the histories of particular peoples. Who can understand America, for instance, if he does not take into consideration decisive events that have made us self-consciously a *people:* the Revolutionary War, the struggle between North and South, the expansion of the frontier, and our rise to a position of world leadership? Similarly other groups—the British, the Russians, the Chinese—have become peoples because of unique events in which they find a common memory and purpose. History, then, is not concerned with abstractions which are independent of time, place, and circumstance; it is concerned with events which happen at a particular time, in a particular place, and in the circumstances of a particular community. If, therefore, God reveals himself in history, his special revelation will find expression in the "scandal of particularity." We may not be able to explain *why* God's revelation came when it did, where it did, and to the people it did; but that his purpose *was* identified with one people is what we must expect in the case of historical revelation.

In times past liberal Protestants have had great difficulty with the doctrine of Israel's election largely because they have started out from an unbiblical understanding of the meaning of "revelation." If the Bible sets forth abstract truths or universal principles, as has often been assumed, then of course any claim of special revelation in history cannot be taken too seriously; for it is characteristic of abstract truths and universal principles that they have no *necessary* connection with the historical factors of time, place, and circumstance. For instance, Einstein's mathematical theories which led to atomic fission are true and understandable when divorced from the historical situation of Einstein himself. It is interesting to know something about the man, and it is more interesting to know the historical repercussions of his physics in the twentieth century; but historical considerations are accidental, or at least incidental, to mathematical truth. Now, if the Bible presents us with abstract information about the nature of God or with universal principles of moral behavior, then plainly it would be presumptuous for the men of the Bible to claim a corner on these truths, for other men in different historical circumstances would inevitably stumble upon them during the course of their cultural evolution. The logic of this would drive one eventually to the position of Tindal, an eighteenth century Deist who maintained that "Christianity is as old as the Creation" (that is, as old as the rational pattern of nature) and that Jesus merely "republished" truths that reasonable men had known, or could have known, all along. On this premise, the "scandal of particularity" must be rejected.

Our purpose is not to criticize philosophical attempts to reach suprahistorical truth or to state universal ethical principles. Our primary concern is to let the Bible speak to us in its own terms, rather than in the terms of, say, a Plato or a Kant. The men of the Bible do not tell us about grasping principles or propositions; they tell us about being grasped by God himself in the midst of crucial events of their history. They do not tell us about their knowing God as an object of reflective thought; rather, they tell us about being *known by God* down at the "grass roots" level of their existence where they faced the immediate issues of daily life. As we have said before, the Word of God to Israel was primarily an interpretation of history—not in the first instance the history of mankind in general, but the concrete historical situations of a particular people. The "scandal of particularity" is indigenous to a religion which takes seriously the claim that God has revealed himself in historical events.

Chosen for a Task

Having discussed the character of historical revelation, let us now examine the implications of God's election of Israel. Here we shall attempt to project ourselves imaginatively into the chosen community and hear the testimony of those for whom God's election was not a matter for discussion, but an inescapable affirmation of faith.

First, the election of Israel was, according to biblical witness, an expression of the mystery of God's way in history. If we find it impossible to understand why God should have chosen *this* people to be the bearer of his special revelation, we must remember that sensitive prophetic spirits of Israel experienced the same bafflement. Sometimes we hear the suggestion that God's revelation was given to Israel because these people had a "genius for religion," just as the Greeks had a genius for philosophy, or as Americans have a genius for action. But Israel's prophets found no evidence that their people were more religiously discerning or that they were in any way "better" than other peoples round about. In fact, the historical evidence suggests that from the very first these people were fickle, dull, insensitive, rebellious, and idolatrous. Likewise the Church of the New Testament was composed of "saints" whose sinful humanity was more obvious than their godliness.

Therefore, God's choice of Israel, as the word "choice" implies, was an act of freedom. Prophets were perplexed over Israel's fateful destiny, just as they were baffled as to why God had singled out a particular one of them—like Moses or Jeremiah—for a special vocation. The idea of the chosen people was never arrived at reflectively or by comparison of

Israel's status with that of other peoples; rather, it was affirmed confessionally by those who were grasped by God's claim in historical crises. As the book of Deuteronomy indicates (9:4-6), God's choice of Israel was a free act of grace—love bestowed without consideration of the worth of its object. Just as Napoleon is said to have raised his generals from the mud, so God raised this people from slavery in Egypt as an expression of his sovereign freedom and unmerited love. As a matter of fact, if we could give a reason for God's election of Israel, we would make God's action conditional, and thereby reduce it to something less than an expression of divine freedom and grace.

In the second place, the conviction that Israel was God's elect did not, at least in the message of the prophets, bring the accompanying assurance that his people would be given preferential treatment. To be sure, there were always patriots who too readily identified God's purpose in history with Israel's national interests, just as Americans at the end of World War II claimed that "God and uranium are on our side." We know from the book of Amos that people in the middle of the eighth century B.C. optimistically anticipated the great "Day of the Lord" when Israel would receive the blessings of victory, prosperity, and prestige which a chosen people thought they deserved. But the prophets thundered against this popular pretension, condemning it as the supreme expression of sin (see Amos 5:18-20). Instead of drawing from the premise "*You only have I known* of all the families of the earth" the popular conclusion "therefore no harm will come upon us," they drew the conclusion "therefore you will be punished for all your iniquities" (Amos 3:2).

Certainly the chosen people did not tread upon a path of roses. Wedged in between two centers of political strength, Egypt and Mesopotamia, Palestine was caught in a world struggle as gigantic in its time as the present contest between East and West. Only for brief periods did the Israelites enjoy real political independence, and then because international factors made foreign interference impossible. The history of Israel was punctuated by a succession of foreign empires that swept over Palestine, wave after wave: Egypt, Assyria, Babylonia, Persia, Greece, and Rome. Israel's land was an international battleground, her people were carried into foreign captivity, her country was policed by armies of occupation, and resurgent nationalism was put down with the harshest measures. So severe was the fate of the chosen people that prophets eventually began to grapple with the problem of why Israel's lot was so much more terrible than that of other wicked nations. Thus it is plain that whatever else Israel's election meant, it did not mean that she was given the advantages of a pampered favorite.

Prophets interpreted the events of Israel's tragic history as moments of engagement with God, Israel's Judge and Redeemer. According to their testimony, to be "chosen" by God was to be "known" by God, and to be known by God was to be exposed uncomfortably to his penetrating judgments. As a New Testament writer puts it:

> The word of God is living and active, sharper than any two-edged sword, piercing to the division of soul and spirit, of joints and marrow, and discerning the thoughts and intentions of the heart. And before him no creature is hidden, but *all are open and laid bare to the eyes of him with whom we have to do.*
>
> —Hebrews 4:12-13

The revelation granted to God's elect is not the kind men normally covet. It is the knowledge which men humbly accept as an inescapable word laid upon the heart and conscience.

Finally, the Bible makes it clear that Israel was chosen for a task, and that task was nothing less than being the servant of God in the accomplishment of his purpose for all mankind. It is a grave error to suppose that God's election of Israel meant a narrow concern for one people. God's sovereignty is not provincial or exclusive; it is actually the sovereignty of the one God who is Creator of the heavens and earth and Lord of all mankind. This universal perspective is presented in the stories at the opening of the Bible (Genesis 1-11)—stories which concern not Israel alone but "all people that on earth do dwell." For instance, at the end of the Flood story, God is described as making a covenant with Noah and his three sons, Shem, Ham, and Japheth (Genesis 9:8-17). The author of this passage supposed that these three sons were the ancestors of all the principal nations and peoples of antiquity. This is undoubtedly erroneous anthropology; moreover, it is more accurate historically to say that God's Covenant was first made with Israel. Nevertheless, the religious truth is basic to Israel's faith: God is sovereign over all peoples, and therefore his Covenant embraces all mankind, as the men of the Bible increasingly came to realize.

It is the biblical witness, however, that God manifests his sovereignty over the whole world through the history of a particular people. Therefore, against the background of "world history" presented in Genesis 1-11, Abraham—the father of the Hebrew people—steps upon the stage in Genesis 12 as the one chosen by God to perform a special task. The promise is given that in him (that is, in the people which shall spring from his seed) all of the nations of the world will find blessing. Thus Israel, we are told, was elected to a world responsibility. To be sure, Israel often misunderstood her vocation or, refusing to perform it, sought refuge in nationalism that was intent only upon the preservation of the Jewish people (see the book of Esther). But when prophets most profoundly interpreted Israel's status as a chosen people they insisted that special revelation had been given her, not that it be a lamp hidden under a bushel, but that it be a light to the Gentiles (see Isaiah 40–55 and the book of Jonah). Eventually the Christian Church became the inheritor of the Promise to Abraham (Galatians 3:8-9), and accepted from her Risen Lord the commission to go into the whole world and proclaim the gospel that all nations might know the blessing of God.

The Removal of the Veil from History

We have said that the heart of the biblical faith is the affirmation that God acts in history. All history is the general scene of his activity, but his activity is uniquely exposed in that strand of history called Hebrew-Christian. Therefore the central theme of the Bible is God's special revelation through a chosen people, the working out of his redemptive purpose in a series of unique events.

In succeeding chapters we shall follow the biblical drama through its several stages of development. It is important to point out here, however, that Christians believe the drama extends throughout *both* Old and New Testaments, that it comes to its climax with the appearance of the Messiah in the person of Jesus, and that the New Testament gives the key to the understanding of the whole. As one reads the Old Testament he cannot help sensing the forward-moving character of events. According to the prophetic view, history does not spin in endless circles; rather—to use familiar words—"time marches on," each event carrying history nearer to the realization of God's purpose. In many passages are anticipations of that which will come to pass "in the latter days." Then in the New Testament on every hand appears the proclamation that history has reached its "crowded climax," that prophecy has been fulfilled, and that, in some sense, God's purpose has been realized. From the Christian standpoint, the figure of the Messiah constitutes the unity of the two Testaments: the Old Testament points toward the Messiah's coming; the New Testament exuberantly proclaims that he has come.

The coming of the Messiah was so decisive that it not only brought the previous history to a denouement but also transformed its meaning by opening men's eyes to perceive the purpose of God, theretofore understood only partially or dimly. In the light of God's revelation in Christ the drama of the Old Testament period was seen with a deeper understanding, in fact with a *new* understanding. As Paul said, speaking of the Jews' misunderstanding of their own Scriptures: "Their minds were hardened; for to this day, when they read the old covenant, that same veil remains unlifted, because only through Christ is it taken away" (II Corinthians 3:14). We should observe, by the way, that it was not Gentiles but Christian Jews who first claimed that Jews failed to understand the Old Testament. Even yet, Christians and Jews read the Old Testament differently because, using different keys of interpretation, they disagree on the meaning and outcome of the biblical drama. The Christian claims that the Old Testament by itself is incomplete, and that the clue to its meaning is given by Jesus Christ who lifts the veil from the past, enabling men to perceive the working out of God's purpose in history.

Christian theologians sometimes speak of the Bible as the "History of Redemption," "Sacred History," or—to use the German word—*Heilsgeschichte*. This is proper for, as we have seen, the Bible bears witness to God's action in the unique series of events beginning with the call of Israel and culminating in the coming of Christ and the birth of the Christian Church. However, we must use these terms cautiously, lest we fall victim to the false notion that biblical history is completely independent from the normal course of human affairs. As a matter of fact, the history of Israel, when viewed by a purely secular historian, would not be substantially different from the histories of other peoples. What makes biblical history different is the *unique perspective* which prophets had upon "the normal course of human affairs." The Bible does not present a special "sacred" drama set aside from ordinary "secular" history; rather, it discloses what the history of any people would look like viewed *sub specie aeternitatis*, under the view of Eternity. Therefore the Christian will supplement the above statement to the effect that Christ lifts the veil from the Old Testament with an equally important affirmation: Christ also lifts the veil from the history of peoples like the Greeks or Romans, French or British, Russians or Americans.

That is to say, he gives the clue to the meaning of all history.

The most vexing issue of our time is the problem of the meaning of history. This is, of course, the inescapable question of every era, but the question has been raised with more earnestness in our day because of the dawning realization that we are living at the end of an epoch and perhaps—if man continues in his hell-bent folly—near the end of civilization. Moreover, we are coming to realize that the meaning of history cannot be determined as objectively as a scientist can calculate the distance to a star. Our primary religious differences arise not from theoretical arguments about God or an after-life, but from disagreement as to the vantage point from which our history is to be viewed. A Hindu, for instance, finds no eternal meaning in the daily round of events and seeks eventual release in a mystic experience. This is one way to deal with the historical problem. Toynbee describes it as the attitude of "detachment." A devout Moslem will insist that the meaning of history has been disclosed in the life of Mohammed and the Prophet's teachings codified in the Koran. A humanist, viewing the human scene from the standpoint of the doctrine of evolution, will describe man as a product of nature with no other problem than that of making the most satisfactory adjustment to his natural environment. And so on. The so-called "ideologies" of the twentieth century actually are, in effect, pseudo religions which offer men an understanding of their history. For instance, according to a Communist writer, the Communist front in 1941 was fortified by the conviction that "Hitler had not, nor could have, history's right to victory. To imagine for a moment the possibility of Hitler's victory meant to forego all reason; if it were to happen, then there would be no truth, logic, nor light in the development of human society; only chaos, darkness, and lunacy."[2] Many Americans, who self-righteously identify God's purpose with "our side," would feel the same about a possible Communist

[2] The reference is given by Martin Wight in *The Ecumenical Review,* Vol. 1, No. 1 (1948), p. 37.

victory. The most frightening aspect of the contemporary strife between Communism and "the American way" is that fundamentally men are involved in a religious war.

Why do reasonable men disagree? Something other than faulty logic must account for our basic differences. It is increasingly apparent that men disagree because their minds look out upon history through different spectacles of faith. Unfortunately we cannot ascend to a cloud and look down upon the human scene with the unbiased objectivity of an angel. We must see life from a human standpoint, from our involvement in events that have no obvious interpretation readily acceptable to all rational men. We must decide where we will take our stand, and our decision must be made in faith. One becomes a Communist, for instance, not by a logical examination of the "facts" but by something amounting to a "conversion," the result being that all moral values, artistic expressions, and scientific endeavors are seen from a *new* perspective. Similarly, conversion is necessary in becoming a Christian, and the prelude is the realization that every other alternative is a dead-end street.

Early Christians took their stand on the faith that God had revealed the meaning of man's life at one point in human history: the life, death, and resurrection of Jesus Christ—viewed as a single event—and the biblical drama which led up to that climatic, eternal moment. So central was the event of the coming of the Messiah that for them it became the turning point of history, the pivotal center of the whole human drama, the vertical line which divided the horizontal plane of world history in two. From this point of vantage they looked backward into "B.C." and forward into "A.D.," finding everywhere the evidence of God's hand in human affairs. Even the tragedies that engulfed whole civilizations were meaningful events when viewed from this standpoint. This was the position of Augustine who, when the great Roman Empire was crumbling to ruin in the early fifth century, wrote the classical and probably greatest Christian interpretation of history, *The City of God.* Likewise in our time we have witnessed the appearance of a number of historical works, especially Arnold Toynbee's massive *Study of History*, which rest upon the conviction that the Christian faith is the most realistic platform from which to survey the whole range of human history.[3] The Christian will claim that the Christian interpretation of history makes sense, and that it most adequately deals with all dimensions of human experience. We must hasten to add, however, that this claim—like any interpretation of history—rests initially upon faith and otherwise is unconvincing.

If it is true that the Bible bears witness to God's revelation of the meaning of human history, then it follows that men cannot realize true peace and security until they are united in the worship and service of him who is Israel's God and the God of our Lord Jesus Christ. The New Testament is uncompromising in its claim, set forth in the name of Jesus, that "No one comes to the Father, but by me" (John 14:6; see also Matthew 11:27; Luke 10:22). These words, and others like them, should not be construed to mean that people who live by some other faith are left wholly in the dark. There is no basis in Christian theology for a sharp disjunction between Christianity and other religions. If, as the Bible assumes, all men are made in the image of God and, furthermore, if God is active in all history, then the Christian will expect to find evidence of God's work everywhere. The ancient Greek's search for the good and true and beautiful, the Hindu's devotion to religious duty without consideration for the consequences (as beautifully expressed in the *Baghavad Gita*), the Confucian humanist's desire for the realization of man's true moral nature, the Communist's passion for social justice—all of this, and much more which could be mentioned, will be regarded as evidence of the grace of God that pursues men and leads them to direct their lives toward him even when

[3] See the stimulating lectures by Herbert Butterfield: ***Christianity and History*** (Scribner, 1950).

they are ignorant of his special revelation.[4] To such people the Christian may say, as Paul said to ancient Greek people in his sermon on Mars Hill: "Whom therefore ye ignorantly worship, him declare I unto you" (Acts 17:23). Moreover, the Christian is told that on the final day of reckoning there will be some surprises in store, for then it will be discovered that those who thought they had been serving Christ actually had rejected him, and those who were ignorant of Christ actually had ministered unto him (Matthew 25:31-46). Since all mankind is comprehended within the sovereignty of God, the Christian will refuse to make God's judgments for him or to probe into the mystery of how the entire historical drama ultimately will be summed up in his purpose.

Having said this, however, the Christian historian cannot escape making the bold claim that Christ is the clue to the meaning of history in general, just as Christ gives the key for the understanding of the biblical history in particular. It is he who lifts the veil from history and exposes the activity and purpose of God. Therefore to know the God who reveals himself in the biblical drama is to know the deepest meaning of man's history. When the scroll of history is completed—so we read in a well-known messianic poem of the Old Testament (Isaiah 2:2-4 and Micah 4:1-4)—all peoples will experience their true unity and blessedness by acknowledging the sovereignty of the God of Israel. In God's good day they will beat their swords into plowshares and will "study war no more." The "peace" of God's rule, however, will be more than the cessation of hostilities. It will be a faith-relationship with God in which men experience the disclosure of life's deepest meaning and the final fulfillment of all historical striving.

---

[4] For further discussion of this matter, see Alan Richardson, *Christian Apologetics* (Harper, 1947), chaps. 5 and 6.

3

The Days of Israel's Youth

IN THE PREVIOUS CHAPTER it was pointed out that the election or special call of Israel is basic to the message of the Bible. Now we must turn our attention to those momentous events in which the chosen people discerned the action of God and responded to his high calling. One event in particular looms through the mists of the past: the exodus of the Israelites from Egypt. Hosea refers to the period of the Exodus as the time of Israel's youth, and affirms that Israel's future blessing will be a re-enactment of that historic moment of her first encounter with God.

> Therefore I am going to persuade her,
> And lead her to the wilderness,
> And speak to her heart . . .
> And she shall respond there as in the days of her youth,
> As in the day when she came up from the land of Egypt.
>
> —Hosea 2:14-15

Properly speaking, Israel's history begins with the Exodus. At this point the curtain rises on the first main act of the biblical drama. To begin our study of the Bible elsewhere is to ignore the witness of prophets and psalmists who point to this crucial event as God's creative and redemptive act which brought Israel upon the stage of history with a sense of mission and destiny.[1]

---

[1] See Amos 3:1–2; Hosea 11:1; 13:4–5; Micah 6:3–5; Jeremiah 2:5–6; Ezekiel 20:5–6; Deuteronomy 26:5–10; Psalms 106:6–12; 135:8–12; 136:10–22.

The memory of Israel's past was eventually preserved in literature now found at the beginning of the Bible. This is not easy literature to read, as many will testify who, having started with Genesis, bravely set out to read the Bible through. The primary reason for the difficulty is that as we read the Bible two different worlds come into conflict. One is the *ancient* world of the *Orient*. Its thoughts are not our thoughts, neither are its ways our ways. Judged by the standards of our science, it is a very capricious world where men seemingly find no trouble in believing that Moses could perform wonders with his magic rod, that Joshua could command the sun to stand still, or that Elisha could cause an axe-head to float on water. Measured by the standards of our morality, it is often a barbarous world in which the coarsest brutalities are endorsed by religion. According to our sophisticated standards of thinking, it is a naive world where God is described in the most human terms and where thought is clothed in the bizarre idiom of the Semitic mind. This is the world of the Bible. The other world is our world, *modern* and *occidental*. Our ways, so we think, are more advanced; our thought has attained a stature of logical consistency; and, above all, science reigns as king over us. We smile at the well-known comic strip which describes a caveman shuttling back and forth between the Stone Age and the twentieth century by the aid of a "time machine." Seriously, however, we find it difficult to shuttle back and forth between our modern, occidental world and the ancient, oriental world of the Bible.

The Age of Miracle

In this chapter we shall concentrate on only one aspect of the modern difficulty with the Bible: the problem of miracle in the opening books of the Old Testament. Modern man finds it difficult, if not impossible, to accept the naive belief that when the Israelites were in dire straits God would "ra'ar back an' pass a miracle," as in *Green Pastures*. This goes against common-sense wisdom and certainly against the scientific understanding of nature as being governed by law-abiding processes which can be stated in precise mathematical formulae. The modern scientific view may leave little room for "supernatural" intervention into human affairs, and God himself may be "lost among the stars"; but at least the reign of natural law allegedly is more "democratic" than the ancient view according to which, seemingly, God capriciously suspended the operation of nature's laws for the benefit of a favored few.

Governed by the modern view, some people attempt to dismiss the biblical miracles as expressions of prescientific ignorance. After all, it is pointed out, these people lived in an age when they could not have known better. They were children of their time; thus the Scripture they wrote inevitably betrays a naive and mistaken understanding of nature. Just as they uncritically accepted the prevailing view that the earth was flat and the center of the universe, so likewise they credulously inherited the common belief in miracles. Since Scriptural truth comes to us wrapped in the swaddling clothes of a prescientific age, so the argument goes, we must seek for the spiritual truth and ignore the outgrown wrapping.

This approach places us in the position of having to disregard the central witness of the Bible itself. If we could overcome our mental bias and listen attentively to the testimony of prophets and apostles of the Bible, we would recognize clearly that at least for them miracle was not incidental to their message. In fact, according to the Bible, the sacred drama moves forward from the Old Testament through the New Testament by virtue of divine miracle. Every new development of the plot is marked by a new act of God: the Exodus from Egypt, the return from Babylonian exile, the resurrection of Jesus, and the Spirit-led expansion of the Church. It is especially noteworthy that a great number of miracles cluster around the two great epochs of the Bible: the Exodus which marked the initiation of the Old Covenant of Moses, and the career of Jesus Christ which inaugurated the New Covenant.

Of course, some of us insist that the biblical account might have been written differently if a modern observer, equipped with the knowledge which science has given, had been at the scene of the so-called miracle. This theorizing cannot change the fact that none of us were at the scene, while those who were involved in the events testified that extraordinary things had taken place, prompting them to exclaim with the psalmist:

> Thou art the God that does wonders;
> Thou hast made thy strength known among the peoples.
> Thou didst by thy power redeem thy people,
> The sons of Jacob and Joseph.
>
> —Psalm 77:14-15

Since past events cannot be brought into the laboratory of the present for examination, it would seem best to approach the question of miracle not from the standpoint of a modern prejudice, but from the standpoint of the historical evidence itself. Above all, since these people had no idea of the law of cause and effect and therefore would not have understood our definition of a miracle as something which disrupts "natural law," we must investigate the character of the experience which lies at the heart of the miracle tradition.

In a later chapter we shall have occasion to discuss the miracles of the New Testament. Now we shall confine our attention to the great Old Testament era of miracle: the period of the Exodus.

Unraveling the Strands of the Pentateuch

The application of the method of historical criticism to the Bible has greatly facilitated our task of interpretation. It has liberated us from the false notion that we are dealing with a completely accurate record of the past, a record which describes what actually and literally happened in all cases. We are no longer obligated to believe that in Elisha's time God miraculously sent bears to eat up mischievous children; nor do we have to wonder about the cosmic implications of Joshua's commanding the sun to stand still; nor do we have to search the seven seas for an aquatic specimen in whose belly Jonah—à la Pinocchio—could have lived for several days. Once the Bible is not regarded as a supernaturally dictated book, these things can be understood in the light of the historical circumstances and the religious context in which they were written.

This does not mean, however, that the whole miracle tradition of the Old Testament must be consigned to the museum of a primitive and unenlightened age, or treated as a mere folk embellishment to the biblical account. On the contrary, historical criticism enables us to distinguish more clearly between what is *peripheral* and what is *central* in the miracle tradition, and thereby to come to a deeper understanding of Israel's faith. The question of miracle in the Old Testament cannot be settled by concentrating on curiosities like axe-heads floating on water, staffs turning into snakes, or the healing of a leprous hand. There is a greater miracle at the center of the whole miracle tradition, and to which the very existence of the people named Israel bears witness. Before we can deal properly with this issue, we must consider the historical evidence at our disposal for the study of the beginnings of Israel's history.

Let us turn our attention to the first five books of the Old Testament. These books collectively are called the Pentateuch—from a Greek word signifying a writing divided into five parts. Together they tell the story of the Hebrew people from their early beginnings down to the time when they were stationed in the plains of Moab, poised for an attack upon the Promised Land, Canaan. The book of Genesis gives a preface to the main story, which begins with Moses. After an account of the primeval beginning of things, the thread of continuity is traced through a long "family tree," until eventually the great figure of Abraham steps onto the stage. Then we read about his direct descendants, Isaac and Jacob, and learn how during a time of famine Jacob and his sons went down to Egypt, where Joseph occupied a position of authority second only to the pharaoh. The book of Exodus begins at this point with a description of the sad fortunes of these Semites in consequence of the rise to power of "a pharaoh who knew not Joseph" (perhaps Seti I, 1319-01 B.C.).[2] There follows a series of vivid stories describing Moses' divine commission to lead the Hebrews out of Egypt, his contest with the pharaoh, the successful escape across the Red Sea, and finally, after a long journey through the wilderness, the arrival at Mount Sinai. Next comes an account of the giving of the Law and the making of a covenant between *Yahweh* and his chosen people.[3] Then we read the tragic sequel to this dramatic moment: the idolatrous worship of the Golden Calf.

At about this point the story definitely bogs down for the modern reader. The last part of Exodus, all of the book of Leviticus, and the first part of the book of Numbers give long and dreary descriptions of how the chosen people are to live and worship. We are told about the exact specifications of the Tabernacle, the making of priestly vestments, the types of offerings which must be presented to Yahweh, laws relating to clean and unclean foods, and many other details important especially to priests. But in the tenth chapter of Numbers the story begins to move again. We read about the departure of the Israelites from Sinai, their march around through Trans-Jordan, and their preparations for the conquest of Canaan. Finally, the book of Deuteronomy presents us with a series of sermons which Moses supposedly delivered to the Israelites as they stood at the very threshold of the Promised Land. With the intention of reminding the people to be faithful to their covenant with Yahweh, Moses rehearses Israel's history

---

2 See the discussion of the historical background of the Exodus in Wright and Filson, *The Westminster Historical Atlas to the Bible* (Westminster, 1945), pp. 37 ff.

3 The special Hebrew name for the deity is "Yahweh" (usually translated "the Lord"). The word "Jehovah" is an artificial word which represents a combination of the consonants of *Yahweh* with the vowels of *Adonai* (Lord), the latter being employed as a substitute for the ineffable Name.

from the time of the Exodus and also restates the laws that are to regulate God's people as they settle down in a new country. Deuteronomy concludes with an account of the death of Moses and Joshua's appointment as his successor.

The Jews called these five books or scrolls the *Torah.* Usually this is translated "Law," but the English translation is scarcely an adequate equivalent, for actually *Torah* means "teaching" or "instruction" which God gives his people either in the form of statutes (law) or the lessons of history (narrative). As can be seen from the above summary of the Pentateuch, the Law is really legislation clasped in the framework of historical traditions. Judaism of the late Old Testament period developed the dogma that the Law in its entirety (including even the account of Moses' death and burial!) was delivered by God to Moses. The belief was accepted by early Christians (see Matthew 8:4; Luke 24:27) and persisted in the Christian Church down to the modern era.

If the "Five Books of Moses" were truly of Mosaic composition, our approach to the story of the Exodus would necessarily have to begin with the consideration that this literature comes to us from an eyewitness, one who was actually involved in the events of the thirteenth century B.C. However, it is now the unanimous verdict of critical biblical scholarship that these traditions *in their written form* come from a much later period. Space does not permit us to treat the fascinating romance of Pentateuchal criticism that began when early rabbis first called attention to passages which seemed to presuppose a time much later than Moses, like the account of his death or passages like Genesis 12:6. It is sufficient to say that scholars now believe that the Pentateuch, rather than being of Mosaic authorship, is actually a "mosaic" of several documents blended together editorially. The earliest document, to which the symbol "J" is given, was composed in the Southern Kingdom, Judah, sometime after the death of Solomon—perhaps about 850 B.C. A century later, about 750 B.C., another document was composed in the Northern Kingdom, Ephraim or Israel. This document, embodying many of the same traditions, is designated by the symbol "E." Sometime after the fall of the Northern Kingdom in 722 B.C., these two documents were combined by a Judean editor in such a manner that the material of both was preserved in so far as possible, even though this resulted in repetitions and inconsistencies. Then about the middle of the seventh century B.C. a law code was composed that became the basis of King Josiah's Reform in Judah in 621 B.C., just on the eve of the collapse of the nation (see II Kings 22-23). The nucleus of the present book of Deuteronomy evidently was officially recognized at that time, and all the literature of this period which was imprinted with the Deuteronomic viewpoint is called "D." Later on, after the Jewish people had returned from Babylonian exile and had compensated for their loss of political independence by establishing a religious community, a group of priests in about 500 B.C. composed a religious history of the Jews, giving due stress to priestly interests such as rituals, genealogies, Sabbath observance, and so on. This Priestly Code is known as "P." Finally, in about 400 B.C Jewish editors blended "P" with both "JE" and "D" to produce the Pentateuch as we now have it. Since the final editors lived in the priestly community of Judaism, it was natural for them to make the P Code the framework into which the earlier sources were inserted. We can visualize the result by imagining what would be involved in weaving together the Four Gospels of the New Testament in such a manner that virtually nothing was lost.[4]

It is important to recognize that the above analysis of the Pentateuch is a hypothesis based on literary criticism. These sources have been found only within the confines of the Pentateuch; they have not been found by archaeologists in search

[4] Interestingly, in the middle of the second century A.D. Tatian did this in his *Diatessaron.* Like the final editors of the Pentateuch, he made the last and latest Gospel, John, the framework of his composition. Like the Pentateuch, too, the result was a kind of literary patchwork in which appeared repetitions, inconsistencies, and differences of theological expression.

of ancient documents. Like all scientific hypotheses, this one is subject to continuing examination in the light of the evidence. But up to the present this hypothesis, perhaps slightly modified, has been generally accepted as the best explanation of the problems of the Pentateuch. We do encounter repetitions, as for instance in the two stories of the Creation (Genesis 1:1-2:4a and 2:4a-25) and the two versions of the Ten Commandments (Exodus 20 and Deuteronomy 5). We find numerous inconsistencies, as for instance in the Flood story where J and P materials have been dovetailed. And we encounter differences of style, vocabulary, and religious expression, as may be seen from a careful comparison of the narrative of Genesis 1 with the picturesque story found in Genesis 2 and 3. In the light of the cumulative evidence, the old dogma of the Mosaic authorship of the Pentateuch has to be scrapped.[5]

How the Past Speaks to Us

Several conclusions are evident from this critical study of the Old Testament. In the first place, we are dealing with documents which are considerably removed, in point of time, from the period of the events described. The traditions about the beginnings of Israel were passed down orally for centuries before they were first reduced to writing by J and E. The situation would be comparable if we had no early records concerning the migration of the Pilgrims to America, but had to rely solely upon traditions (poems, legends, anecdotes, and so on) passed down orally to the historian of the twentieth century. Even when we consider the remarkable power of memory of the ancient Semites, we must make due allowance for the fact that the traditions come to us through folk channels in which the interest was in the telling of the story, not

---

[5] A readable account of the history of Pentateuchal criticism and an outline of the Documentary Hypothesis is given in E. R. Trattner, *Unravelling the Book of Books* (Scribner, 1931).

the communication of accurate factual information. In this connection, scholars often point out that narratives written down by an eyewitness of the events, like the account of David's domestic affairs in II Samuel 9-20, usually give a comparatively straightforward and unadorned presentation, while narratives that are dependent upon an oral tradition are replete with miracle tales, as in the case of the Elijah-Elisha cycle of stories. This does not mean that we should dismiss the miracle faith as an invention of the popular imagination, but it does mean that we should study it in terms of the folk mind in which it took shape and evolved.

Again, we must be clear about the attitude toward the past reflected in these documents. We may be sure that J and E, the earliest historians, did not write down the traditions of Israel because of a curiosity about what actually happened "back there" in the days of long ago. We can hardly imagine these writers, after the manner of modern historians, carefully checking all the available sources and objectively weighing the evidence in order that the past might be reconstructed accurately. This was not the Hebrew way of writing history. For these writers the past was not so much "back there" as it was a present reality in the memory of a people, giving meaning to daily events and casting its light ahead into the future. In other words, we are dealing with what Nels Ferré whimsically described in a university chapel sermon as "the is-ness of the was," the presentness of the past in the life of a historical community. Each of us knows how within himself he bears his own past. This past is not written down in a diary, or represented by photograph albums containing pictures of what actually took place. Rather, it is held in the remembrance of the present, thereby giving each of us a unique outlook upon the actions of the day and the aspirations for tomorrow. Likewise in the case of Israel we are dealing primarily with *remembered* events. The traditions of the past were preserved in the oral memory and eventually written down in various documents, not because of historical curiosity but because the meaning of these events was a vital part of the life of each generation. Through the remembrance of the past God continued to speak in the present (see Amos 2:9-16; Jeremiah 2:1-19). So, for instance, the annual observance of the ancient rite of the Passover kept alive and fresh the memory of the Exodus.

The fact that the past is not treated in textbook fashion helps to explain something which bewilders us about the composition of the Pentateuch. What led the editors to piece together various documents in disregard of plagiarizing others' work and forging Moses' name, and above all in seeming unawareness of the inconsistencies resulting from such a "scissors-and-paste" method? The answer is that writing under a pseudonym was a widespread and respectable practice in antiquity, and "authorship rights" was hardly a consideration when authors and editors were unconcerned about their personal autograph. While the editors of the Pentateuch were probably aware of inconsistencies resulting from their work, their governing consideration was not logical consistency but the preservation of the tradition in all its richness. These writings, in other words, must be understood primarily as a continuing proclamation of Israel's faith. And since all generations were linked together in the chain of witnesses, the voices of the past were summoned to testify in the present as the traditions were subjected to a fresh editorial revision. The incorporation of J, E, D, and P into a single work is perhaps analogous to our hymnbooks in which hymns of different ages are conserved and used, despite differences among them, as witness of a common faith.

Finally, all these sources are unanimous in their emphasis upon miracle. Obviously there are real differences between the various writings of the Pentateuch. J and E seem to reflect the prophetic viewpoint of the ninth and eighth centuries B.C., D seems to represent an alliance of prophets and priests, and P definitely views the past through the eyes of priests. J and P begin with the Creation, E starts with Abraham, and

D is concerned primarily with the Mosaic period. Each writing reflects different historical circumstances that prevailed at the time of its composition and employs a characteristic style, vocabulary, and theological language. But despite these and other differences all the sources agree that miracle stories are indispensable in the proclamation of Israel's faith.

Moreover, if we were to pursue our investigation beyond the *written* sources of the Pentateuch back into the period of the *oral* transmission of the faith, we would discover that the experience of miracle lies at the very heart of the tradition. In recent years a great deal of light has been thrown on this point by a school of study known as "Form Criticism." [6] Accepting the basic outline of the Documentary Hypothesis, these scholars have attempted to study the preliterary forms into which the tradition was cast and the life situations of the community in which the small fragments were remembered, long before they were incorporated into the literary cycles of J and E. They have isolated certain units, now embedded in the literary strata of the Pentateuch, and have found after careful analysis that they bear the marks of being heirlooms handed down from an ancient time, shortly after the period of the Exodus. As an example we may cite the confession of faith which, according to Deuteronomy 26:5-10 (cf. 6:20-24), the worshiper makes at the sanctuary in connection with his offering of the first fruits:

> A nomad Aramean was my father; he went down to Egypt to reside there, with a small company, and there he became a nation, great, mighty, and numerous; the Egyptians treated us harshly, oppressed us, and imposed hard servitude upon us; but we cried to the Lord, the God of our fathers, and the Lord heard our cry, and seeing our affliction, our toil and our oppression, *the Lord brought us out of Egypt with a strong hand and an outstretched arm, with great terrors, signs, and portents;* and bringing us to this place, he gave us this

---

[6] See chapter 7 for the application of this method to the New Testament. This approach was first used in Old Testament study and was known as *Gattungkritik,* the study of the *Gattung* or unit as to its "form" and history.

land, a land flowing with milk and honey. And now see, I have brought the first of the produce of the soil, which thou, O Lord, hast given me.

This ancient cultic confession is really a recitation of the "mighty acts" of God which brought the Israelite community into being and which were remembered by succeeding generations as the basis of the community's ongoing life. A narrative like J is actually only an elaboration of the theme of *Heilsgeschichte* or the Drama of God's Redemptive Acts—a theme that was a part of the oral tradition from an early time.

Of course, this study of the folk mind of Israel, aided by the comparative examination of other folk traditions, has helped us to understand how the tradition was embellished as the years went by. It would be rash, however, to assert that miracle stories were foreign to the authentic tradition of Israel or that they were mere inventions of popular imagination. On the contrary, both a literary examination of the Pentateuch and a form-critical study of the oral transmission of Israel's faith lead to the conclusion that the experience of miracle was native to Israel's faith.

The Significance of the Exodus

We have attempted to prepare for the consideration of our question by recognizing that the Pentateuch does not provide us with an on-the-scene report of events, and that the motive for remembering and eventually writing these stories was not the historian's desire to produce an accurate textbook of history. Now we must face the central issue: what is the nature of the miracle faith which was stated anew as each generation retold the stories, and as various editors gave the tradition fresh statement by reworking the literary sources?

The book of Genesis gives us the impression that God's special action in history began with his calling Abraham to leave Mesopotamia and to go out by faith into the Land of Promise

(Genesis 12:1; cf. Hebrews 11:8). Thus the God who called Israel out of Egypt is, as the documents of the Pentateuch testify, "the God of the fathers": Abraham, Isaac, and Jacob. In a sense this is profoundly true. God's deliverance of the Israelites from Egypt was preceded by his providential guidance of their ancestors in the past. This claim, however, was made *in retrospect,* just as one who is called into Christian service looks back from the standpoint of faith and sees that in his earlier years God was guiding and preparing him for his vocation. Therefore the prevailing interpretation of the book of Genesis, including the "call" of Abraham, is probably a projection backward of the meaning discerned in later events of Israel's history, especially the Exodus. We can understand how the ancient traditions have been treated if we imagine American historians beginning with an interpretation of American history derived, say, from the Revolutionary War and, by backward projection, viewing everything from Columbus' discovery of America on as preparation for the signing of the Declaration of Independence.

The stories of the patriarchal age are folk stories which were preserved, in the first instance, for their enthralling interest, not for their historical value. Admittedly, they contain a measure of historical accuracy, as archaeologists are now pointing out. Excavations at Ur, Abraham's native city, and other places in the Near East have enabled us to see the patriarchal narratives against the background of ancient civilization and the movement of population across the coveted arc of land which has been called the "Fertile Crescent." [7] Abraham's migration from Ur to Haran and from Haran into Palestine was undoubtedly a phase of a great movement of population which occurred sometime between 2000 and 1700 B.C. The discovery of the names Abram and Jacob in the records of these peoples clearly indicates that Semitic elements

[7] The "Fertile Crescent" is J. H. Breasted's designation of the fertile strip of land which skirts the Mediterranean coast (Palestine-Syria) and bends around, following the valley of the Tigris-Euphrates down to the Persian Gulf.

were involved. But the question as to what actually motivated Abraham to go into Palestine cannot be answered merely by reading the story in Genesis 12. We must remember that the patriarchal traditions of Genesis are governed by a religious view which, properly speaking, came from the period of Moses and later. The light of God's revelation to Moses and the prophets shone backward into the period of the patriarchs and even into the mythological period of "prehistory" (Genesis 1-11). Thus J projects the worship of God under the special name "Yahweh" back to the time of Adam's grandson (Genesis 4:26), contrary to E and P, which emphasize the special revelation in the Mosaic period (see Exodus 3:14-15[E]; 6:3[P]).[8]

Turning to the period of the Exodus, immediately the question arises: why should the Exodus have this pivotal significance in Israel's faith? Viewed by itself the flight of a handful of slave-laborers from the borderland of Egypt is nothing extraordinary. To be sure, the book of Exodus in its present form gives us the impression that the presence of Hebrews in Egypt constituted a real political threat to the country and that their petition to leave caused reverberations throughout the land. Again we must remember, however, that these events are described in documents of a much later period, and from an Israelite point of view. Unquestionably the historical situation was considerably magnified in the folk tradition owing to the profound significance of the Exodus in Israel's faith. In Egyptian records of the period the event is passed over in complete silence. We learn from Egyptian sources that it was customary for Egyptian officials to admit Asiatics into the Delta region (Goshen) especially during a time of famine, and moreover we are told that pharaohs like Rameses II used *'Apiru* (evidently the Egyptian equivalent of "Hebrews") to

---

[8] The J source employs the word "Yahweh" throughout the book of Genesis, while E and P refrain from using the special name until the time of Moses. This alternation in the use of divine names was one of the chief clues which led to the unraveling of the sources of the Pentateuch.

do hard labor on public projects. But the flight of this particular group of Hebrews was, from the Egyptian standpoint, an event of such minor significance that it did not even receive official mention, so far as we know. This is no argument against the historicity of the Exodus. It is only an indication of the different standpoints from which the event was viewed. To Egyptians this was only a minor border incident; to the Hebrews involved it was a "mighty act" of Yahweh.

This difference in standpoint should warn us immediately against assuming that the extraordinary wonders and signs attending the Exodus were proofs which compelled people to acknowledge the power of Yahweh. Today many people suppose that the performance of miracles in the biblical period is an argument which should convince all rational people of the truth of the Bible. How could these marvelous things have occurred, it is asked, without the supernatural intervention of God? If, however, a modern skeptic had been on hand at the time, he would not necessarily have seen what the Israelites saw, and certainly he would not have found proofs that compelled his reason to acknowledge the redemptive activity of God in history. The miracle of the Red Sea was no proof to hostile Egyptians or to ficklehearted Israelites who longed for the "fleshpots" of Egypt. But to those who saw *in faith*, it was the assurance that God was with them, fighting for them against impossible odds. This is the conviction expressed in an ancient scrap of poetry which scholars believe was composed by one who witnessed the cataclysm of the Red Sea:

> Sing ye to the Lord, for he hath triumphed gloriously,
> The horse and his rider hath he thrown into the sea!
>
> —Exodus 15:21

Here we are up against the tantalizing problem of election, the mystery that some men see the action of God while other rational men, beholding the same outward manifestations of his sovereignty, are spiritually blind. We cannot properly discuss the question of what happened at the Red Sea until we have grappled with this more basic issue, for it is commonplace knowledge that one's attitude makes all the difference in what he sees. Israel's election consisted in the gift of spiritual sight which enabled this people to trace the working of God's hand in human affairs. Why *they* saw God's action in history, when others about them did not, can be explained only by saying that God caused them to see—which, of course, is no explanation at all. But apart from this spiritual discernment of the chosen people we are at a loss to understand why Israelites saw the hand of God everywhere, even in things we would regard as commonplace or capable of some scientific explanation.

Consider, for instance, the miracle of the Red Sea. For many people the biblical story has lost its glamour because scholars have pointed out that: (a) the body of water referred to is not the Red Sea but the shallow "sea of reeds" or Marsh Sea further north; (b) the miracle occurred during a violent storm when the wind reached such a velocity that the shallow waters were temporarily held back, as the J narrative suggests ("a strong east wind," Exodus 14:21); and (c) this "natural event" has been witnessed in more recent times in this area. This very plausible theory fails to explain the perfect timing: the strange coincidence of the natural phenomenon with the emergency of the fugitive Hebrews. (Compare the modern exodus from Dunkirk!) But even if it could be proved beyond a shadow of doubt that such a natural phenomenon actually underlies the biblical tradition we would not necessarily arrive at an understanding of the biblical meaning of the event. Suppose, says the skeptic, the Hebrews *were* lucky enough to get across the Marsh Sea during a wind storm. So what? After all, nature is full of freakish things, as any modern scientist knows. So after discussing what might or might not have happened we come again to the stubborn fact that what to one person may be a sign of God's providence to another may be interpreted quite differently, depending on his sight, his perspective upon history. This leads one scholar to state that "there is no Miracle except to the eye that perceives it: we might add that to the eye which perceives it, it ceases in one sense to be a 'Miracle' at all," for all things are touched by the hand of God.[9]

The Role of Moses

In any discussion of the Exodus, and the extraordinary signs and wonders that accompanied it, we must begin with the supreme miracle of Israel's election and the unique outlook of this people upon history. Moreover, we must give due attention to the role of Moses, whose call is inseparably related to the call of Israel. To the historian Moses presents a tremendous problem, a problem greater than the much discussed issue of the "historical Jesus." Anything said about Moses must be qualified by the caveat that his career antedates the earliest written documents of the Old Testament by at least four centuries, and that he is known to us only in the framework of the faith of the Israelite community.

The account of Moses' call is given in the vivid narrative found in Exodus 3. Moses was tending the flocks of his Midianite father-in-law, so the story goes, when he came to the slopes of Horeb, otherwise known as Sinai. There, while he was brooding over the plight of his fellow men in Egypt, "the Angel of the Lord" appeared to him in a flame of fire out of the midst of a bush. Knowing that we are dealing with a story which in its written form is much later than Moses' time, and knowing furthermore that in the Old Testament faith finds expression in the rich imagery of oriental symbolism, we should not fall into the error of rationalizing this as a portrayal of something which took place objectively, as though the burning bush could have been pictured with a movie camera or the Voice recorded by a phonograph had someone been around with those modern instruments. To ask the question "Did this

---

[9] W. J. Phythian-Adams, *The Call of Israel* (Oxford, 1934), p. 177.

happen just as it is described?" betrays our inability to under stand the Hebraic mode of thinking, which makes no sharp dis tinction between what we would call the inner and the outer the subjective and the objective, the world of imagination and the realm of hard fact. To us of the West these are two separate dimensions; to the oriental mind, however, they blend together as one. Therefore, literalism kills the meaning of the story. Of course God did not actually reveal himself in fire; but how could the truth be stated more vividly that God, though hidden from mortal sight, makes known his glory in commonplace situations? Likewise, God did not literally carry on a conversation with Moses; but is it not profoundly true that this dialogue has been repeated again and again when men have encountered God? Just as the poet addresses himself to the poet within us, so the narrative of Exodus 3 speaks from faith to faith.

It is important to recognize that God's word came to Moses in a moment when he was acutely conscious of the historical situation of his people in Egypt. We cannot properly consider Moses as a mystic who had a private experience of God's presence out in the silence and solitude of the desert. In Moses' case, as indeed with all the prophets, our attention fastens first upon the historical situation in Egypt which was integrally related to what was taking place in the ancient world during the second millenium before Christ. Moses' role was not that of telling his countrymen about a private religious experience; it was, rather, that of mediating to them the meaning of a specific historical crisis in which they were all involved. He was, of course, the leader who took the initiative in setting his people free; but, like the prophets, he was also the divine spokesman who interpreted the signs of the times. In this sense Hosea is correct in saying: "By a prophet the Lord brought Israel out of Egypt" (12:13).

God's revelation to Moses, then, came as the interpretation of a historical situation: Israel's bondage in Egypt. One conviction dominates all the narratives of the Pentateuch: the completely wonderful outgoing of God's love toward Israel, his stooping down mercifully to rescue his "son" from the house of bondage (Exodus 4:22). "And the Lord said, I have surely seen the affliction of my people which are in Egypt, and have heard their cry by reason of their taskmasters; for I know their sorrows, and I am come down to deliver them. . ." (Exodus 3:7-8). What made the Exodus crucial for Israel was not the bare events, like the escape from Egypt or the crossing of the Marsh Sea, but the meaning revealed in those events. To the outsider the Exodus was only a phase of the continual shifting of population in the ancient world; to Israel, however, this was the event which revealed God as Lord and Redeemer. Looking out from this standpoint of faith, miracles were seen on every hand, giving assurance of his mercy, his protection, his guidance, and his faithfulness.

Did the Miracles Happen?

Up to this point we have said that the supreme miracle was wrought by God in history: his creation of a people to be his own in a special sense.

> I will take you as my own people, and I will be your God, and you shall know that it is I, the Lord your God, who shall free you from the burdens of the Egyptians.
>
> —Exodus 6:7

It is wrong to detach a miracle story from this context of faith and study it in isolation. The miracle stories, collectively and individually, must be viewed in the light of the central affirmation of faith: God's call of Israel. The deliverance of the infant Moses from the pharaoh's massacre, the plagues in Egypt, the crossing of the Marsh Sea, the pillar of cloud and fire, the sending of the manna and quails, the striking of the rock to obtain water, the defeat of Amalek—each one of these incidents, viewed from the standpoint of faith, was an assurance or sign of the saving activity of God in the history of his people, Israel. We could go so far as to say that even though any one of these stories could be shown on historical grounds to be an inaccurate or legendary account of the actual situation, the truth of the miracle tradition as a whole would not be affected in the slightest. For it is precisely the central element of the tradition, namely the call of Israel, which lies beyond the scope of historical or scientific inquiry. Israel's faith did not rest merely upon the Exodus and accompanying incidents, which are open to historical or archaeological study; rather, Israel's faith rested upon the experience that the Exodus was *God's redemptive act.* A people had been created by God's sovereign activity in history! This was the miracle that "happened."

We insist, however, upon pressing the question as to whether a particular episode, which illustrates this central truth, actually took place. This is a matter for discussion in terms of historical criticism. For instance, the story about the infant Moses floating down the Nile in a basket is so obviously based on familiar legends that we may conclude that here the tradition has been embellished by a folk motif.[10] Even so, the folk story in this case expresses the religious truth that God's redemptive purpose was at work even before Moses' later awareness of it. In the providence of God the evil design of the pharaoh actually became the means whereby Egyptians trained the future leader of the Hebrews! Similarly, the stories concerning Moses' wonder-working rod (for example, Exodus 7:10-13) betray the interests of the folk mind. But in every case these popular superstitions not only add vividness to the story but also imaginatively express the truth of God's sovereignty over the priestly wizardry of Egypt and over all powers that would oppose the accomplishment of his purpose in history.

Other stories may be imaginative exaggerations of natural occurrences which attended the Exodus, the wilderness wan-

---

[10] The birth story of Moses strikingly resembles the legend of the famous Sargon, king of Akkad. See G. A. Barton, *Archaeology and the Bible,* 7th ed. (American Sunday School Union), p. 375.

dering, and the invasion of Canaan. Some scholars believe that most of the plagues can be explained on the basis of a natural catastrophe: the inundation of the Nile River. We have already noticed that some explain the crossing of the Red Sea in terms of a violent windstorm which occurred at the critical moment; others theorize that a volcanic explosion caused the sea-bottom to be raised up and produced other extraordinary phenomena, such as the pillar of cloud and fire.[11] The quails in the wilderness present no great problem, for we are told that during the course of their migration northward in the spring they are numerous in the area and, when exhausted, can easily be caught. Similarly the "manna" from heaven may have been a honeylike substance from a kind of tamarisk tree that grows in the region (Arabs still call it *mun*). And so on. These "explanations" should be taken with a critical grain of salt. Historical criticism impresses us with the difficulty of reaching back through the haze of the oral tradition and reconstructing what actually happened. It also warns us of the impossibility of sharply separating fact from interpretation in a literature concerned primarily with proclaiming Israel's faith.

Whatever natural events accompanied the Exodus we may be sure of this: the book of Exodus is not concerned primarily with telling about freakish natural events which took place in seeming disruption of what we would call "natural law." These stories were remembered not because men were interested in nature as such, but because nature also manifested the glory of the God of history. We find it difficult to understand the Bible on this matter because today nature is something we look at "out there," something we control by means of our science, something which is indifferent to the history in which men are involved. According to the Bible, however, nature is

---

11 On the assumption that Sinai at this time was an active volcano, W. J. Phythian-Adams (*op. cit.*, pp. 137-172) rather fancifully accounts for the plagues, the cataclysm of the Red Sea, the pillar of cloud and fire, and the awe-inspiring phenomena experienced at the sacred mountain.

involved in history because God is Lord of both nature and history. Nature is, as it were, a mirror which reflects the meaning of man's life in history. This is the case in the book of Exodus. Stories which to us seem to describe abnormal natural events are really manifestations of the supreme miracle: God's saving activity in the history of his people, Israel. God is described as fighting for Israel by using the forces of nature to protect and sustain his people (Exodus 14:25). Here is an interpretation of history which recognizes that the course of events is affected by something more than natural or human factors.

Is this miracle faith true? Did God speak to Moses and did he lead Israel out of Egypt "with a strong hand"? This question, as we have said, lies beyond the boundaries of natural science and historical inquiry. It can be answered only by the decision of faith. As Alan Richardson reminds us, however, any denial of the miracle faith of the Bible will be made from the standpoint of a rival interpretation of the meaning of man's life, and that interpretation itself will be based on faith, not on an impartial and neutral study of the facts.[12] Historical criticism has clarified our problem by liberating us from the false notion that the Bible is an accurate and infallible record of the past, and by helping us to understand what the men of the Bible were saying when they used the language of miracle. It is no longer necessary to choose between either the Bible or the assured conclusions of the natural sciences. The alternative is the biblical understanding of man's history or some other view. Christianity takes its stand upon the conviction that God manifested his love and purpose in that unique series of historical events which began with the Exodus and culminated in the coming of Jesus Christ. This is the miracle which "happened"; and this is the abiding experience of the miracle stories. For in so far as, by faith, we look out upon history from this biblical standpoint, our eyes are opened

---

[12] *Christian Apologetics* (Harper, 1947), p. 173.

to behold the mystery and majesty of God's redemptive love. The miracle stories then occasion no difficulty; in fact, they express the faith of one who sees all of life touched by divine miracle. As Elizabeth Barrett Browning writes:

> Earth's crammed with heaven,
> And every common bush afire with God;
> But only he who sees takes off his shoes.

4

Israel Comes of Age

WE HAVE ALL had the frustrating experience of being absorbed in a radio serial, only to hear an announcer cut into the story at the moment of greatest expectancy with the abrupt announcement: "Listen tomorrow, same time, same station, for the next exciting episode." We have a similar feeling when we come to the end of the first unit of the Old Testament, the Pentateuch. To be sure, the Jewish Church has said that the Law stands alone in sacred grandeur, like the holy Mount Sinai itself. Ever since this literature was canonized (declared sacred Scripture) in about 400 B.C. it has been first in the hearts of the Jewish people, so much so that all other literature has been regarded as mere commentary on its meaning. Nevertheless it is evident that the Pentateuch by itself is incomplete. It breaks off at the moment of greatest expectancy in the movement of the sacred drama. The book of Numbers carries the story up to the time when the Israelites were poised on the east bank of the Jordan River, waiting for their great "D-Day" to arrive. Deuteronomy, we have noticed, purports to be Moses' final briefing of the people. Everything is in readiness for crossing over to possess the land which, according to the book of Genesis, God had promised to give his chosen people in order that they might fulfill their destiny in history.

The story is continued in a series of historical books found in the second unit of the Old Testament: the Prophets. In the Hebrew Bible the canon of the Prophets, officially recognized as sacred Scripture in about 200 B.C., is subdivided as follows:

FORMER PROPHETS:	Joshua, Judges, I and II Samuel, I and II Kings
LATTER PROPHETS:	Isaiah, Jeremiah, Ezekiel, the "Twelve" (minor prophets).[1]

In this chapter we shall be concerned with the "Former Prophets." These books carry the story, which broke off abruptly at the end of the Pentateuch, from the invasion of Canaan to the fall of the nation. To fully appreciate the story we must view this cavalcade of events against the background of the larger international scene of population movements and imperial expansion in the Fertile Crescent.[2]

The book of Joshua describes the conquest of Canaan under the military leadership of Joshua, a conquest which was providentially possible because of the weakness of Egypt and the absence of interference from Mesopotamia. The book of Judges describes various episodes that took place during the period of the settlement in Canaan, when champions or "judges" arose from time to time to defend the cause of Israel against their enemies. In this period the greatest threat came from the Philistines (see the Samson legends), a people who entered Palestine as a result of a population upheaval in the Aegean world about 1200 B.C. and who by 1050 B.C. had expanded from their base on the coastal plain throughout much of Palestine. The books of Samuel describe the founding of the Hebrew monarchy in this crisis, and tell how David was able both to push the Philistines back against the Mediterranean Sea and to build up a vast, though temporary, Israelite empire. Finally, the books of Kings, after describing Solomon in all his imperial glory, tell how the empire fell apart after

---

1 Notice that in the New Testament (for instance, Matthew 5:17) "the Law and the Prophets" is a designation of the two major units of Jewish Scripture.

2 The fascinating account is admirably presented by T. H. Robinson in *A History of Israel* (Oxford, 1932), Vol. I: "From the Exodus to the Fall of Jerusalem, 586 B.C."

Solomon's death, being split into two rival kingdoms which continued their troubled independent existence until first the Northern Kingdom was destroyed by Assyrian invasion (722 B.C.) and later the Southern Kingdom was conquered by Babylonians who carried away the cream of the population into exile (586 B.C.). Thus these books deal with Israel's coming to the maturity of nationhood through the acquisition of a land, the establishment of self-government, and participation in the political rivalries of the ancient world.

The Immorality of Scripture

The modern reader finds this phase of the biblical drama very difficult. This is not because the books present us with a dry-as-dust chronicle of the past. Actually all the narratives are governed by a religious theme, especially as a result of Deuteronomic editing of the traditions. Nor is it because the stories are uninteresting. With the exception of a few passages —like Joshua's allotment of the tribal territories or the specifications of Solomon's Temple—these stories are vivid and exciting and have provided the dramatic motifs for artistic works such as *Samson and Delilah*, Browning's *Saul*, and Mendelssohn's *Elijah*. The real obstacle is that measured by the standards of our age many of the stories seem to be so crudely primitive, so downright immoral. We find it hard to justify Joshua's merciless annihilation of whole cities to the last man, woman, and child in the name of the Lord. The Song of Deborah (Judges 5) seems to express fierce delight in the hammer-murder of the Canaanite Sisera by the hand of a woman, the pathos of which is heightened by the description of a soldier's mother waiting for a son who would never return. Samson's amours and exploits among the Philistines make interesting reading but seem no more inspiring than the feats of Tarzan. And what can one say in defense of the prophet Samuel who, when Saul showed mercy on an Amalekite king, hunted down the enemy in the sanctuary itself and "hewed

Agag in pieces before the Lord"? The list of objectionable passages is a long one. Moreover, our problem is accentuated by the consideration that when Jesus said he came not to destroy but to fulfill the "Prophets," his words had reference to the whole prophetic canon, including these objectionable books of the Former Prophets.

Our problem is not a new one. Actually it is as old as Christianity itself. The Christian Church treasured the Scriptures of the Jewish people not because of their lofty moral character, but because of the conviction that the sacred drama inaugurated at the time of the call of Israel had come to its climax in the career of Jesus Christ. A serious attempt to discard the Old Testament in the second century was put down as heretical for this very reason, as we shall see in chapter 7. Nevertheless, intelligent Christians who came into the Church from a Gentile background continued to find many passages of the Old Testament puzzling and repulsive. This was true above all in the case of Origen of Alexandria, a keen Christian thinker who wrote many sermons and commentaries on biblical books in the first half of the third century A.D. As Fosdick says: "No modern ever recognized more clearly or handled more frankly than he did the fact that the Old Testament contains ideas, laws, customs, and ideals which cannot stand the test of developed thought and morals." [3]

The ancient way out of this dilemma, and one which was vigorously defended by Origen and his school, was through allegory. God has put many puzzling and seemingly naughty things into Scripture, said Origen, for the purpose of stimulating the intelligent mind to look for the allegorical meaning, the mystic significance hidden beneath the surface of the letter. Perhaps Origen's most famous example of allegory is his treatment of the story of the Israelite spies who were given hospitality by a prostitute, Rahab (Joshua 2). Taken by itself the story is not particularly edifying, but Origen ingeniously

[3] *The Modern Use of the Bible* (Macmillan, 1929), p. 74. All of chapter 3 is valuable in this connection.

extracted from it a profound meaning: the red cord which Rahab was instructed to hang from her window represents the saving blood of Christ; and the fact that this signal was to guarantee protection to Rahab's household indicates that only in the household of the faithful, the Church, is there salvation through Christ's blood. Just as the Greeks found Greek philosophy in the Homeric literature by allegorizing the shocking loves and quarrels of the gods, just as Hindus found in the stories of Lord Krishna's promiscuous relations with the cowgirls an allegory of the soul's longing for union with Brahma, so also Christians were able to satisfy their conscience and intelligence by seeking out the hidden sense, moral and spiritual, which is veiled in the figurative language of Scripture.[4]

This solution of the problem satisfied the brilliant mind of Augustine (see his *Confessions* VI, 4) and dominated most of the medieval period. It had the advantage of enabling intelligent people to revere the Scriptures as the Word of God and to make the Bible relevant for their living. Christian allegorists rightly recognized that the Bible is a unity, and that the Christian must interpret the Old Testament in the light of the New. Moreover, their flexible and imaginative treatment of Scripture is a pleasing relief from the wooden literalism which too often plagues the Church. We, however, can no longer use this method of interpretation in good conscience. For one thing, allegory is really a disguised form of biblical literalism, the assumption being that if God dictated the words they must have a hidden divine meaning. This view of the content of revelation is no longer tenable in the light of historical criticism and the best Christian theology. Moreover, it can scarcely be denied that allegory actually reads meaning into the biblical text, meaning which was never intended, as in the case of Origen's allegory concerning Rahab. Using this method, the

[4] The Song of Songs presents an illustration of allegorical interpretation. These sensuous love lyrics were given a place in Scripture because Jews found in them an allegory of God's love for Israel, and because Christians found in them an allegory of Christ's love for his Church.

Bible can be made to say anything. We know too well that many biblical interpreters of our day are ventriloquists, as it were, who cleverly project their own words into Scripture and give the impression that their opinions are the Word of God. Thus it has become proverbial that "the Bible proves anything." From this kind of fanciful and subjective interpretation we seek to be delivered. The prerequisite for hearing God's Word in the Bible, rather than our own prejudice, is the recovery of the historical sense of a given passage of Scripture.

This modern attitude toward the Bible has been profoundly influenced by Luther and Calvin. Both of these Reformers condemned allegory in the strongest terms. They never intended that the right of every individual to read the Bible should mean that the individual has the right to stand in judgment upon Scripture or to make the Bible accord with his own private interpretation; rather, they insisted that every individual must make a *personal response* to God's Word which is contained in Scripture. He must hear the Word that stands in judgment upon him. Therefore the Reformers insisted upon recovering the one original meaning of a Scriptural passage and letting the Bible speak for itself. Luther, for instance, wrote these words which might have been written by any modern biblical critic:

> It is necessary if one will understand the prophecy, to know what the situation was in the land, what events were happening, what the people thought, what the relationships were which they sustained to their neighbors, friends, and foes, and especially what their attitude was toward their God and toward his prophets.[5]

Biblical criticism of the nineteenth and twentieth centuries has contributed immeasurably to the fulfillment of this ambition which the Reformers could never attain completely due to the limitations of their period. We can now read the Bible with a fairly thorough understanding of the human sit-

---

[5] Quoted by Fosdick, *op. cit.*, p. 87.

uation in which men heard God's Word and can come much closer to a knowledge of the original meaning of the biblical writer. But this knowledge has only magnified our problem: how can we read this literature for our inspiration and profit when so many passages contain coarse ideas and repulsive immoralities?

For the modern age the problem is made even more acute for another reason: we tend to identify morality with religion, or, more accurately, modern man's faith is devotion to certain moral values. Matthew Arnold's definition of religion as "morality tinged with emotion" has won the assent of many Americans who have drifted away from Christian theology, but have adhered to its moral by-products. Many have said that their "Christianity" consists of being a good sport, giving the other fellow a "break," and being a respectable citizen who lives according to the Golden Rule. Consequently, in colloquial usage "Christian" has come to mean "a decent, civilized, or presentable person" (see *Webster's Collegiate Dictionary*). Indeed, some suggest that the solution to the world's problems lies in burying the dead theologies which in the past have led to dissension, and spreading abroad a religion of kindness and goodwill. Whoever wrote the following words has given simple expression to the prevailing moralism:

> I have no need of any creeds,
> They but confuse the mind,
> For all the creed this old world needs,
> Is that of being kind.

Having this attitude, many people adopt a kind of pick-and-choose approach to the Bible, especially the Old Testament. The Latter Prophets seem to talk the modern language, inasmuch as they thundered against the social vices of their day and demanded social justice. But the books of Joshua, Judges, Samuel, and Kings are frowned upon because of their shocking barbarism.

Lest there be any misunderstanding of what follows, let us

recognize that the Bible gives a certain support to the concern for "moral values." In other religions of antiquity, religion did not necessarily produce the fruits of ethical conduct. The gods were often regarded as capricious beings who had to be propitiated by the proper performance of the right ceremonies. This view, which reduced religion to a form of magic, was vehemently attacked by the prophets who proclaimed God's sovereignty over the whole of life, especially in the area of human relationships (see Amos 5:21-24; Isaiah 1:1-20). Obedience to God, they said, does not mean the performance of magical rituals or the visiting of sacred shrines; rather it means caring for the orphan and widow in their affliction and ordering the society of Israel in such a manner that every individual may have a place of dignity in the community. Thus in Israel's faith *religion and morality were inseparable.* But to say that they were inseparable is quite another thing than saying that they were identical. A morally good person is not necessarily a God-fearing man (he may be like Oliver Alden in George Santayana's *The Last Puritan*) and, vice versa, a God-fearing man may be "immoral" in the eyes of his contemporaries.[6] Therefore we must seek for an understanding of the biblical message which on the one hand does not deny its social relevance, and on the other hand does not leave us with a watered-down moralism. Specifically, we must inquire into the meaning of "faith" and "sin," two words whose usage is controlled by the basic concept of the Bible: the Covenant.

The Faith of the Covenant

The unfortunate translation "Testament," with which we are familiar in the titles of the two major sections of the Christian Bible, conceals from many of us the underlying conception of "covenant," which is a more accurate rendering of the Hebrew and Greek words. One theme runs throughout the

[6] See the essay by S. Kierkegaard, *Fear and Trembling,* which illustrates this point by a kind of poetic treatment of the story of Abraham's sacrifice.

whole Bible: Israel is the people of the Covenant. The Bible is the book of two covenants: the Old Covenant and the New Covenant, the Covenant of Sinai and the Covenant sealed at Calvary.

According to the present arrangement of the Pentateuchal narratives, all the early stories of Genesis point toward God's covenant with Abraham, and this in turn is treated as a preview of the main covenant at Sinai. We have already observed, however, that the narratives of Genesis are governed by a religious viewpoint which has been projected backward upon the patriarchal period. Historically the Covenant was first made at Sinai after the miraculous deliverance from Egypt.

The ceremony of the making of the Covenant is described vividly in Exodus 24. Animals were sacrificed on an altar at the base of the mountain. Half the blood was sprinkled on the altar (a representation of Yahweh's participation), and the other half was dashed out upon the assembled people. Thus "the blood of the Covenant" sacramentally joined together God and his people in close relationship. The story contains elements which suggest that the account is substantially accurate as a description of this dramatic moment in the Mosaic period. However, the fact that the Covenant is central in all the sources—J, E, D, and P—indicates that we are dealing not with the mere chronicling of a distant event but with an experience which was a vital part of the ongoing life of the chosen people. Each generation could testify with a Deuteronomic writer:

> The Lord made not this covenant with our fathers, but with us, even us, who are all of us here alive this day.
>
> —Deuteronomy 5:3

This covenant between God and his people has several important characteristics. In the first place, it was not a natural relationship; rather, it was a relationship entered into by decision. Perhaps we can see the difference if the natural relationship which results from being born into a family is compared with the relationship which exists on entering marriage. In the former case biological (that is, natural) factors beyond the child's control are determinative, and unless the child is an orphan it is impossible for him to imagine a time when a natural relationship with parents did not exist. In the latter case, however, two young people leave their natural relationships and on the basis of free decision create a new home. Thus marriage, at its deepest level, is a covenant—a relationship based upon commitment, trust, and loyalty "till death us do part." Similarly in the case of Israel: the Covenant was *freely* entered into at a particular historic moment and became the beginning of Israel's history, the time of her creation as a historical people. It was not a matter of continuing in a natural relationship which had existed all the while; rather, it was a matter of God's choice and Israel's response at a definite moment. Like Abraham, who left his native country and kindred (his natural environment) and faithfully responded to God's call to go into a new country, Israel also severed previous loyalties and made her supreme decision of faith.

Again, this was an exclusive relationship. Israel was to worship God alone according to the special Name which he had disclosed to Moses (Exodus 3:15; 6:3).[7] Loyalty in personal relationships is inescapably narrowing. Some time ago there was current a popular song to the effect that "you can't marry ten pretty girls" for "your heart picks one." Like-

---

[7] According to Semitic idiom, a person's name is filled with his inner self; therefore, to know the personal name is to enter into relation with another. The *religious* meaning of the disclosure of the sacred Name can be seen within this Semitic context. Notice that E and P, both of which stress the introduction of the new Name in the Mosaic period (see page 54), do not suggest that Israel began to worship a new deity, for Yahweh is actually "the God of the fathers" and the Lord of history; rather, the new name symbolizes God's unique revelation to Israel, his special claim upon the people created by his saving acts. For a discussion of the historical question as to the origin of the Name itself, see T. J. Meek, *Hebrew Origins* (Harper, 1950), pp. 92-118.

wise, in Israel's case, commitment involved a narrowing of loyalty. God had "picked" Israel and, in grateful response, Israel had "picked" God. Henceforth he was to be the only center of her allegiance, and her destiny was to be realized in serving and glorifying him alone. So Israel's first commandment was "thou shalt have no other gods before me." For this reason, Yahweh is described frequently as a "jealous" God, the God who will tolerate no other rivals for Israel's loyalty (see Exodus 34:14). He was to be Israel's God, and Israel was to be his faithful people.

Finally, Israel was to acknowledge God's lordship over her life by giving him her complete obedience. According to the traditions now preserved in the book of Exodus, the Covenant was made on the basis of God's law. "All that the Lord hath said will we do, and be obedient," said the people in chorus as they participated in the covenant ceremony (Exodus 24: 3-8). Scholars are agreed that not all of the laws now found in Exodus come from the Mosaic period. Many reflect the circumstances of a later period in the land of Canaan and show the influence of patterns of law which the Israelites borrowed from their neighbors. Probably, however, a summary of God's requirements upon his people was a part of the covenant tradition from the earliest times, and it may be, as some scholars argue, that the Ten Commandments (in shorter form) were issued by Moses. In any case, on God's part the giving of the Law signified his jealous demand upon the total allegiance of his people. There was to be no division between "sacred" and "secular." Every aspect of Israel's life—cultic and civil, social and personal—was to be ordered according to his demand, as one can see from reading the Covenant Code (Exodus 20:22—23:33). And on Israel's part acceptance of the divine law was to signify the spontaneous expression of an inner bond which united the people, collectively and individually, to Yahweh. This ideal, however, proved too difficult for Israel to realize. Eventually Jeremiah, disillusioned over a later attempt to legislate faith in God, looked toward the time when God would make a New Covenant—one in which there would be an inward and spontaneous acknowledgment of God's sovereignty over the whole of life, and one which therefore would truly fulfill the original meaning of the Mosaic covenant (see Jeremiah 31:31-34). As R. B. Y. Scott rightly observes, Jeremiah learned like Paul that what the Law could not do, God could and ultimately would do. Thus the deepest insights of the Old Testament point toward their fulfillment in the Christ who came, as he said, not to destroy but to fulfill the Law (Matthew 5:17).

The Bible, then, applies the word covenant to that depth of personal, historical experience which is the meeting place between man and God. Speaking in the first person, God addresses man in personal terms: "*I* am the Lord, thy God, who brought thee up out of the land of Egypt; *thou* shalt have no other gods before me." [8] It is in the context of this divine-human relationship that we must understand the meaning of the important biblical words: faith and sin. For the men of the Bible faith means the trustful acceptance of God's sovereignty, glad obedience of his will, faithfulness to his covenant. And sin is the very opposite: it is the rejection of God's claim to rule supreme in the heart, it is deliberate rebellion and disobedience, it is unfaithfulness to his covenant. Sin is not so much the transgression of specific moral laws (that may be involved) as it is the denial of God's *right* to give the law and exert his sway over every aspect of life. This matter is put forcefully by D. R. Davies, who compares sin in the religious life to treason in the political sphere.[9] When a man breaks the laws of the state, he does not lose his citizenship. "He remains a citizen, however many the laws he breaks, *so long as he recognizes the state and its right to make laws,* whether he obeys them or not. But when he pro-

[8] See Martin Buber, *I and Thou* (Clark, 1937).

[9] *Down Peacock's Feathers* (Macmillan, 1946), p. 49. This book is an excellent exposition of the prayer of General Confession.

ceeds to challenge the right to power of the state, he is challenging the very foundations on which both state and law rest, and there is a qualitative difference between that action and his violations of the law. It is the difference between crime and treason." So, as Davies observes, sin is treason, not crime. It is the willful repudiation of the sovereignty of God whose will is the basis of law and order within the covenanted community. It is not so much breaking a law as breaking a relationship.

We can best understand the biblical language concerning faith and sin in terms of our own personal encounter with God in moments of worship. As Christians we do not pray to a God who, like "Uncle Sam," is only an imaginative personalization of our social ideals. Rather, when we express our faith we acknowledge a genuine personal relationship into which God has graciously invited us. We know that we are his creatures who are dependent upon him. We say and sing that we rely on him, that we trust in him more than any other person, and that our hearts are restless until they find rest in him. And likewise when we confess our sin we do not say that we have violated moral values, or ethical standards, or the code of human decency. Obviously these things make our estrangement from God externally visible. Fundamentally, however, we say that we have broken our relationship with God. "Against thee, thee only have I sinned and done this evil in thy sight" (Psalm 51:4)—so runs the deepest cry of the human spirit. In the strict sense, there is no sin where there is no faith relationship, even though there may be the moral evil of which most people are aware. Sin presupposes a personal relationship with God, in the light of which one discerns the true character of social acts. It is necessary to put the accent in the right place if we are to deal with the problem which we have raised in this chapter.

History Viewed from Within the Covenant

It is from the viewpoint of this personal relationship between God and his people that the books of Joshua, Judges, Samuel, and Kings recall the past. These books, edited at the end of a tumultuous history which issued finally in the destruction of the nation, raised the question: what does the past say to us now about the meaning of the present and the prospect for tomorrow? The question was answered by an interpretation based on the Covenant: faithfulness to God is Israel's security and salvation; rebellion against God's lordship inevitably brings ruin. History, therefore, is the scene in which God confronts man in acts of judgment and mercy. From this standpoint, the past was viewed as a long series of "ups and downs," moments of faith and periods of rebellion. The book of Joshua opens with the reminder that success in the land of Canaan depends not primarily on military might but on humble and faithful obedience to God's will. But so alluring were the temptations in the new land that just before his death Joshua found it necessary to summon all Israel to renew their covenant with Yahweh (Joshua 24). The book of Judges in its present Deuteronomic edition describes the history of the period as a rhythm of rebellion against, and return to, the God of the Covenant (2:11-3:6). A tradition in I Samuel regards the founding of the monarchy as Israel's rejection of God's kingship—an act which led to the later tyranny of kings and to Israel's feverish participation in power politics (I Samuel 8; cf. Hosea 8:4; 13:9-11). And in the books of Kings every king is measured in terms of whether or not he gave exclusive loyalty to Yahweh, as this was understood by Judean editors (see, for example, I Kings 16:21-28).

In a strict sense, this kind of historical writing is inaccurate in important details. On critical grounds we know that Joshua's conquest of Canaan was not a swift blitzkrieg which put him in control of the whole land. The account of the crossing of the Jordan River and the walls of Jericho that "came tumbling down" at the shout of Israel is unquestionably a heightened version of the event itself.[10] We know that the "judges" did not follow one another in succession as rulers over a united Israel, and there is evidence in I Samuel that Samuel gave prophetic support to the founding of the monarchy, rather than opposing it on the grounds that Israel was rejecting God's kingship. Moreover, in the books of Kings important rulers, like Omri and Jeroboam II, are passed over with a brevity which is out of proportion to their historical significance. The person who wants to know the facts concerning the reign of a king is referred to the royal archives. So the resumé of the reign of a king of Israel or Judah invariably ends with this formula: "Now the rest of the acts of [the king], and all that he did, are they not written in the books of the chronicles of the kings of Israel [or of Judah]?" (I Kings 16:27, and so on). In this way the writers plainly say that they are not concerned with colorless facts, but with the interpretation of Israel's history in terms of the key categories of faith and sin. The only "history" which matters to these writers is the history of God in relation to Israel and Israel in relation to God. For them, history is not the scene of mere human striving; it is the arena where God is continually meeting his people in crises that have as their meaning, "Give in, and admit that I am God" (Psalm 46:10; Moffatt translation).[11]

This is *interpreted* history, but that does not necessarily condemn it, even though certain facts are neglected or glossed over. Anyone who writes history will have to interpret; he will select some facts and neglect others according to the

---

[10] Archaeologists have excavated Jericho and have found in the walls of the ruined city evidences of earthquake activity which is not unusual in the geological fault of this region. It seems, then, that seismic disturbance may have dammed up the Jordan allowing the Israelites to cross on dry land, and also that an earthquake ruined the city allowing the Israelites to take possession easily. Our approach to this miracle, however, would be the same as the treatment of the Red Sea in the previous chapter.

[11] This dynamic (and, as we shall see, prophetic) interpretation of history lies behind the somewhat static framework of the Deuteronomic historians who are governed by a legalistic point of view, to be discussed in chapter 6.

pattern of meaning he sees in the past. This is just as true with modern history books as it was in the case of Joshua, Judges, Samuel, and Kings. The question of the meaning of the past is answerable only from a point of view taken in the present, whether it be the conviction that the past was a long preparation for a democratic way of life, or the belief that history is the scene of a class conflict which some day will be resolved in a Communist utopia. Let us be fair to the Hebrew historians even though we may question the adequacy of their point of view. They were not concerned primarily with setting forth moral principles, social ideals, or new ideas about God. They were concerned with proclaiming the truth that history is the scene of the making and breaking of the Covenant. It is the arena of a continuing encounter with the God who says to his people:

> I call heaven and earth to record this day against you, that I have set before you life and death, blessing and cursing: therefore choose life, that both thou and thy seed may live: that thou mayest love the Lord thy God and that thou mayest obey his voice, and that thou mayest cleave unto him: for he is thy life, and the length of thy days.
> —Deuteronomy 30:19-20

Here is the testimony that man finds "life," that is, the true meaning of his history, in a personal relation to the Lord of History. In God there is blessing and salvation; separated from him man's days become a curse and a futility. In the crises of the twentieth century many people are finding that indeed this is the only truth of history that matters.

Revelation Within the Limitations of History

In the preceding section we have viewed the history of Israel in terms of the chief category of the Bible: God's Covenant with his people. Faith, we have seen, is not devotion to moral values or ideal social ends, as in modern humanism; it is personal acknowledgment of God's sovereignty, and surrender to his demand. Such faith finds expression in "good works," to use New Testament language. On the other hand, sin is not immorality or the commission of social crimes; it is rebellion against God's lordship—a traitorous rebellion against the covenant obligation, which often results in the violation of the moral code. Now we are in a position to deal more fairly with the so-called barbarities and crudities which offend our moral sensitivity as we read the Old Testament. What should we say about the savage wars of conquest that entrenched Israel in the land of Canaan? Was God actually a "man of war" who led the armies to victory and even punished Israelites when they failed to annihilate the enemies ruthlessly? These are practical questions, for some of us have heard people attempt to justify modern offensive war or the use of the atomic bomb by appealing to divine precedents in the Old Testament.

Let us keep in mind a basic point in biblical theology: God's revelation takes place in history and therefore is subject to the limitations of history itself. Previously we have questioned the notion that revelation consisted in the transference of God's ideas to man through some private "pipeline," or the mechanical taking of Scriptural notes at divine dictation. If this were the case, it would seem that God said things to Joshua which he later repudiated in the time of the prophets and Jesus. The men of the Bible, however, are much more concerned with God's action, his intrusion into their daily affairs in acts of judgment and mercy. They do not testify that by tuning to the proper wave length they received information or doctrines broadcast by God; rather, they tell us that in specific crises they encountered God himself and were drawn into a relationship in which they were known, judged, and loved. To them, God was their ever present Lord and Companion. "Be strong and of good courage; be not afraid, neither be thou dismayed: for the Lord thy God is with thee whithersoever thou goest" (Joshua 1:9).

If, then, history is the sphere in which God confronts man with his demand ("I am the Lord thy God") and his promise

("I will be with thee"), obviously this "I-Thou" relationship will be described and understood in the particular historical situation of a man's life. Man can hear God's Word in only one place: the place where he is standing. Joshua, for instance, could not hear the Word of the Lord in the later situation of the prophets, or in the period of the New Testament, or in the situation of the twentieth century. He had to hear it in the limitations of the cultural, social, and political situation of his own day. What seemed right for him in his time may have been wrong for another man in a quite different historical situation. The God of the Bible does not speak to men from an ivory tower above the rough-and-tumble of ordinary life; he reveals himself in the concrete situations where men are living. To ask that the Bible be free from the historical realities of the periods of Moses, Joshua, or Samuel is to misunderstand the nature of historical revelation. Just as the Incarnation presupposes God's revelation in a particular human person, so likewise the election of Israel presupposes his revelation within the historical limitations of a particular people.

Consider the conquest of Canaan. Looking back upon that period of fierce warfare we are apt to question whether it was right for the Hebrews to take Canaan by the power of the sword. Put yourself, however, into the life situation of Joshua and his successors. The first problem the chosen people had to face before they could fulfill God's purpose for the world was that of obtaining *Lebensraum,* "living space." These fugitive slaves had to fight for every inch of the precarious toe hold they were able to secure in the hill country of Palestine. The nations opposing them were fierce and ruthless, and the Hebrews fought according to the accepted moral standards of the day. This was a life-and-death struggle for survival against tremendous odds. Actually our dispossession of the American Indians in some ways presents a far greater ethical problem. But just as Americans maintain that God's providence was behind the events of early American history, despite the tragic wrongs that were committed, so in a more special sense it can be said retrospectively that God's purpose was at work in the savage wars of conquest in Canaan. In a profound sense God gave the land to Israel for an inheritance.

In this bitter struggle it was natural for the Hebrews to describe their relationship with God in terms of their own cultural and historical situation. Not only were they confident that God was giving them a homeland in Palestine, but they unhesitantly viewed every military operation, even the most ruthless kind, as being inspired and guided by God himself. Their bitterness toward the Amalekites, who had decimated their numbers in the wilderness period, was shared, they believed, by God, who vowed eternal hostility against the enemy until they were to be blotted from the face of the earth (Exodus 17:14; I Samuel 15). The oldest poem in the Old Testament, the Song of Deborah (Judges 5), vividly describes Yahweh majestically coming in the fury of a storm to aid his embattled people. There was not a chance that the Canaanite commander could have won for, says the poet,

> From the heavens fought the stars,
> From their courses they fought with Sisera.
> —Judges 5:20

The Hebrews of this early period understood their covenant relation with God in terms of their own cultural limitations. Moreover, they tended to do what all of us do in our sinful self-centeredness; they identified their own ambitions and interests with the purpose of God. The military successes which led up to the building of the empire of David and Solomon fostered the illusion, later attacked by the prophets, that because the Israelites were the chosen people God would guarantee them continuing prosperity and success. Too easily was the purpose of God in history identified with the preservation and glorification of the Hebrew people. Yet these people, despite the limitations of their culture and their sin, knew that history is an expression of the will of God. Man proposes;

God disposes. So the book of Joshua gives an impressive story about the great military commander of the Hebrews bowing himself humbly before the holy and righteous will of God just before beginning the war against Canaan:

> And it came to pass, when Joshua was by Jericho, that he lifted up his eyes and looked, and, behold, there stood a man [a divine visitor] over against him with his sword drawn in his hand: and Joshua went unto him, and said unto him, Art thou for us, or for our adversaries? And he said, Nay; but as captain of the host of the Lord am I now come. And Joshua fell on his face to the earth, and did worship, and said unto him, What saith my lord unto his servant? And the captain of the Lord's host said unto Joshua, Loose thy shoe from off thy foot; for the place whereon thou standest is holy. And Joshua did so.
>
> —Joshua 5:13-15

Commenting on this passage, Alan Richardson writes: "Wherever God is known and obeyed, there is always the possibility that the simple identification of our own interests with right and justice will be avoided and our actions will be judged by a higher, more objective purpose than our own convenience dictates." [12] Obviously Joshua's understanding of the will of God was limited by the historical situation in which he stood, but—if the above passage is typical of him—in moments of genuine worship he acknowledged allegiance to a purpose higher than Israel's military ambitions. The full implications of this were not brought out until the prophetic period, but all the later development which came to a climax in the New Testament was incipient in the covenant relationship from the very first.

Measured by our standards, Joshua and his soldiers were immoral people. But in so far as they acknowledged their absolute responsibility to the will of God as they understood it and gave obedience according to the moral development of their day, Christians include them in the roll call of the

---

[12] *Preface to Bible Study* (Westminster, 1944), p. 84. This book, written out of Canon Richardson's experience in the British Student Christian Movement, is an excellent introduction to biblical theology.

faithful (Hebrews 11:30 ff.). And in so far as they disobeyed the righteous will of God as they understood it, they knew themselves to be sinners and, like Achan and his household, felt the terrible divine judgment (Joshua 7). We shudder at the cruelty and savagery of the age and thank God for the deeper understanding of his will which men received in the following centuries; but mark this: *in principle* this conception of faith and its opposite, sin, is never outmoded in the Bible. These stories were preserved not because they bear witness to an absolute "moral right," but because they testify to a basic conviction of the whole Bible: *the life of the chosen people stands under the judgment of the God who has entered into covenant with them.* To be known by God is to be exposed to his searching criticism, with the result that no action can be performed with an easy conscience, regardless of its approval in terms of the moral standards of the day. As George Ernest Wright remarks, "This is the conviction which is the connecting thread of the Old Testament, and as a result Israel's history is 'holy history.'"[13] It is the application of this "critical principle," to use the words of Paul Tillich, which makes the history of Israel unique and puts the Bible in a category by itself among all the sacred literature of the world.

Israel's Spiritual Development

We cannot ignore the fact that there was development in Israel's religion. It would be foolish to say that there is no difference between the insights of Joshua and Jeremiah, or that the Old Testament stands on the same spiritual plane as the New. The Bible is not static; it is dynamic. We could speak unhesitantly of the "progress" within the Bible were it not for the fact that this good word has been taken captive by those who advocate an evolutionary interpretation of his-

---

[13] *The Challenge of Israel's Faith* (University of Chicago, 1944), p. 32.

tory. The Bible "progresses" because God initiates the sacred drama and through the power of his new action in a succession of historical crises carries it forward toward its conclusion. In this sense it is justifiable to speak of "progressive revelation." On Israel's part these God-initiated crises in her history led to a maturing understanding of the covenant obligation and a deepening awareness of the character and scope of God's redemptive purpose.

It is a common human experience that the years bring a deepening understanding of the meaning of a personal commitment. This is true, for instance, with respect to the covenant of marriage. The personal relationship remains constant throughout the years, but its meaning deepens as two people together face the successes and hardships of life. Likewise this is true in the case of a personal commitment to Jesus Christ. Christians who first made that commitment years ago will testify that their understanding of the lordship of Christ has deepened as each passing year brought a maturing appreciation of the revelation of God's love in Christ. Within the enduring relationship of this commitment, Christians "grow in the grace and knowledge of our Lord and Savior Jesus Christ" (II Peter 3:18).

The life history of an individual is comparable to the life history of a people. What we recognize to be true in the area of our individual commitments was also true with respect to Israel's covenant with God. The covenant relationship remained constant as the basis of Israel's life through the years, the generations, and the centuries. It was constant, however, not in the same sense that the Hebrew monarchy continued through many generations. It was constant in the sense that, as the deep and inescapable basis of Israel's ongoing life, every generation had to renew the covenant and enter into a personal relationship with God. This truth is illustrated in the story of Joshua summoning all Israel to the sanctuary at Shechem for the purpose of renewing the covenant of Sinai.

> Therefore, stand in awe of the Lord, and serve him faithfully and loyally; remove the gods whom your fathers served. . . . However, if you find it obnoxious to serve the Lord, choose today whom you will serve. . . . But as for me and my house, we will serve the Lord.
>
> —Joshua 24:14-15

Thus in later generations prophets reiterated the call to repentance. Each crisis served as a time of decision, as though Israel once again stood before the Mount of the Covenant. Through all of these generations, as the Covenant was given new application in new historical crises, there was a maturing understanding of the will of God. When Israel left the nomadic situation of the wilderness and adopted the agricultural ways of Canaan, it became necessary for her to understand anew the implications of the Covenant in a more complex civilization. When Israel had built up a strong and prosperous empire under David and Solomon, again it became necessary to hear the covenant demand. And when, finally, Palestine was engulfed in a maelstrom of world events, which both enlarged Israel's horizons and intensified her suffering, the Covenant was more profoundly understood.

As we shall see, the prophets gave Israel a deeper insight into the meaning and implication of the relationship between God and his people. They found in the Covenant both a basis for condemning social injustice and a motivation for ethical obligation. In widening vision they perceived the purpose and scope of God's redemptive activity in history. And, above all, they saw with clearer eyes the role of God's chosen people. Thus the advancing years brought a deepening understanding of God's will and a higher understanding of how men should serve him.

It is a far cry from Joshua, claiming to serve God by ruthlessly annihilating his enemies, to the time when Christian missionaries went out into the uttermost parts of the earth to preach the gospel of the Cross. A great distance must be traveled from the patriotic period of the Judges, when men lustily sang the war songs of the Lord, to the time when prophets like Isaiah and Jeremiah envisioned God raising up a foreign nation to bring judgment upon the chosen people. It is important to notice, however, that this spiritual development took place within a unified framework of experience: Israel's covenant relation with God. Regardless of the change of moral customs, the development of law to meet the increasing complexity of society, the widening of international horizons, it is the same God who speaks through the pages of the Bible. The God of Abraham, Isaac, and Jacob is also the God and Father of Jesus Christ. Throughout the Bible faith is always a personal surrender to his will, even though men's understanding of his will matures; and sin is always rebellion against his claim to reign supreme in the human heart, even though the ramifications of sin are traced more clearly in economic, social, and political life.

Thus the Old Testament men of faith—like Abraham, Moses, Joshua, Gideon, Jephthah, Samuel, and the prophets—form a "great cloud of witnesses" (Hebrews 12:1). They surround the Christian like a vast throng of people in a stadium. From a distance they watch the Christian run his race, and their shouting urges him on. The faith of the men of old anticipates fulfillment and completion in the New Testament where God's will is revealed in stainless purity and where his purpose is embodied in Jesus Christ. So the writer of the Epistle to the Hebrews ends his famous roll call of the Old Testament heroes of faith by saying:

> These all, having obtained a good report through faith, received not the promise: God having provided some better thing for us, that they without us should not be made perfect (Hebrews 11:39-40).

5

The Day of the Lord's Anger

"THAT WAS BEFORE God became a Christian!" The exclamation came from a Sunday School girl, so the familiar story goes, in a class that was studying a lesson from the Old Testament, in particular a passage describing the terrible wrath of God. Of course, with simple eloquence she was echoing the opinion of her seniors. How often it has been pointed out, alas from the pulpit itself, that the God of the Old Testament is a jealous God, a God of wrath and judgment. Usually this glib observation carries the insinuation that such a conception of God is primitive and pre-Christian. By contrast, it is said, the God of the New Testament is the God of love and forgiveness.

The Wrath of God

This false understanding may easily arise from a superficial reading of the writings of the so-called Latter Prophets, which we shall discuss in this chapter. But let us recognize that this is no new issue. In the middle of the second century A.D. a man named Marcion caused quite a stir in the Christian Church by boldly rejecting all the Old Testament and drawing up a canon of selected writings, consisting of some of the books now contained in the New Testament. While we cannot consider here all the reasons for Marcion's negative attitude toward the Jewish Scriptures, one of his arguments was that the God of the Old Testament is different in nature from the

God of the New. Whereas the Christian God is the God of love, the Old Testament God, he argued, is the God of jealousy and wrath, of law and justice. Marcion came to the curious conclusion that the two Testaments contain the revelation of two different deities. The Old Testament, he claimed, records the revelation of an inferior, non-Christian deity who created the world and spoke by the prophets. Only in the New Testament era did the true "Christian" God reveal himself: the God and Father of our Lord Jesus Christ.

We cannot follow Marcion all the way in his thinking. Nevertheless on the issue of the wrathful God of the prophets we tend to be Marcionites. We look back with a certain amazement upon the period of the eighteenth century when Jonathan Edwards was able to preach sermons like "Sinners in the Hand of an Angry God," and started a religious reawakening which spread like wildfire through respectable New England. We understand, however, why Edwards eventually had to quit his pastorate in Northampton, Massachusetts, and go off and preach his message of hell-fire to the Indians. For most Americans such a conception of God is too stern, too demanding, too fear-inspiring, too undemocratic. A recent best-seller advises that the time has come to forsake the older conceptions of God which reflect a more totalitarian view of the divine sovereignty, and to refashion a God-idea which will accord with the brave freedom-loving spirit of democratic Americans.

It is good that the "hell-fire and damnation" preaching is disappearing, for most of it was based on a literal interpretation of Scripture and a self-regarding appeal to individuals to "get religion" as the best insurance policy against the possible terrors of eternity. Nevertheless, the idea of the wrath of God cannot easily be discarded from the biblical witness. Against Marcion and his kind, traditional Christianity has insisted upon the unity of Old and New Testaments and has proclaimed that the God who spoke by the prophets is the same God who speaks through Jesus Christ (Hebrews 1:1). Moreover, even though the Bible discloses a deepening understanding of God's purpose and also an increasing refinement in theological expression, it is improper to say that the God who speaks in the Old Testament is different in *character* from the God who reveals himself in Jesus Christ. If the God of the Old Testament displays wrath, he also manifests mercy and forgiveness. One of the great sentences in the J narrative is the description of God's revelation to Moses:

> And the Lord passed by before him, and proclaimed, The Lord, the Lord God, merciful and gracious, long-suffering, and abundant in goodness and truth, keeping mercy for thousands, forgiving iniquity and transgression and sin, and that will by no means clear the guilty . . .
>
> —Exodus 34:6-7

If, on the other hand, the God of the New Testament freely offers men his forgiveness, the revelation of his love also prompted Christians, like Paul, to say that "the wrath of God is revealed from heaven against all ungodliness and unrighteousness of men" (Romans 1:18). Wrath and forgiveness are not mutually exclusive terms: both are united in men's deepest experience of God's love. Without the awareness of divine wrath (judgment) the experience of God's love easily lapses into a kind of sticky sentimentality, as in too many modern hymns; and without the hope of divine forgiveness the knowledge of God's wrath loses its redemptive significance.

A word should be said about the meaning of "wrath" and "mercy" when used with reference to God. These terms are not intended as attributes which describe God metaphysically (as the philosophers would say), or abstractly, as he is in himself. For the men of the Bible, God is not the object of reflective thought, the Being whose existence must be demonstrated and whose nature must be defined. God is, rather, the Subject who addresses men and establishes a relation with them. So, for instance, the "atheism" referred to by the Psalmist (14:1; 53:1) is not doubt about God's existence, but doubt about his relation to the world, as though he does not see or care what men do. Therefore, words like "wrath" or "forgiveness" are symbols drawn from human experience to describe the relation between God and his people. If we are to do justice to the Bible, we must always give due stress to the Other-ness, the transcendence, the holiness of the God who remains hidden from the sight of finite and sinful human beings. "I am God and not man, the Holy One in the midst of you" (Hosea 11:9). Yet in so far as the holy God acts in history, revealing himself in what he *does*, obviously the language of human experience must be used to communicate men's encounter with him. What other language could be used? Hence the Bible, which consistently emphasizes God's holiness and warns men against making any image or likeness of him, boldly uses the most human language in speaking of God. God is described as having relations with men after the fashion of a man, as in the Garden of Eden story. He speaks, sees, acts, decides, repents, sorrows, gets angry. He is called King, Judge, Shepherd, Father, Warrior, Redeemer. Often these human features (anthropomorphisms and anthropopathisms) are subdued in the interests of refining theological expression and giving stress to God's holiness (as in Genesis 1), but they are never completely eliminated, least of all in the New Testament where it is claimed that God was incarnate in Jesus Christ. Moreover, since the religious experience which men communicate is essentially a personal "I-Thou" relationship, metaphors and parables drawn from human relationships are indispensable. Thus the Bible speaks of men's relationship with God in such terms as the relation between a king and subject, a husband and wife, or a father and son. Only in the height and depth of human experience can men find adequate symbols to communicate the meaning of being confronted by God.

In our deepest human relationships we know the meaning of wrath and forgiveness, for we have experienced the human love in whose judgment we suffer guilt and yet in whose forgiveness we are renewed and recreated. The meaning of this rarest human friendship is discerned at an even deeper level in man's knowledge of God. To know the wrath of God is to stand under the judgment of the divine love we spurn; and to know the mercy of God is to accept the forgiveness which, though not sparing us from the consequences of our sin, does not allow our offense to be a barrier separating us from fellowship with him. It was in the light of the Cross that men of the New Testament beheld the fullness of God's love (see Romans 5:6-11), but this revelation was anticipated by the prophets who interpreted the meaning of the Covenant in the crises of Israel's history.

The Prophets of Israel

We have already observed that the books of Joshua, Judges, Samuel, and Kings are included in the prophetic canon of the Old Testament. One of the chief reasons for "historical" books being included in this category is that their final editors viewed the crises of Israel's past as engagements with the God who both punished his people for breaking their covenant with him and repeatedly bestowed upon them the renewal of his mercy. These are prophetic writings in the sense that history is regarded as the scene in which God works out his righteous and redemptive purpose for Israel. Actually, however, the Deuteronomic editors of the historical books were profoundly influenced by the classical prophets who went before them, men whose writings are preserved in the Latter Prophets.

The most distinctive aspect of Israel's religious history was the appearance of a line of prophets whose influence eventually stamped almost the whole of the Old Testament. Hebrew prophecy was unique both in the content of its message and in the persistence of the prophetic witness throughout the greater part of Israel's history. As R. B. Y. Scott points out, here we are dealing with "an apostolic succession of prophetic voices for which there is no parallel in the ancient world."[1] Thanks to the labors of biblical critics, we can now put the prophets in their proper relative position in this "apostolic succession" and view their message in terms of the historical realities of their time.

The classical period of Hebrew prophecy began in the middle of the eighth century B.C. with the appearance of Amos in Bethel. However, it is clear from the book of Amos that already prophecy had become a deeply established function in Israel, so much so that it was often regarded as a profession. Space does not permit us to deal with the antecedents of the prophetic movement, in particular the "sons of the prophets" or prophetic schools (see Amos 7:14) which existed as early as the time of Saul (I Samuel 10:5-12). It is sufficient to notice that Amos did not want to be associated with these popular, professional prophets who went about in bands, excited themselves into ecstatic frenzy, and invariably were "flaming firebrands" of nationalism. In that sense, Amos insisted, he was no prophet. But on another occasion he recalled that from time to time in the past Yahweh had raised up prophets whom the people had silenced (2:11-12). These were the prophets whose badge was not professional standing, but an authentic commission from God. In this more noble succession we may include such figures as Nathan (II Samuel 12), Elijah (I Kings 17, 19, 21), Micaiah (I Kings 22) and many of the prophets whose writings, like those of Amos, are now preserved in the books of the Latter Prophets. These men were not servants of popular desire or defenders of the status quo. Like Micaiah they testified, "What the Lord saith unto me, that will I speak," even though it usually invited ostracism, ridicule, and persecution. It is one of the strange facts of biblical history that although the prophets were an unpopular minority in their day, the whole Old Testament—reflecting as it does a dominant prophetic viewpoint—bears witness to the

[1] *The Relevance of the Prophets* (Macmillan, 1944), p. 57. This well-written and discerning book is one of the best on the subject.

inescapable realism of their message. The uniqueness of Israel's faith is the uniqueness of the prophets.

At this point, two misconceptions of the role of a prophet should be cleared up. Frequently the prophets are regarded as men of great religious experience, and too often this experience is likened to the subjective piety of modern man. For many of us, God is a "feeling" that wells up in the mystic depths of the soul, "a Presence which disturbs us with the joy of elevated thoughts," either when we are enthralled by the beauties of nature or when we are put into the mood of worship by the pleasingly esthetic atmosphere of a beautiful church. Therefore, with our modern bias we are tempted to think of the prophets as mystics who apprehended God's reality in the depths of the soul. The prophets do describe intense religious experiences which catapulted them out into society, but these experiences were not subjective mystical rapture. It is rather striking that the prophets invariably appeared at a critical juncture of Israel's history to proclaim "the Word of the Lord." They encountered God not in the privacy of their own souls or even primarily in the grandeur of nature, but in the historical events taking place. Had there been no historical event, no prophet would have arisen to confront his countrymen with "thus saith the Lord"! The sovereign activity of God in history was objectively and openly manifest for all to see, but only an Amos in the Tekoan wilderness or an Isaiah in the Temple of Jerusalem had the eyes which enabled him to discern the signs of the times.

Again, the prophets are frequently misunderstood as clairvoyants who were able to peer into the future and predict things scheduled to come to pass according to God's timetable. Webster's Dictionary defines "prophecy" as "a prediction of something that is to happen; the power or act of predicting the future." So we speak of weather prophets, political prophets, and the like. It cannot be denied that Old Testament prophets made predictions; some of them came true and some did not. They were profoundly obsessed with the future.

Moreover, their major "prediction" was that in spite of all opposing forces God would accomplish his redemptive purpose in history. But for them the future was always an immediate tomorrow, the "next moment" of history whose meaning embraced the present and charged it with great urgency. The old cliché that the prophets were not *fore*tellers but *forth*-tellers is perhaps an oversimplification, but it helps to put the accent in the right place. The prophets were men who spoke forth God's Word for the present, a Word which was on the verge of being realized in God's tomorrow. As a matter of fact, our word "prophet" once had this primary meaning, for it was derived from a Greek word signifying "to speak for, in behalf of," and this in turn was a fairly accurate translation of the underlying Hebrew word which seems to have referred to one's being commissioned as a spokesman of God, a messenger who speaks in behalf of the deity.

Thus the prophets were not fortunetellers who gazed into God's crystal ball and predicted the shape of things to come or the date of "the end of the world." [2] This view would presuppose that the future is "cut and dried" long in advance, that it is prearranged in the plan of God. No place would be left for man in his freedom to "make history." The prophets, however, did not address their message to future ages; they spoke to their contemporaries, declaring the meaning of the events in which they were involved. To understand their message we must project ourselves imaginatively into their world, stand where they stood in the concrete crises of Israel's history, and thereby recover in some degree the immediacy of their historical moment. If the prophets also speak to us in the twentieth century, it is not because they were able to forecast in mysterious language the headlines of our day, but because the essential meaning of our situation in relation to God is

[2] Predictions of the "end of the world" have been based on the book of Daniel and similar literature in the Bible. It is noteworthy, however, that Daniel is not even included in the canon of the Prophets. It belongs in a special category of literature (apocalyptic) which flourished in the period of late Judaism when, it was believed, the voice of prophecy had ceased.

precisely the same today, even though the local and temporal setting has changed.

Wars and Rumors of Wars

The period of the great prophets was a tumultuous one. In the middle of the eighth century B.C.—the time of Amos and Hosea—the shadow of Assyria was lengthening across the world, threatening to bring to an end the peace and security of the peoples of Syria and Palestine. A century before, Assyria had made a bid for world power and had fought a great battle at Karkar (853 B.C.) against western allies, among whom Israel was represented in strong force. Shortly after this battle Assyria declined. During the years of the sleeping giant, Israel and Judah enjoyed the military success and economic prosperity which created an atmosphere of confidence and expectancy. But beginning in the year 745 B.C. once again the Assyrian was on the march. This dreadful menace caused the hearts of petty kings to "shake like trees in the wind," and prompted them feverishly to enter into last-minute alliances with the hope of checking Assyrian aggression. However, the flood from the Euphrates River could not be held back. During the last half of the eighth century, roughly during the time of Isaiah of Jerusalem, the Assyrians appeared in Palestine. In 734 B.C. they defeated a confederacy composed of Syria and the Northern Kingdom of Palestine (see Isaiah 7). In 722 B.C. the Northern Kingdom was destroyed (both Isaiah and Micah were prophesying in the Southern Kingdom at this time), and in 701 B.C. "the Assyrian came down like a wolf on the fold," encamping before the gates of Jerusalem. Although the Southern Kingdom was spared from destruction at that time, it was at the price of becoming a vassal to Assyria, a situation which existed throughout most of the next century. When Jeremiah came to the prophetic ministry in 626 B.C. the Assyrian power was exhausted. Hence the Judeans revived their hope that once again the nation might regain independence. But this hope was in vain. From the ashes of the Assyrian empire rose an even more terrible nation, Babylonia, which by the end of the seventh century B.C. had defeated all other rivals, especially Egypt, and had asserted her supremacy over the Near East. After quelling periodic nationalistic uprisings in Judah, the Babylonians eventually conquered Jerusalem and carried away the cream of the population in two major deportations (597 and 586 B.C.). Both Jeremiah and Ezekiel were prophesying during the final death throes of the nation. The following diagram gives a visual summary of the succession of the prophets before the Exile.

Northern Kingdom	*Southern Kingdom*	*Dominating Foreign Empire*
Amos, ca. 750 B.C. Hosea, ca. 745 B.C.		ASSYRIA 745-610 B.C.
(Fall of Northern Kingdom in 722 B.C.)	Isaiah, 740-700 B.C. Micah, ca. 725	
	(Composition of nucleus of Deuteronomy, ca. 650 B.C.)	
	Zephaniah, ca. 630-624 B.C. Jeremiah, 626-585 B.C. (Josiah's "Deuteronomic" Reformation, 621 B.C.)	
	Habakkuk, ca. 605 B.C. Ezekiel, 593-571 B.C. (Fall of Southern Kingdom in 586 B.C.)	BABYLONIA 610-538 B.C.

Thus the prophets prophesied during a period filled with wars and rumors of wars. In this stormy era the people of Israel lost everything they had strived to obtain: their self-government, their land, and, above all, their sense of prestige and destiny. Seemingly these things meant the death of hope. In popular thought the belief in Israel's election had nourished the expectation of a coming "Day of the Lord" which would be a time of "light," that is, prosperity and victory over enemies (see Amos 5:18-20). But instead of light, darkness fell. Why, then, did God allow these things to happen? Had he forgotten his ancient promises? Had he called his people out of Egypt, led them triumphantly into Canaan, and established them securely under David and Solomon, only to let them down in the hours of their greatest need? This was the poignant question these tragic events occasioned. In specific crises the prophets appeared as God's interpreters, his messengers.

> Surely, he will do nothing,
> the Lord God,
> Except he reveal his purpose
> to his servants the prophets.
> —Amos 3:7

The Broken Covenant

In reading the prophetic literature, one notices that certain themes recur constantly, almost to the point of monotony. We must remember that the oracles or utterances of the prophets were originally given in short inspired outbursts in particular life situations; it was only later that these oracles were strung together, like beads on a string, to form the prophetic books as we now have them. For instance, when we read a book like Amos we do not find a carefully worked out logical argument running through all the chapters; we find, rather, a series of small poetic units (see 4:1-3) in which the prophet confronted the people with God's demand for the moment. In a variety of ways and in many different circumstances the pre-Exilic prophets spoke a message that was old yet always new.

The central prophetic theme is stated magnificently by the prophet Jeremiah:

> Be aghast, O heavens, at this;
> Be shocked, O earth, beyond words,
> Is the oracle of the Lord.
> For my people have committed two crimes:
> They have forsaken me, the fountain of living water,
> To hew for themselves cisterns, broken cisterns,
> That can hold no water.
>
> —Jeremiah 2:12-13

The poetic figure was well understood by the people of Jerusalem who, lacking an adequate source of fresh spring water, had to rely upon rain water stored in cisterns cut out of rock. The situation would appear ludicrous if the people were attempting to store water in cracked and leaky cisterns, especially if spring water were within reach! Yet, said Jeremiah, that was Israel's folly: she had rejected the true Fountain upon which her life depended and in proud self-sufficiency was seeking to contain the meaning of her life within cisterns of her own making.

"They have forsaken Me." Jeremiah's words clearly refer to the covenant relation between Israel and God. According to each one of the prophets, Israel's trouble was due to a perverted will, a misuse of the freedom that was her divine endowment. Instead of being faithful to the God of the Covenant, her life story was one of continual and deliberate revolt. Instead of accepting him as her sovereign Lord and the true center of her life, she insisted upon going her own way, with his name upon her lips, but with her heart far from him. It was not merely that social injustices were being committed, not merely that an unwise foreign policy was being pursued, not merely that strong statesmen were lacking; more basically the trouble was in the realm of the spirit—in that area where God makes his demand upon the will and where man, in free decision, must say Yes or No. Resolutely, firmly, stubbornly, Israel had said No to God. She was the faithless wife whose harlotry had led her to pursue other lovers; she was the child who had rebelled against the parent; she was the subject who had committed an act of treason against her King. This was Israel's sickness unto death.

When the prophets talk about "sin" they do not capitalize the word and turn it into a generalization. They refer to specific sins, each of which individually and all of which collectively illustrate concretely the perversion of Israel's will. In many pulpits today preachers can easily get a hearing by speaking in glittering generalities about God, sin, and redemption. But when the discussion of man's broken relationship with God is focused upon the outward symptoms of the spiritual sickness—race relations, nationalism, economic inequalities, and so on—they are in danger of being reprimanded with the advice to "keep politics out of the pulpit." The prophets were never popular preachers, precisely because in their message the divine criticism of Israel's life was so boldly specific.

Symptoms of Sickness

In at least three areas the prophets found unmistakable evidence of the *broken* covenant. First, they turned their attention to the area of men's social relationships. One of the most obvious, and to the modern mind most commendable, aspects of the prophetic message was their fierce attack upon the social injustices of their day. The rich were selling the poor "for a pair of sandals," wealthy landlords were swallowing up the holdings of independent farmers, the rights of defenseless orphans and widows were violated, and the inequalities of a corrupt status quo were defended by kings, priests, and legal administrators. This was especially true in the eighth century when Amos and Hosea prophesied in the Northern Kingdom and Isaiah and Micah prophesied in the Southern Kingdom, during the long and prosperous reigns of Jeroboam II in the North (785-744 B.C.) and Uzziah in the South (780-740 B.C.). Owing to the quiescence of Assyria and the weakness of Egypt, it was possible for the people of these kingdoms to build a commercial society which outwardly was brilliant but inwardly was characterized by the extremes of wealth and poverty, power and exploitation. Such a society could not long endure.

It is important to understand clearly why the prophets pronounced the sentence of death upon Israel's social order. The "justice" of which they spoke was not a universal rational concept that would be self-evident to all men of reason, if only a Socrates were around to lead men dialectically to apprehend it. Nor was it an ideal, a moral "value," a humanitarian standard, or an ethical norm. The justice demanded was obedience to the divine Person; it was submission to the will of God in the covenant relation. This is the meaning of the statement in Micah 6:8 which is often considered the epitome of the prophetic message:

> What doth the Lord require of thee, but to do justice,
> to love *faithfulness*, and to walk humbly with thy God.[3]

Man's chief end in life is humbly to accept God's lordship over his life, and so to live among his fellow men that all his actions will express obedience to the will of God. It is in this sense that Amos insists that justice must roll down like a never failing stream, rather than being like the brooks of Palestine which quickly dry up when the rainy season is over (5:24).

According to the prophetic analysis, Israel's social life was corrupted by pride and self-sufficiency. The ruling factions of society were ordering affairs in their own interest. The powerful people were led by their inordinate ambitions to get more power and to keep that power by amassing still more

[3] By translating "faithfulness" instead of "mercy," I have departed from the usual translation. Actually the Hebrew word, *chesed*, cannot easily be rendered into English. Whether used of God or man, the word refers primarily to faithfulness to a covenant. "Israel's true *chesed* to Jehovah involves primarily Knowledge of God, and issuing from that, loyalty in true and proper worship, together with the proper behavior in respect of the humanitarian virtues." Norman H. Snaith, *The Distinctive Ideas of the Old Testament* (Westminster, 1946), p. 155.

power—always, of course, at the expense of those who did not have power: the economically poor, the socially disenfranchised, the legally helpless. They were desperately seeking the security which man can provide, the order which man can impose, the peace which is the precarious achievement of power. The wealthy, according to Amos' vivid description, were "at ease" in their palaces, lying upon ivory couches and indulging in sensuous comforts, but completely unmoved by "the ruin of Joseph" (Amos 6:1-7). Like a careless French monarch, they would have exclaimed lightheartedly, "After us, the deluge." Thus man, by his cunning exercise of power and by his acquisitive hoarding of the wealth of society, had exalted himself arrogantly to the point of forgetting, forsaking, and rebelling against God. In this grotesque situation, the only criterion for justice was the will of the strongest, and the only measure for the meaning of life was man's vain self-sufficiency.

To be sure, these men were "social prophets." Notice, however, that they approached the problems of social injustice by going to the root of the matter: when men in pride and self-confidence separate themselves from God, disastrous consequences follow. Estranged from God, men are separated from one another. A broken relationship with God inevitably results in fractured relations with one's fellow men. When there is no "knowledge of God"—that is, faith in him and fidelity to his Covenant—cursing, lying, murder, theft, and adultery follow one after the other, and the whole land is plunged into universal mourning (Hosea 4:1-3). It would be wrong to suppose that the prophetic attack was based on the consideration that the social crimes of Israel were more atrocious than those committed in neighboring countries. Measured by comparative standards the social conditions in Israel were probably better, or at least no worse, than conditions in Moab, Ammon, or Edom. In the prophetic analysis, however, these social conditions were intolerably worse within the chosen community for the simple reason that they were symptoms of a betrayed trust, a violated Covenant, a broken relationship with God (Amos 3:2). Israel was unique among other nations in that her life was measured and tested by the plumb line of the God of the Covenant.

Israel's spiritual sickness was manifest in a second area: popular religion. There is an element of truth in the words of Karl Marx that the beginning of all criticism is the criticism of religion. The prophets knew that truth, and understood it more profoundly and realistically than did the revolutionary Jew of the nineteenth century The prophets hurled God's judgment against popular religion, for they saw clearly its basic idolatry. With prophetic insight a modern writer has pointed out that man is never so sinful as when he is religious.[4] If man's secret desire is to put himself at the center of life, religion can become the subtlest method of accomplishing that objective. Religion too easily degenerates into magic: man's attempt to control life in his own interests, and to establish his relationship with God on his own terms. With his religion man attempts to "make friends and influence people," to obtain peace of mind and integration of personality, and to ward off unseen dangers in order that he may enjoy security and well-being.

From the prophetic viewpoint, this was the character of the popular religion of their day. Space does not allow a consideration of the "Baal" religion which the prophets incessantly attacked, a Canaanite nature religion that was essentially a deification of the reproductive forces of nature. The basic assumption of this religion of magic was that by engaging in the proper ritual man could bring fertile increase to his family, his flocks, his land. In fact, the pursuit of the Baal religion in those days had something of the meaning which science holds for us today: it was an effective means of controlling nature. Such a religion was man's bid for security, prosperity, and well-being in an environment where life was precarious and uncertain. So far had the process of accommodating the inherited faith of Sinai to the Canaanite cult

[4] Joseph Haroutunian, *Wisdom and Folly in Religion* (Scribner, 1940), chap. 1.

gone, that Yahweh and Baal were almost equivalent words in popular usage (Hosea 2:16).

To all outward appearances the people of Israel were very religious. They were zealous in performing the proper sacrifices, observing the great feast days, and making pilgrimages to the ancient shrines. It is probably wrong to infer from some of the strong prophetic denunciations that the prophets were against the use of ritual, and were advocates of a "nonliturgical" free church. The prophets denounced the cult because of its basic idolatry. The cult was an outward symptom of man's self-sufficiency. For the masses such an innocuous religion was an opiate; for those in power it was a means of justifying a social order inherently corrupted by selfish ambitions. For this reason the prophets describe God's loathing of the scenes of so-called worship (Amos 5:21-27; Isaiah 1:10-17). God cannot be controlled by priestly rituals or moved by pious songs; nor can the uncleanness of Israel's heart be removed by ceremonials. Worship must be the expression of a will directed toward God in genuine repentance and wholehearted faithfulness, for as Hosea tersely said, Yahweh delights in *chesed* (faithfulness), in "the knowledge of God" rather than sacrifices (6:6). So Jeremiah dared to stand in the gates of the Temple as the people were entering to pay their respects to God, and exclaim:

Thus says the Lord of hosts, the God of Israel: Amend your ways and your doings, that I may establish your home in this place. Trust not in deceptive words, such as The temple of the Lord, the temple of the Lord, the temple of the Lord is this! For if you but amend your ways and your doings—if you practice strict justice toward one another, if you do not oppress the resident alien, the orphan, and the widow, nor shed innocent blood in this place, nor run after other gods to your own hurt—I will establish your home in this place, in the land which I gave to your fathers for all time. But, as it is, you trust in deceitful words, that are of no avail. What? Steal, murder, and commit adultery, swear falsely, offer sacrifices to the Baal, and run after other gods, whom you do not know, and then come and

> stand before me in this house which bears my name, and say, We are safe—only to practice these abominations! Has this house which bears my name become a robbers' cave in your eyes? Lo! I see through it, is the oracle of the Lord.
>
> —Jeremiah 7:1-11

According to the prophets, Israel's only security was faithfulness to the God of the Covenant—faithfulness which is expressed in proper worship and translated into all social relationships.

The third area in which the prophets found evidence of the broken covenant was the realm of politics. Owing to the military successes of the period, the kingdoms of the North and South could not resist the temptation to magnify their national prestige in the eyes of the world. Consequently, national policy was directed toward enlarging Israel's boundaries through military conquest and strengthening her political position by means of foreign alliances. In more favorable times this policy fostered the kind of political confidence which Amos attacked (6:13); in more uncertain periods the same nationalism led to feverish attempts to find security by courting the protection of other nations (Hosea 7:11; 12:1). The prophets regarded these political machinations as another symptom of rebellion against the God of the Covenant. Just as those who held power attempted to maintain that privilege domestically by means of legal chicanery and ruthless exploitation of the underprivileged, so also they attempted to maintain their position by playing the game of power politics. The prophets insisted, however, that this was to rebel against God and to pursue the way of the world. Through the prophets Israel was warned that it was not God's purpose in choosing Israel to make her a great nation, as other nations measured greatness. "In quietness and confidence shall be your strength, in returning and in resting shall you be saved," was Isaiah's reminder to his countrymen in a tense military crisis (Isaiah 30:15). To trust in chariots and horses was to attempt resistance against events which were the judgments of God. To fight against Assyria or

Babylonia was to fight against God himself whose sovereignty controlled the movements of these nations. This was the theological basis of Isaiah's passivism (not pacifism!) and of Jeremiah's seemingly traitorous policy of collaboration with the foe.

In these three areas—social relationships, popular religion, and political policy—the prophets found concrete evidences of Israel's sin. Just as a doctor regards a fever not as the disease itself but as its symptom, so likewise the prophets found in these things symptoms of a chronic sickness. Their diagnosis went much deeper than a mere attack upon social injustices, magical cult practices, and foreign policy. They perceived that the *root* of these expressions of sin was a fundamental distrust of God which, because of a long history of habitual acts, had been so deeply ingrained in Israel's life that it was no longer a matter of conscious intention. As Hosea tersely said: "A *harlotrous spirit* has led them astray, and they have become apostates from their God" (4:12). R. B. Y. Scott has summarized the matter in these words:

> The basic attitude of man was thus optimistic confidence in himself and in the way of life he had devised to secure his satisfactions. He felt himself autonomous. He was sure that the exercise of social power after the fashion of other nations, together with divine favor insured by many and costly sacrifices, were adequate to attain his ends. He refused to face the facts of human suffering and social degeneracy, or to believe that calamities which came were warnings of final doom. He gave to the world of his own scheming the trust that was due alone to Yahweh, the Maker of Heaven and earth and men. For in his heart of hearts he believed that he, and not Yahweh, was in control. The other gods whom he acknowledged as real divinities though subsidiary to Yahweh were fit symbols of his self-sufficiency. For them, too, his hands had made, like the cities where their proud shrines were built.[5]

Thus the prophets were iconoclasts, men who sought to smash the idols in which Israelites placed their trust, to the

[5] *Op. cit.*, pp. 114 f.

end that Yahweh might be the sole center of Israel's allegiance. The prophets did not think of themselves as innovaters who introduced new ideas or social changes. Doubtless they would have been shocked if they could have known that centuries later they would be caricatured as social reformers, spiritual geniuses who were ahead of their times, or primitive philosophers whose insights contributed to the development of monotheism or the enrichment of the God-idea. We must be on guard against modernizing the prophets in our desire to accommodate them to our world of thought and concern. Without exception they took their stand upon the platform of one controlling conviction: Yahweh had chosen Israel and had entered into special covenant with this people. To be sure, their message contributed a deepening understanding of Israel's election as the covenant demand was focused anew in each historical crisis. But their primary role was that of summoning revolting, rebellious Israel to the covenant loyalty which was the inescapable basis of her life in history. Elijah's return to the sacred mountain of the Covenant (I Kings 19) is a symbol of the spirit of the whole prophetic movement. Israel was summoned to return to Sinai, not in the sense that the people must turn the clock backward to the nomadic conditions of a more primitive age, but in the sense that the Covenant of Sinai must be renewed in the contemporary cultural and historical situation. The prophetic message could be summarized in the words of Jeremiah, spoken in the name of the God of the Covenant:

> Return, apostate children!
> I will heal your apostasy!
>
> —Jeremiah 3:22

The Inescapable Punishment

"You only have I known of all the families of the earth; *therefore* I will punish you for all your iniquities" (Amos 3:2). This was the "peal of thunder," as George Adam Smith says, with which "the storm of prophecy" began. To be *known* by God in this intimate sense was to have all of life exposed to the divine scrutiny (see Psalm 139). No cultic rites could cover up the real motives which led Israel to the temples; no commercial prosperity could conceal the spiritual sickness of a people bent on independence; no military alliance could hide Israel's trust in "flesh" (Isaiah 31:1-3). Contrary to popular belief, the prophets proclaimed that the Covenant did not guarantee inevitable victory and a rosy future; rather, it gave promise of a dark day when God's anger would break upon his people. Literally there would be no hiding place, not even at the altar of the temple, from his dreadful presence (Amos 9:1-4; cf. Jeremiah 23:23-24).

Given the persistence of Israel's rebellion, God had to act. Sin against God is a serious offense that cannot be passed over lightly; for God is a jealous God. He will tolerate no rivals to his claim to rule supreme in the human heart. "No man can serve two masters. . . . Ye cannot serve God and Mammon," as Jesus said, similarly expressing God's demand for undivided allegiance. The "monotheism" of the Bible does not provide men primarily with an intellectual belief in terms of which they can understand all of life as being comprehended in a pattern of order and unity; rather, the one-ness of God derives its meaning from the recognition that the Lord of heaven and earth makes a peremptory claim upon man's will. "Hear, O Israel, the Lord our God is one Lord, and thou shalt love the Lord thy God with *all thine heart*, and with *all thy soul*, and with *all thy might*" (Deuteronomy 6:4-5). Jealously the one God demands everything; nothing is to be held back. This is the very nature of the covenant relationship.

Measured by this "plumb line," Israel could not stand approved before her God. It was not that her allegiance was halfhearted; rather, as we have seen, the trouble lay with the falseness of her heart, the harlotry of her ways. Every aspect of her life was symptomatic of treason against her King. Therefore disaster was inevitable, as all the pre-Exilic prophets testified unanimously. Moreover, the inescapable disaster was not understood as the mere consequence of disobeying an impersonal moral law which, like the physical law of gravitation, indifferently hurts those who foolishly oppose it. To be sure, in the words of the oft-quoted proverb, "they sowed the wind, and they shall reap the whirlwind" (Hosea 8:7). Israel, in her freedom, was held responsible for sin and its consequence; but when the consequence came it was the expression of God's will, the manifestation of his terrible presence. Israel was to be *punished*—a word which implies intention and personal relationship. Outwardly other nations might be engulfed in the same catastrophes as Israel, but for Israel the event would have the inner meaning of divine judgment owing to her unique, personal relation to the God of history.

The point bears emphasis again that in the prophets' message the wrath of God does not stand in contradiction to God's infinite concern for his people, any more than parental discipline of a child means the cessation of love. The anger of God is not the heartless cruelty of a tyrant, or the sentence of a judge who coldly metes out punishment to a criminal. The punishment God inflicts upon his people is redemptive in nature. Its purpose is that Israel, in despair, will come to her senses and acknowledge the foolishness of her ways. This is most beautifully illustrated in the message of Hosea where the prophet, using a metaphor derived from the family relationship, describes God's concern for Israel as that of a father who had taught his son to walk, who had tenderly held him in his arms, and who, when the growing son rebelled, suffered when it was necessary to discipline the boy.

> When Israel was a child, I came to love him,
> And from Egypt I called him.
> The more I called them,
> The more they went away from me. . .
> But it was I who taught Ephraim to walk;
> I took them up in my arms;

> But they did not know that I cared for them. . .
> How can I give you up, O Ephraim!
> How surrender you, O Israel! . . .
> My mind turns against me;
> My sympathies also grow hot.
> I will not carry out my fierce anger;
> Nor will I again destroy Ephraim;
> For I am God and not man,
> The holy one in the midst of you;
> And I will not destroy.
>
> —Hosea 11:1-3, 8-9

In symbolism drawn from human experience, the prophet proclaims that both wrath and mercy struggle together in the heart of God. But the love of God is not a pampering and indulgent affection. "Whom the Lord loveth he correcteth, even as a father the son in whom he delighteth" (Proverbs 3:12; cf. Hebrews 12:6). Before Israel could understand the depth of God's forgiveness, his people had to know the reality of their sin, the fact of their estrangement from him. And for some strange reason, people do not readily acknowledge their need of God's love and their dependence upon him until their self-centered and self-sufficient way of life has been shaken to its foundations. Israel had to discover, as Paul did later, that God's strength is made perfect in man's weakness.

According to all the pre-Exilic prophets, God's punishment was to come in the form of an invading nation. In Isaiah's day Assyria was approaching the zenith of its power. In a vivid passage, the prophet describes the Assyrian dictator coming into Palestine at the command of God for the purpose of punishing the sin of his people:

> O Assyria, rod of my anger,
> And staff of my fury!
> Against a godless nation I send him,
> And against the people of my wrath I charge him. . .
>
> —Isaiah 10:5-6

The prophet recognizes that the Assyrian is unaware that he is being used as God's instrument; he is intent only upon fulfilling his own proud ambitions. Therefore, "when the Lord has finished all his work on Mount Zion and Jerusalem," the Assyrian "rod" will be cast aside and his pride too will be shattered. In the meantime, God is using the terrible suffering perpetrated by the invader to bring judgment upon the self-sufficiency of his own people. The day of God's wrath is as near as the rumbling of Assyrian chariots. On that Day, proclaims the prophet, "the haughtiness of man will be humbled, and the pride of man will be brought low; and the Lord alone will be exalted" (Isaiah 2:5-22). As Zephaniah said in a later period, the imminent divine event would be a day of darkness and gloom when the whole land would be "devoured by the fire of his jealousy" (1:14-18). It would be folly to resist the foreign nation which God commands (as Isaiah and Jeremiah advised Judah's rulers) because such resistance would be tantamount to an attempted escape from God's righteous judgment. Therefore, submit and pay tribute. Let the invader come! Military crisis is not primarily a call to arms; it is a call to repentance.

The dreadful manifestation of God's presence, said the prophets, would mark the end of Israel's rebellious history and the beginning of her acknowledgement of his righteous rule. Then the meaning of Israel's tragic history would be luminously clear; for when nations, appalled at the destruction of Jerusalem, would ask "Wherefore hath the Lord done thus unto this great city?" they would know the answer: "Because they have forsaken the covenant of the Lord their God, and worshiped other gods, and served them" (Jeremiah 22:8). According to the prophetic view, history is not the scene of mere human activity or the trampling march of blind power; it is the arena in which God makes known his sovereignty through acts of judgment. And it is the arena of suffering and frustration because man's attempt to live as though he were God always defeats itself.

It is noteworthy that whatever else the pre-Exilic prophets had to say about God's ultimate restoration of his people they were, first of all and without exception, prophets of doom. Indeed, the readiness to speak God's word of judgment, and thus to criticize or negate the accepted "values" of society, seems to have been the primary credential of a true prophet of Yahweh. This point is vividly illustrated by a passage in the book of Jeremiah that deals with Jeremiah's controversy with the popular prophet Hananiah (chapter 28). Standing in the Temple precinct, the latter patriotically was promising a happy issue to the military crisis, even though the Babylonian king Nebuchadnezzar had already looted the Temple treasury and had carried away one group of exiles into foreign captivity. Jeremiah, however, reminded Hananiah that the prophets of Yahweh who had preceded them had prophesied "of war, and of evil, and of pestilence" (verse 8). So, true to this apostolic succession, Jeremiah refused to prophesy of peace, victory, and prosperity. The first task of God's prophet, as he came to know at the time of his divine commission, was "to root out, and to pull down, and to destroy and to throw down"; only after God's word had accomplished its destructive intention was he "to build and to plant" (1:10). Thus the prophetic Word, in its initial impact upon society, was a negation of all false securities and counterfeit values. Out of their experience of encounter with God the prophets testified that when men are truly known by God, judgment is inescapable. There is no hiding place from his wrath, which is none other than the holiness of his love.

We may pause to recognize that this prophetic note is basic to the faith of the Bible. Christianity is unique among all the religions of the world because it sees God's judgment falling not only upon other peoples, but first and foremost upon the chosen community itself. The Church which bears Christ's name is fundamentally a community of sinners who know the reality of divine judgment, even though this community also knows the grace of divine forgiveness. From this standpoint,

Christians may view the terrible world conflicts of our period as being in a profound sense the work of God even though, at the same time, these catastrophes are the consequences of the sins of modern men. Just as Isaiah could call the Assyrian the rod of God's anger, as Jeremiah could say that the Babylonian conqueror was the chosen instrument of God, or as early Christians could see in Titus' final conquest of Jerusalem God's judgment upon Israel, so the Christian will say that God "raised up" Hitler to bring judgment upon the corruptness of Western civilization, or that he "raised up" Stalinite Communism to bring judgment upon the failure of Christian nations. Though these sinful agents, in both cases, are destined to be cast aside, they come at the command of the righteous will of God.[6] No man, regardless of his power, can successfully boast independence of the Lord of history, and no society, whether Western democratic or Eastern Communistic, can set up a social order which stands outside of the judgment of God. The history of the past bears eloquent testimony to the element of judgment in human affairs.[7]

According to the prophets, the imminence of God's judgment was not just a prediction about the future; primarily it was a call to repentance and faith in the present. Just as a man, warned by his doctor that his days are numbered, is suddenly confronted with the crisis of the present, so the knowledge that God is about to act in the future makes today a day of crisis. It is an eternal Now, with an intensity of urgency and a quality of meaning that cannot be measured by the beat of the pulse or the hastening shadow of the sundial. *This* day—not tomorrow or the day after—is the time when God makes his demand; *this* day he sets before man the alternative of life or death, the blessing or the curse. Each event becomes an engagement with God, and in that dynamic mo-

---

[6] See the sermon by Harry Emerson Fosdick, "God Talks to a Dictator," in *Living Under Tension* (Harper, 1941), pp. 172-181.

[7] For a Cambridge historian's discussion of this matter, see Herbert Butterfield, *Christianity and History* (Scribner, 1949), chap. 3.

ment a man is asked to repent, to make the wager of faith, to act as a responsible person. Thus the prophets spoke to their contemporaries out of the urgency of events which were hastening toward God's Day of Victory. To them the real tragedy was that the people were "at ease in Zion" and blind to the character of the crisis in which they were involved. Their message was a sharp rebuke to a complacent generation: "Prepare to meet your God, O Israel" (Amos 4:12).

The prophets were not at home in their age because, unlike the usual patriots, they saw life under the judgment of God. But precisely because they were not at home in their age, they speak to every age, exposing the "eternal dimension" of the present. The prophetic message, with its acute urgency, is profoundly relevant in our own catastrophic day, even though outwardly the historical circumstances and cultural setting have changed in the intervening centuries. The prophets shatter our complacency and expose the meaning of the crisis in which we are involved. They face us with our responsibility to God and lay bare our refusal to hear and obey his demand. It is not difficult to translate their message into our contemporary situation, but the land cannot bear their words today any more than in Amos' time. When those with power insist upon ordering society according to their own selfish interests, reducing human beings to the position of slaves who make men rich and comfortable, then God will manifest himself as the champion of the weak and disinherited. When the Church becomes the ally of the status quo, harboring outrages like racial segregation within the institution and salving her conscience by preaching an innocuous gospel of "personal salvation," then God's indignation at the scenes of worship blazes forth no less furiously than in the day of Isaiah. And if in pride and sufficiency those who hold power and guide the making of national policy refuse to hear and obey the demand of God in the atomic age, the Day of the Lord's anger again will strike terror upon the earth. Surely the prophets are contemporaries—for him who has ears to hear.

Beyond the Judgment

In the prophetic message the Day of the Lord's wrath is described as coming inevitably. This was no fatalistic inevitability, no predetermined *kismet* which had to be because God's prearranged timetable could not be altered. The prophets spoke to *responsible* people who, at least in principle, had the freedom to avert the full fury of God's destruction by a redirection of the will toward him. We are not saying that the Assyrian armies would not have devastated Palestine if only the eighth century prophets had been given a favorable hearing. Israel's change of attitude would not necessarily have prevented Assyrian aggression, but it would have made a difference in the way the people faced the political situation. By repentance the people would have been prepared to receive the divine mercy and forgiveness which would be evident in a time of disaster. Even Amos, in whose prophecy there is scarcely a ray of hope, insisted that *if* Israel would only seek Yahweh in repentance and faithfulness *perhaps* he would be gracious to a remnant (5:14-15). But the prophets did not pin their hopes on Israel having a change of heart. Too clearly did they see that the decisions the people were making had behind them the habitual ways of the past, indelibly inscribed into Israel's society. Too realistically did they see that Israel's history had gathered such a momentum of evil that no human power was adequate to stop its inexorable movement toward the precipice of destruction. The prophets were not idealists. They were not optimistic about the possibilities, humanly speaking. Just as the J writer in Genesis pictured a mythological flood coming as divine judgment because of the sinful corruption of history ("the imagination of man's heart is evil from his youth. . ."; Genesis 8:21), so also the prophets envisioned the immediate consequence of the spiritual condition of their society as being God's inescapable judgment. Though God had given man his freedom, man could not misuse that freedom without suffering disastrous consequences.

Scattered throughout the prophetic writings, however, are many passages which anticipate the coming of a New Age.[8] Scholars believe that some of these passages have been added by later editors in the interests of toning down the harsh statements of the prophets and making their literature more readable and usable in religious services. This is unquestionably the case, for instance, with the Appendix to the book of Amos (9:9-15). But not all the passages of hope, by any means, can be eliminated from the prophetic books. The prophets believed that God's punishment was disciplinary or redemptive in nature; therefore beyond the manifestation of God's judgment would be a new disclosure of his mercy and forgiveness. Running through the biblical message is the "two-beat rhythm," as C. H. Dodd aptly puts it, of judgment and renewal, threat and promise, doom and hope.

This twofold theme is set forth magnificently in the prophecy of Hosea, who found in his relation with his estranged wife a parable of the relationship between Yahweh and Israel (chapters 1-3). Just as Gomer had proved unfaithful to the marriage vow, so likewise Israel—described symbolically as Yahweh's wife—was unfaithful to the covenant with her God. But just as Hosea reinstated Gomer in his home, despite the fact that he had every legal right to cast her out, so Yahweh once again would betroth Israel unto himself. The meaning of Israel's suffering, according to this prophet, was that Yahweh was leading her back to the "wilderness" (a symbol for the despair resulting from the loss of self-government and political self-sufficiency) in order that he might "persuade her" and "speak to her heart" (Hosea 2:14). It was not God's purpose to destroy utterly; his purpose in punishing Israel was to shatter her pride so that "as in the days of her youth, as in the day when she came up from the land of Egypt," she might respond to his love in faithfulness and obedience.

---

[8] We shall return to the prophetic doctrine of the "last things," both the Final Judgment and the New Creation, in chapter 10.

Israel would then find her perfect freedom in capitulating to the sovereignty of God.

In the prophecy of Isaiah, the hope in God's mercy led to the formulation of the doctrine of the Remnant (Isaiah 10:20-23). Though God's judgment would fall severely upon the nation, a remnant would be preserved as an expression of the new beginning made possible by divine grace. Here, for the first time, the distinction was made between the visible Israel ("Israel according to the flesh") and the true Israel which Yahweh, ever faithful to his Covenant, would not abandon. In a profound sense, the formulation of Isaiah's doctrine was "the birth-hour of the Church," that is, the company of people who, by repentance and faith, bear witness to the New Age which God would inaugurate. Moreover, Isaiah seems to have been the first prophet to anticipate the coming of a Messiah—an "anointed One"—who, blessed with divine endowments, would rule over reconstituted Israel (see Isaiah 9:2-7; 11:1-9).

The pictures of the messianic age are idyllic. There will be no more war, every man will sit in security under his vine and fig tree, and there will be a kind of "peace" in which every man in the redeemed community will stand in dignity before God (Isaiah 2:1-4 and Micah 4:1-5). Even nature will be marvelously transformed, so much so that it will no longer be "red in tooth and claw," and once ferocious animals will be friendly to man (Isaiah 11:6-9). In other words, the anxieties, insecurities, and corruptions of history—which, according to the Semitic idiom, nature mirrors—will be removed in consequence of man's change of heart, the redirection of his will toward God. As Isaiah writes, "The land will have become full of the knowledge of the Lord, as the waters cover the sea."

Finally, Jeremiah, in various oracles and dramatic acts, gave expression to the hope that beyond the day of punishment would be a day of renewal and restoration. Probably his greatest utterance was his description of the "New Covenant" which would lie on the other side of the manifestation of God's wrath (31:31-34). The background of this prophecy seems to have been Jeremiah's disillusionment over the "Deuteronomic" Reformation of King Josiah in 621 B.C. (see II Kings 22, 23). In his youthful idealism he had evidently sympathized with the effort to bring about Israel's regeneration through the official enactment of laws which were strongly influenced by prophetic teachings. He came to see, however, that a formal relationship is not necessarily a real relationship with God, and that obedience to laws written in a book cannot settle the question of whether there is a genuine inward response to God's demand. So, said the prophet, at the "End" the old Mosaic Covenant would be superseded by a Covenant in which God's Law would be written on the heart. No longer would knowledge of God be a matter of mere repetition of a creed or routine instruction in a past religious tradition; rather, man's knowledge of God would be direct and personal, even as Hosea had prophesied earlier (2:19, 20). It is wrong to regard Jeremiah as the prophet of "individualism," if one means that he was the precursor of a point of view that has dominated the modern period from the Renaissance on. The New Covenant, like the old Mosaic Covenant, was to make the people once again a "whole family." The ancient schism which had separated the Northern and Southern Kingdoms would be healed, and "the whole house of Israel and the whole house of Judah" would be united in their common relationship to Yahweh. Jeremiah stressed the *inwardness* of the covenant bond which, ideally, had united God and Israel from the first, but which had been broken by people who substituted ceremony and tradition for faith and trust.[9] Above all, said Jeremiah, in the age of the New Covenant Israel would know the deepest dimension of God's love: his forgiveness.

[9] It is true, of course, that this message, delivered at a time when the temple system and the national matrix were collapsing, stressed the role and the responsibility of the individual. But the individual is never understood apart from the community, either in the Old Testament or the New (where there is emphasis upon the Church).

"For I will pardon their guilt, and their sin will I remember no more." Thus God, by healing men's broken relation with him, would heal the wounds and divisions of Israel's society. No longer estranged from God, men would not be alienated from one another.

Similarly, Ezekiel looked toward the time when God in his grace would gather together the scattered bones of Israel and breathe into them his life-giving spirit (chapter 37). Beyond Israel's doom lay her resurrection. Like Jeremiah, Ezekiel stressed the changed inward attitude which would characterize the restored community as a whole and every individual member of it. To the people a "new heart" would be given and, faithfully obedient to God, they would enter into everlasting security and peace (36:25 ff.).

Let us gather together the threads of this discussion in three general observations. First, the New Age toward which the prophets pointed could not be ushered in by man's efforts. The prophets knew nothing of our illusion of progress, with its assumption that man—by means of education, science, and good intention—can build a better world. The prophets looked upon a society which was incurably ill, spiritually destitute, and, save for the grace of God, hopelessly lost. It was not that Israel's intentions were bad. On the contrary, the people thought they were worshiping God and the rulers were engaging in political actions aimed at protecting the country from ruin. Israel's trouble was that she had so completely strayed from God, following the devices and desires of her own heart, that she did not know the nature of her spiritual dilemma, and even the prophetic message seemed to have the effect of confirming the people in their set ways. Tragically, Israel appeared to have lost her freedom, the capacity to respond to God's demand. "Their deeds will not permit them to return to their God," said Hosea (5:4). Like a pathetic man who is the victim of amnesia, Israel had lost her memory: she had forgotten Yahweh. Therefore, nothing that the amnesia victim could do would change the situation. Divine action was necessary to bring Israel to her senses. Her lost memory could be restored only by the severest "shock treatment."

In the second place, the prophetic message of hope for the future was not based upon an estimate of the political probabilities of the day. It was based solely upon their firm belief in God's faithfulness (*chesed*) to his Covenant. To be sure, Yahweh was not bound legally or mechanically by this Covenant, for, as Amos pointed out, the divine purpose in history was not necessarily tied up with the survival of Israel, as though Yahweh were a mere folk-god who had to save his people in order to save himself from oblivion (9:7). Yahweh had freely chosen Israel, and could freely reject his people. If, then, God was to spare a remnant and ultimately restore Israel, this would be an expression of his grace, his unmerited love. Though Israel's faithfulness was fickle—"like a morning cloud, or like the dew that leaves early" (Hosea 6:4)—God's faithfulness was sure and constant. This was the basis of the prophetic hope.

Finally, the prophetic message shows an understanding of God's love as including *both* wrath and mercy, judgment and renewal. Admittedly, these two dimensions are never completely harmonized until the New Testament, but it is not a simple question of either-or in the message of the Old Testament. The prophets proclaimed that up to the moment of their speaking God had spared Israel because of his long-suffering and tender concern for his people. And while Israel could no longer escape the consequences of her rebellion, she could be saved from its tragedy if in repentance she would acknowledge the justice of God's judgment and hope for the new beginning which his grace would make possible. In the prophetic message, God's punishment is essentially redemptive. It is like a refiner's fire which purges out the dross. When Israel's pride is humbled and she stands in the wilderness of despair, then God's anger will vanish and he will "speak to her heart," bestowing upon her all of the blessings of his love (Hosea 2:14-15). Like the fugitive from the "Hound of

Heaven" in Francis Thompson's poem, Israel would then realize that all things betray her when she betrays the Lord of her life, and at the end of her long road of rebellious flight she would yield to his chastening love.

> All which I took from thee I did but take,
> Not for thy harms,
> But just that thou might'st seek it in My arms.
> All which thy child's mistake
> Fancies as lost, I have stored for thee at home:
> Rise, clasp my hand, and come!
>
> Halts by me that footfall:
> Is my gloom, after all,
> Shade of His hand, outstretched caressingly?

Thus the prophetic message points toward the future. According to the Christian witness, the prophetic hope was not finally realized until God's love, including both judgment and forgiveness, was given its deepest manifestation in the Cross of Jesus Christ. It was he, the long promised Messiah, who came to gather together the Remnant from all nations into the New Israel. It was he who gave men the new heart and the inward Law. And, above all, it was he who fulfilled Jeremiah's prophecy by uniting God and men in a New Covenant.

6

The Valley of Death's Shadow

DURING A DARK HOUR OF World War II, the celebrated Austrian writer, Stephen Zweig, committed suicide. Having been exiled from his own country and having seen the foundations of European civilization swept away, he incarnated the tragedy of many individuals who faced the prospect of survival in a world where cherished securities had been destroyed. On the day before his death, he wrote a letter explaining the reason for his suicide: "After one's sixtieth year unusual powers are needed in order to make another wholly new beginning. Those that I possess have been exhausted by long years of homeless wandering." [1]

When the Pillars of the State Fall

We who have seen the pillars of nations fall, and who have heard the anguished outcries of individuals made homeless and spiritually destitute by these tragic events, can appreciate imaginatively Israel's desolation of spirit in the dark days of the Babylonian conquest. The fall of the nation in 586 B.C. was a disaster which cut to the very quick of Israel's life. Jeremiah, who suffered sensitively with his people and wished that it were possible to escape the prophetic task, was an embodiment of the tragedy. Though the book of Lamentations was not written by him, it is understandable how later tra-

[1] Quoted by J. L. Hromadka in *Doom and Resurrection* (Madrus House, 1945), p. 26.

dition could ascribe to him these disconsolate poems, most of which are written in an elegiac meter appropriate to the mood of sorrow. These songs of lament vividly describe the conditions, physical and spiritual, which prevailed after the destruction of Jerusalem. Nowhere do we find a more poignant cry of anguish than these lines in which the bereaved City pleads for pity upon a people suffering under overwhelming affliction:

Is it nothing to you, all ye that pass by? behold and see
If there be any sorrow like unto my sorrow, which is done unto me,
Wherewith the Lord hath afflicted me in the day of his fierce anger.
—Lamentations 1:12

Like the writer of the twenty-third Psalm, the victims of the tragedy knew what it was to walk through the valley of the shadow of death.

It is a measure of the vitality of Israel's faith, however, that the chosen people were able to find the "unusual powers" necessary "in order to make another wholly new beginning" after long years of homeless exile. Indeed, the destruction of Jerusalem marked the beginning of a new chapter in the biblical drama: the chapter of Judaism. Though the historian can find antecedents for this new phase in the period before the fall of the nation, especially in King Josiah's "Deuteronomic" Reformation of 621 B.C., the phenomenon of Judaism, properly speaking, belongs to the centuries after 586 B.C.[2]

Judaism was created in the crisis of the disintegration of Israel's national existence, the destruction of the political matrix of her life. Across the centuries of Judaism fell the

---

[2] For purposes of convenience, the religion of the pre-Exilic period may be called "the faith of Israel." This faith was embraced by those Hebrews known as Israelites, whether living in Samaria (Northern Kingdom) or Judah (Southern Kingdom). Judaism, however, was the religion of the post-Exilic "Jews." Originally, "Jews" referred to residents of *Judah* who claimed that, in contrast to Samaria, the traditions and blood of Israel had been kept pure in their community. In time, the word Jew came to be applied to all those who adhered to Judaism, whether in the Holy Land itself or in the Dispersion.

shadow of this most disastrous event of her history. With deep anxiety Israel was forced to wrestle anew with the question of the meaning of her history. Prophets had warned of the terrible disaster, but scarcely anyone believed that the doom would fall so "pitiless and dark." When the heavy blow fell, shattering the foundations of the sacred City and scattering the people into a foreign country, faith was strained almost to the breaking point. The fact that Judaism produced the pessimistic book of Ecclesiastes, which announced in melancholy language that there is no discernible meaning in the tangled skein of human experience, is sufficient evidence of the enormity of the problem of suffering in this period.

The book of Lamentations takes a stand with the pre-Exilic prophets: the terrible disaster was the judgment of God upon a faithless people. This book affirms that the judgment is just; no one should complain about the inevitable consequences of his sins (3:39). Yet God's mercies are "new every morning"; therefore "it is good that a man should both hope and quietly wait for the salvation of the Lord" (3:22-26). But Judaism was not satisfied with this prophetic treatment of her suffering. Previously the prophet Habakkuk, contemplating the monstrous wickedness of the Babylonian power, had raised the question as to why God allowed the wicked to be so prosperous and to carry the punishment of the chosen people to such terrible extremes (chapter 1). Habakkuk was willing to take his stand upon his watchtower and wait patiently for Yahweh's answer to his complaint, an answer which finally came in the words "The righteous shall live by faith [faithfulness]," by trustful and patient acceptance of God's sovereignty (2:1-5). But Habakkuk's question could not be silenced, especially in a period when the old national matrix was gone and the problem of the fate of the individual within the community clamored for attention. As Butterfield observes:

> This whole idea of judgment seems generally to be adapted to peoples regarded in their corporate capacity, and it marks that form

of Old Testament teaching which envisaged, not individuals so much, but rather the solidarity of a whole nation, while at the same time the condemnation is addressed not to this man or that party but to the sins of the nation as a body, the people as a whole. Such an idea might help to explain why great human systems collapsed and why great powers have sometimes been brought to their doom when nothing in the world seemed capable of resisting them; but, far from explaining, it only brings out into greater relief the crucial ethical problem that provoked some of the principal thought of the Old Testament, namely the case of a weak people submerged by cataclysm—the helpless prey of a cruel aggressor.[3]

So Judaism's haunting problem came to be *theodicy*, the problem of the righteousness of God. One of Judaism's most characteristic questions was: why do the wicked prosper and the righteous suffer? The problem is raised in many of the psalms, is present in the book of Ecclesiastes, and reaches its climactic statement in the book of Job. It has continued to torture the religious mind throughout the ages, not least of all in our own time. This chapter will not pretend to give an answer to what will always be an insoluble mystery, but we shall attempt to see why Judaism by its very nature understood the question in this particular way. The discussion will prove relevant to our thinking and living because usually we insist on framing the question in similar terms: why do "good people" suffer?

By the Rivers of Babylon

The evidence from archaeology indicates that the destruction of Judah was complete. During the Babylonian blitz every major city and fortress of Judah was destroyed, at the price of the wholesale slaughtering of people. The renowned archaeologist, W. F. Albright, points out that excavations in Palestine have confirmed the accuracy of the account found in II Kings 24 and 25. He writes:

[3] Herbert Butterfield, *Christianity and History* (Scribner, 1949), p. 62.

> Many towns were destroyed at the beginning of the sixth century B.C. and never again occupied; others were destroyed at that time and partly reoccupied at some later date; still others were destroyed and reoccupied after a long period of abandonment. . . . There is not a single known case where a town of Judah proper was continuously occupied through the exilic period.[4]

All but the poorest people of the land were carried away into Babylonian captivity in two major deportations, one in 597 B.C. and the other in 586 B.C. The kingdom of Judah was blotted off the map.

A later psalmist recalls the mood of despair and homesickness which settled down upon the "displaced persons" from Judah:

> By the rivers of Babylon,
> There we sat down, and wept,
> When we remembered Zion.
> Upon the poplars, in the midst of her,
> We hung up our harps.
>
> —Psalm 137:1-2

The sun of Israel's hope had been eclipsed. Captives who longed for their homeland could neither engage in mirth nor "sing the Lord's songs in a strange land." The spiritual crisis was acute. Had God forgotten his promise to Abraham? Had he deserted his people after subjecting them to the most terrible punishment? Two prophets interpreted the meaning of the historical tragedy to the exiles: Ezekiel and the "Unknown Prophet."

According to the witness of the book which bears his name, Ezekiel, a priest of Jerusalem, was among the exiles carried away in 597 B.C. as a result of the first Babylonian invasion. With a number of other "DP's" he settled down in Tel-abib, a town not far from Babylon, where he seems to have kept in touch with events taking place back in Palestine. Before the fall of Jerusalem (from 593 to 586 B.C.) he was consistently

---

[4] *The Archaeology of Palestine* (Pelican Books A199, 1949), pp. 141-142.

a prophet of doom, like other pre-Exilic prophets. The first part of the book (chapters 1-24) describes the sin of Israel and the imminence of divine judgment. In particular, Ezekiel addressed himself to the growing problem of theodicy by challenging the popular interpretation of the impending calamity summed up in the proverb: "The fathers have eaten sour grapes and the children's teeth are set on edge." Those who detach Ezekiel's teaching on "individual responsibility" from the context of his whole message often caricature him as a prophet of individualism who ignores the fateful influence upon the individual of historical forces and social environment. But here, as in the case of Jeremiah's prophecy of the New Covenant, we must not separate the role of the individual from the destiny of the community. Taken as a whole, the gist of Ezekiel's message was this: Israel was careening wildly toward destruction because of a momentum of evil as old as her history. But Ezekiel's generation could not evade its involvement in the corrupt situation by shifting the blame to previous generations. Every man, said Ezekiel, is responsible for the consequences of his own sin. "The soul that sinneth, it shall die" (see chapter 18). Translated into our language, this would mean that the generation which felt the full brunt of the second World War cannot cynically shift the blame to a previous generation which failed at Versailles. We do, of course, inherit the consequences of past failures, and in any historical reckoning must pay the penalty for ancient wrongs; but every individual is held accountable for his own life—a life which has been fatefully fashioned by the past but which is also his own making. It is easy to see, however, that Ezekiel's emphasis upon individual responsibility would only thrust the problem of theodicy into bold relief, especially if an individual, like Job, were to claim innocence or righteousness before God. We shall return to this in a later passage.

When Ezekiel received the news of the fall of Jerusalem,

his message suddenly changed from doom to comfort and hope (chapters 33-48). During the remaining years of his prophetic career (586-571 B.C.) he proclaimed the restoration and redemption which God in his grace—that is, for his Name's sake (cf. 36:22)—would make possible. The exiles were reminded that God's purpose could not be defeated by Israel's rebellion. Eventually he would restore the remnant of the people, purified by suffering, to their country where they would be given the new heart necessary for fulfilling the obligations of the Covenant. Though there was at the time no basis for this hope, save the confidence that Yahweh was faithful to the Covenant in spite of Israel's disloyalty, Ezekiel assured his countrymen that a new divine miracle would be performed in history: Israel would be resurrected from the grave and would be given new life (37:1-14). In particular, the new order would be a holy community, with an ordered priesthood and regular sacrificial ceremonies. The blueprint of the Temple-centered religious community, found in chapters 40-48, represents the priest's dream of the realization of God's Kingdom on earth. This priestly utopia increasingly became the concern of Judaism. It is not without reason that Ezekiel has often been called "the father of Judaism."

Ezekiel is unique in that his Exilic ministry spanned the cataclysmic years before and after the fall of Jerusalem. In the political convulsions of the time he saw the activity of God who not only wrecks and ruins but also builds and plants. The promise for the future reached an even greater pitch of expectancy in the message of a second prophet of the Exile whose name is unknown. Because his writings are found in the last part of the present book of Isaiah, the Unknown Prophet is usually called "Second Isaiah." If any conclusion of biblical criticism is established beyond dispute, it is that the last part of the book of Isaiah (Isaiah 40-55; some scholars put all of 40-66 in this category) does not belong to the Isaiah of the eighth century B.C., but comes from another prophet who lived during the final years of the Babylonian period when Persia was on the verge of asserting world supremacy, probably about 540 B.C.[5]

Briefly, this is the background of Second Isaiah's prophetic ministry. The Babylonian empire proved to be virtually co-extensive with the long reign of one king, Nebuchadnezzar. His death in 562 B.C. marked the beginning of the end. In 550 B.C. a new figure appeared on the international horizon: Cyrus, king of a small vassal state of Media. In that year he seized the rulership of all Persia and began his invincible march westward. One by one all major fortresses yielded to his armies, and it soon became apparent that the Babylonian line of defense would crumple under his attack. In 538 B.C. he triumphantly entered the city of Babylon, and thus inaugurated the brilliant Persian empire which was destined to last until the battle of Issus (333 B.C.) when Alexander the Great was victorious over Persia.

Against the background of these spectacular developments, and in particular just before Cyrus' deathblow to Babylon, Second Isaiah proclaimed to despairing exiles the triumph of God's purpose in history. In contrast to earlier prophets who had described foreign monarchs as the instruments of God's anger, this poet-prophet hailed Cyrus as God's "anointed one" (Hebrew: "messiah"; cf. 45:1) who would be the instrument in the release and redemption of Israel. The fifteen chapters of his prophecy ring with a tone of comfort and hope. The language is rhapsodic. The keynote of his message is stated at the very opening of chapter 40:

---

5 These chapters cannot be assigned to Isaiah of Jerusalem (740-700 B.C.) for the following reasons: (1) The historical situation is radically different: the Temple is destroyed, the cities of Judah are in ruins, Babylonia—not Assyria—is the world power, and Cyrus, the Persian monarch, is explicitly mentioned (44:28; 45:1). (2) The style of the poems is much more lyrical and the vocabulary is indicative of different authorship. (3) The divine judgment, in contrast to Isaiah's message, lies in the past, and the period of restoration is proclaimed to be near at hand.

Comfort ye, comfort ye my people,
Saith your God.
Speak ye comfortably to Jerusalem,
And cry unto her,
That her warfare is accomplished,
That her iniquity is pardoned:
For she hath received of the Lord's hand
Double for all her sins.

This prophet views the role of the chosen people against the panorama of a world drama governed by the power and purpose of God, and in the perspective of the whole creation which manifests the glory and handiwork of the Creator. If this was Israel's God—the Lord of all history and the Creator of the ends of the earth—then surely there was no need for Jewish exiles to be downcast! His purpose had been manifested majestically in the long range of Israel's history as far back as the time of Abraham; his purpose was evident even in the terrible ordeal of suffering which the defeated people had experienced at the hand of Babylonia; and, above all, his purpose would be declared unto the whole world by the release of the chosen people from captivity in order that, singing and rejoicing, they might return along a supernaturally prepared highway leading to Palestine. This was the religious meaning of the rise of Cyrus! We must emphasize that Second Isaiah's message of hope was not based merely upon an analysis of the political probabilities of the day; it was based primarily upon the belief in God's grace, his faithfulness (*chesed*) to his Covenant with Israel (40:8; 54:10).

Nowhere in the whole Old Testament is there a deeper understanding of the meaning of Israel's suffering. No other prophet of the Old Testament so clearly understands the meaning of the election of Israel and the Promise to Abraham. To Second Isaiah, Israel's journey through the valley of the shadow of death was not merely a sign of God's chastisement of a sinful people, as previous prophets had declared. To be sure, that was part of the meaning of her suffering. At last, however, the divine judgment had fallen and, at the point of despair, Israel was in a position to receive the free gift of God's grace, the renewal of his forgiveness, the opportunity for a new beginning. The deeper significance of Israel's suffering was that in this way God was manifesting the sovereignty of his love over all mankind. Israel's suffering was vicarious; it was borne for others. This is the theme of one of the "Servant" poems—the magnificent passage found in Isaiah 52:13-53:12.[6] Moved by Israel's witness to God's redemptive activity in history, the nations confess that the tiny nation they had scorned was actually suffering all the while in their stead.

> Yet it was our pains that he bore,
> Our sorrows that he carried;
> While we accounted him stricken,
> Smitten by God, and afflicted.
> He was wounded for our transgressions,
> He was crushed for our iniquities;
> The chastisement of our welfare was upon him,
> And through his stripes we were healed.
> All we like sheep had gone astray,
> We had turned everyone to his own way;
> And the Lord made to light upon him
> The guilt of us all.
>
> —Isaiah 53:4-6

The Christian Church later found in this passage a description of the role of Jesus, the true Servant of God who fulfilled the vocation which Israel had rejected. It is probable, however, that in this passage Second Isaiah did not envision a coming messiah; rather, he was plumbing the deep meaning of Israel's pain. The modern Jewish poet, Robert Nathan, has caught something of the meaning of the Suffering Servant in these lines:

> These are the chosen people. He has set
> Upon their brow the diadem of thorn,
> The one imperishable coronet,
> The crown of pain, the briar branch of scorn.

---

[6] The other Servant poems are found in 42:1-4; 49:1-6; 50:4-9.

Around their shoulders He has hung His scrolls,
Dark as the desert, yellow as the light;
His is the voice of ages in their souls,
The burning bush, the pillar in the night.
These are the chosen; He has named them all.
None can escape the poison of His grace,
Or ever ease the everlasting smart.
It is for them, the honey and the gall,
To be the wakeful, the abiding race,
And guard the wells of pity of the heart.[7]

For Second Isaiah, however, the role of the Servant Israel was not merely to "guard the wells of pity of the heart." The Suffering Servant had been given a world mission. God had chosen this people in order that they might be obedient, obedient even unto suffering and death, and thereby be his agent in bringing blessing and salvation to all the earth. This was Israel's high destiny, her true vocation. Here we stand at the highest peak of the Old Testament revelation.

Both Ezekiel and Second Isaiah in different ways exerted a far-reaching influence across the centuries, although with them the classical era of Old Testament prophecy came to an end. Owing to the tragic development of post-Exilic history, Judaism tended to stress the priestly message of Ezekiel and to ignore Second Isaiah's emphasis upon Israel's missionary task. The situation is well described in the "Westminster Bible":

> The former [Ezekiel] summoned his people to become established again as a God-fearing nation; the latter [Second Isaiah] called them to become God's instrument for revealing His glory to all mankind. Taken together, these two callings constitute the fullest Old Testament revelation of the purpose of God for the people of his choice. . . . It was the final tragedy of Israel that in seeking to fulfill the first of these callings in every detail of their individual and corporate life, they gradually lost sight of the second.[8]

---

[7] "These are the chosen people," *Selected Poems of Robert Nathan* (Knopf, 1935), p. 18.

[8] *Westminster Study Edition of the Holy Bible* (Westminster, 1948), p. 12.

This will become clear as we turn from the period of the Exile to the post-Exilic period of the Restoration.

Rebuilding the Foundations

Second Isaiah had given assurance that the Jews would be allowed to return to their own land, rebuild the ruined cities of Judah, and re-lay the foundations of the Temple. All this was made possible providentially under the benevolent rule of Cyrus, who has been called "one of the most enlightened rulers ever to appear in human history." He reversed the severe policy with respect to captive peoples which had been followed by both Assyria and Babylonia, and inaugurated a policy of toleration. Instead of deporting conquered peoples into an alien land, he allowed them to remain in their home countries and permitted them to maintain their cultural and religious traditions. In the case of the Jews, he issued an edict granting them the privilege of returning to Palestine if they so desired. So began the first period of "Zionism," migration to the Sacred City, Jerusalem.

The main historical sources for this period are the books of Ezra and Nehemiah, a continuation of the Jewish history set forth in I and II Chronicles.[9] These books deal with a century of Jewish history, beginning with the reign of Cyrus. This source, supplemented by the books of the prophets Haggai and Zechariah (ca. 520 B.C.), gives us a glimpse of the restoration of religious and social life in Judah. At first the situation of the returned exiles was precarious, owing to poor crops and the constant menace from hostile Samaritans. However, spurred on by Haggai's reminder that no improvement could be expected as long as the Temple was in ruins, and encouraged by Zechariah's glowing promises of the future security and prosperity of restored Jerusalem, the people in due time set about rebuilding the Temple during the years 520-516

[9] Scholars believe that I and II Chronicles, Ezra, and Nehemiah were all written by a Jewish Chronicler in about 300 B.C.

B.C. According to the traditional chronology, Ezra, the scribe, led another expedition of exiles back from Babylonia to Jerusalem in 458 B.C. and soon instigated a great religious reform aimed at purifying the community of foreign elements and integrating it around obedience to the Law of God. Still later, Nehemiah was appointed governor of Jerusalem by the Persian king, and under his administration the walls of Jerusalem were rebuilt (444-432 B.C.).

Unfortunately the Old Testament history of the Jewish people breaks off abruptly at the end of Ezra-Nehemiah. The next two centuries, the fourth and third B.C., are almost a complete blank to the historian. Nevertheless, post-Exilic Judaism produced a vast literature, the study of which enables us to see the major characteristics of the pattern of life that was developing throughout this period. As we noted earlier, the Pentateuch was given a "P" framework and canonized about 400 B.C.; the Prophets, Former and Latter, were annotated by Jewish editors and finally canonized by 200 B.C.; and a third collection of miscellaneous writings was brought together toward the close of the second century B.C., though the extent of this third section of the Old Testament was not finally settled until the discussions of the great Jewish Council at Jamnia in A.D. 90 when controversies with Christians forced a decision on the limits of Jewish Scripture. In the Hebrew Bible the books of the Writings are arranged as follows:

1) Poetical Books: Psalms, Job, Proverbs
2) Five Festal Scrolls: Ruth, Song of Songs, Ecclesiastes, Lamentations, Esther [10]
3) "Prophecy": Daniel
4) History: Ezra, Nehemiah, I and II Chronicles

Thus the entire Old Testament, as we now have it, was a product of the period of biblical Judaism. Of course, much

[10] It is worth noting that three of these books—Song of Songs, Ecclesiastes, and Esther—got into the canon only "by the skin of their teeth," for their inspiration was seriously questioned by the rabbis.

of this literature reaches back to the time before the rise of Judaism. Obvious in the case of the Pentateuch and the Prophets, it is also true in the case of some of the Writings. For instance, the book of Psalms contains many ancient poems, even though the Psalter is properly regarded as the hymnbook of Judaism. Nevertheless, *in its present form* the whole Old Testament—Law, Prophets, and Writings—bears the indelible stamp of Judaism.

Ezra was the great architect of Judaism. Under his influence the returned Jews were bound together into a compact and increasingly exclusive community something like the priestly utopia which Ezekiel had envisioned. Essentially this was a holy community, with the Temple as its focal point and the Law as the norm of authority. There is an important truth in the old cliché that "Israel went into exile a nation and returned as a Church." No longer having a political basis for the common life, the Jews found the matrix of their historical existence in a religious-ethnic community. According to Nehemiah 8, Ezra read "the book of the Law of Moses" (perhaps the P Code) in the hearing of the people, and on the basis of this the people entered into a solemn covenant, resolving to separate themselves from the rest of the world by rigorous obedience to God's commands and strict devotion to the Temple services. Thus in the institution of the Temple, Jews found *security*; in obedience to the Law they found *authority*; in a priestly order they found the basis for *community*. Properly speaking, Judaism of this type was not the accomplishment of any single man, even a leader as great as Ezra. Judaism was essentially created out of the crisis resulting from the fall of the nation.[11] Lest we become hasty in our criticism of the ancient Jews, let us remember that in our own time, when the pillars of various nations have been destroyed, people are seeking security, authority, and community. The United

---

[11] This point is forcefully made by James A. Muilenburg in his treatment of Judaism in *The Vitality of the Christian Tradition*, ed. George Thomas (Harper, 1944), pp. 24-35.

States, faced with the threat of Communism from without and within, is now attempting to preserve "the American way of life" by measures no less harsh than the severe enactments by which Ezra sought to preserve the purity of Israel's tradition in a time of aggressive ideas and enemies.

There were, of course, other currents in Judaism than those represented by Ezra and Nehemiah. Judaism preserved the prophets and eventually canonized them; therefore the prophetic witness was never completely absent, even though prophets of the stature of Isaiah or Jeremiah no longer appeared. Moreover, the Temple, though central, was not the only religious institution of Judaism. Synagogues were located in communities outside Jerusalem and throughout the Dispersion, and in them a distinctive type of Judaism developed which eventually made its contribution to Christianity. In time, two great religious parties arose: the Sadducees who represented the conservative interests of the Temple of Jerusalem, and the Pharisees who represented the more liberal and flexible tradition of the synagogues.[12] Judaism could also produce "wisdom" literature like Job, a missionary tract like Jonah, and "apocalyptic" literature like Daniel. All of this indicates that Judaism in the pre-Christian period was not a static system or a goose-stepping religious totalitarianism. Deep in the life of Judaism were vital forces which periodically burst to the surface and which eventually erupted in the form of Christianity. Nevertheless, the Jewish life that developed in Palestine during the six centuries before Christ increasingly assumed the rigid form of a holy community walled off from the world by ties of blood and religion. During a time when outside pressures threatened to destroy Israel and her religious faith, the men of the post-Exilic community

---

[12] Besides being a kind of priestly aristocracy, the Sadducees also differed with the Pharisees over the question of the "Law of Moses." Sadducees acknowledged only the authority of the Pentateuch, while Pharisees accepted *both* the Pentateuch and the oral interpretations which were built upon it ("the tradition of the elders"; Mark 7:5,9) and which eventually were codified in the Talmud.

believed that their well-being and salvation were dependent upon meticulous observance of the commandments of the Law. Judaism canonized Second Isaiah, but ignored his message. The meaning of Israel's suffering was dealt with from the standpoint of a legalistic religion.

Life Under the Law

Earlier prophets had foreseen that God in his grace would raise up a remnant which, purified by suffering, would become the nucleus of the new order, the divinely established Kingdom. For the pre-Exilic prophets, however, the Kingdom was always *about to come*, and they never speculated on who would be members of the remnant which God would spare. With the post-Exilic Jewish community, the situation seems to have been different. As George Ernest Wright observes:

> The returned exiles were sure that they were the remnant about whom the early prophets had spoken (Hag. 1:12; Zech. 8:6,12), and they believed that if they now turned to the Lord with greater zeal God would establish the "golden age" with them as the principal recipients of its benefits.[13]

The Priestly Code seems to assume that the restored community was in the same state of holiness as was Israel in the idealized period of Moses. We may wonder how the priests could make this tremendous claim when prophets of a previous period, dealing with the same stuff of human nature, would have been apt to say that the whole social fabric was dyed with the scarlet of sin and that there was no health in the body of Israel. The answer is that the men of Judaism had pledged themselves to keep the divine laws as given in the Pentateuch, and believed firmly that these divine ordinances were a part of the inner and outer fabric of the community. In saying this, we are not suggesting that post-Exilic Judaism was or claimed to be perfect in the sight of God. Actually Judaism was pro-

---

13 *The Challenge of Israel's Faith* (University of Chicago, 1944), p. 91.

foundly obsessed with the awful reality of sin, even as it was acutely conscious of the holiness of God. But the point is that Judaism claimed to have in its priestly institutions the ceremonial means for absolving ritual uncleanness and moral trespass, above all on the Day of Atonement (Leviticus 16; 23:26-32; Numbers 29:7-11) when the sins of the people were "covered" and the community was restored to a state of holiness.

Fundamental to this legalism is the assumption that God has revealed his will in a code; he has measured out precisely what man is to do and not to do. Thus Judaism had a yardstick by which to see whether the community measured up to the attainable standard of God's will, and to distinguish between the "righteous" and the "wicked" within the community. Of course, the influence of earlier prophets is discernible in the Law of Judaism. Besides the priestly or cultic requirements are many ethical laws which show the humanitarian concern and social passion of Judaism. For instance, the command "Thou shalt love thy neighbor as thyself," which appears in the New Testament in several places, is a direct quotation from the book of Leviticus (19:18). The priests of Judaism sincerely thought that they were "putting teeth" into the prophetic teachings by incorporating them into the Law, just as in an earlier period King Josiah sought to implement the prophetic-priestly program of "Deuteronomy" by making it the officially enforced law of the land. Notice, however, what happened when the prophetic demands were incorporated in a statute book. Prophetic teachings about justice and mercy became goals of living which men could attain by sincere and devout effort, and thereby receive the blessing of God's approval.

From the perspective of legalism, the meaning of human experience is contained within this simple formula: God rewards obedience to the law by giving prosperity, health, and peace; he punishes infraction of his law by sending suffering, adversity, and untimely death. In other words, good fortune is a sign of God's approval; misfortune is the concrete evidence of his displeasure. This came to be Judaism's orthodox position.

Let us see how this doctrine of rewards and punishments applies in two types of situations: the life of the individual, and the lot of the community as a whole.

The Wheat and the Chaff

The first Psalm beautifully expresses Judaism's doctrine of rewards and punishments. This hymn extols the benefits that come from studying the "Law" day and night. Indeed, the Law itself provides an objective standard of judgment in terms of which the "righteous" are separated from the "wicked," the wheat from the chaff, the sheep from the goats. The righteous man assures himself of God's blessings by diligently keeping the Law. Consequently, he is like a tree firmly rooted in fertile soil; he enjoys security, prosperity, good health, reputation, and influence in the community. The unrighteous man, on the other hand, is the one who foolishly disobeys or ignores God's Law. Consequently he is "like the chaff which the wind drives away"; his life is insecure and his influence passing. Such a man cannot dare to stand in the congregation of the "righteous," and he deserves no blessing from God. Christians who do not accept this easy distinction between good and bad people, and who reject the priestly doctrine of gaining approval before God by good works, will read this Psalm with a deeper understanding than that intended by the original Jewish writer.

Many of the Psalms, for instance 19:7-14 or 119, express gratitude to God for the revelation of his Law and suggest that obedience of the Law makes one the recipient of God's blessings in *this life*. As one psalmist puts it:

> I have been young, and now am old;
> Yet have I not seen the righteous forsaken,
> Nor his seed begging bread.
>
> —Psalm 37:25

The same utilitarian point of view prevails in the book of Proverbs, where Judaism's doctrine of rewards and punishments is stated in a number of homespun maxims (see, for instance, 11:31).

Probably the majority of religious people today approach the problems of suffering with a similar philosophy. When we accept this distinction between good people and bad people, we too find ourselves wrestling with Judaism's problem: why do the righteous suffer and the wicked prosper? The facts of experience do not confirm the view that those who are "righteous" are granted special benefits or are cushioned from the painful shocks of life. Many of the Psalms grapple with this question. The author of one of the most magnificent Psalms (Psalm 73) grasps the nettle of the problem. He points out that his own righteousness seems to be of no avail: he suffers under affliction, while on every hand the boastful wicked prosper. Why is this? In general, he clings to the answer given by orthodox Judaism: the wicked stand in "slippery places"; their comfort is momentary and they will suddenly come to an end. In the meantime the problem receives its immediate solution in the psalmist's deep sense of trust in God. So the storm of his mental turmoil quiets into this spiritual calm:

> Yet I am always with thee;
> Thou holdest my right hand.
> By thy counsel thou leadest me;
> And by the hand thou dost take me after thee.
> Whom have I in the heavens but thee?
> And having thee, I wish nought else on earth.
> My flesh and my heart fail;
> But my heart's rock and my portion is God forever.
>
> —Psalm 73:23-26

In the case of the author of Ecclesiastes, however, the same perplexity led to a sense of futility. Failing to find any discernible meaning in a world where distinctions between virtue and wickedness are seemingly ignored by God, he suggests as a text for his sermon: "Futility of futilities, all is futility." This disillusionment is the logical conclusion of Judaism's legalistic doctrine of rewards and punishments.

It is worth noticing in passing that Judaism, as represented in Old Testament literature, did not attempt to solve its problem of theodicy by postponing the payment of rewards and punishments to a future life. The clearest exception to this is a passage in the late book of Daniel (written about 168 B.C.) where it is stated that in the final day of the resurrection some will awake to everlasting life and others to everlasting reproach and contempt (Daniel 12:2-3; see also Isaiah 25:8; 26:19). The prevailing view of the Old Testament, however, is that when a man dies he goes to the shadowy land of darkness called Sheol, where personality ceases for righteous and wicked alike (see Job 30:23; Isaiah 14:9, 15). Judaism's preoccupation with the problems of this life made theodicy a poignant issue.

The most forceful challenge to the legalistic framework of Judaism was given by the author of the book of Job, a book which may have been written about the time of Ezra and Nehemiah. In the prose prologue, Job—a legendary righteous man (Ezekiel 14:14-20)—is described as the ideal Jew: "perfect and upright, and the one that feared God and turned away from evil." The drama begins with Satan's taunt to the effect that in view of the obvious benefits which Job receives from his obedience, Job's serving God is anything but disinterested and unselfish. "Does Job serve God for nothing?" Convinced that Job's faithfulness is genuine, God gives Satan permission to test Job by afflicting him with a series of catastrophes. In a short time Job loses everything: family, property, health, and above all, reputation in the community. His three orthodox Jewish friends come to comfort him as he sits pathetically on the refuse heap of the village, scraping his sores. At this point the book changes from prose to poetic dialogue. After listening to Job's lament (chapter 3) his friends offer the simple answer to his troubles: Job must have sinned to bring upon himself such divine punishment. Job protests his innocence and, growing bolder and bolder as the friends monotonously repeat their Jewish orthodoxy, defiantly accuses God of perverting justice. His indignant accusations crescendo to a climax in chapter 31, where he reviews his life and claims that, on the whole, he is a man of moral rectitude, righteous according to the Law. Then God answers Job out of the whirlwind (chapters 38-41).[14] By means of a series of ironical questions, Job is reminded that he is creature and that therefore it is presumptuous for him to claim that he has any standard by which he can stand in judgment upon the Creator. So Job is rebuked and silenced. Finally he humbles himself and says:

> I had heard of thee by the hearing of the ear,
> But now mine eye seeth thee:
> Wherefore I abhor myself, and repent
> In dust and ashes.
>
> —Job 42:5-6

This is more than a confession of inability to plumb a mystery that lies beyond the grasp of the human mind. Job's final word was one of *repentance*—acknowledgment of the presumption involved in his attempt to judge God by the standard of human morality, the pride involved in challenging God to use his omnipotence as men would do. This was tantamount to a repudiation of Jewish legalism, which had been the common ground on which Job had argued with his friends. The religious error of Judaism was this: not only did it find in the Law an objective standard by which the "righteous" and the "wicked" could be distinguished; it also provided "righteous" men with an objective standard to which they could demand that God be accountable. This is the final expression of human pride.

---

[14] The Elihu speeches (chaps. 32-37) are believed by scholars to be a later addition to the book. Notice that the cycle of poems comes to a natural ending with the last verse of chapter 31: "The words of Job are ended."

The book of Job does not give an answer to all our questions, but it does challenge the assumptions which govern many men as they raise their questions. There is no neat correlation between good fortune and righteousness, and misfortune and sin. This point was made forcefully by Jesus, according to a story found in Luke:

> There were some present at that very time who told him of the Galileans whose blood Pilate had mingled with their sacrifices. And he answered them, Do you think that these Galileans were worse sinners than all the other Galileans, because they suffered thus? I tell you, No; but unless you repent you will all likewise perish. Or those eighteen upon whom the tower in Siloam fell and killed them, do you think that they were worse offenders than all the others who dwelt in Jerusalem? I tell you, No; but unless you repent you will all likewise perish.
>
> —Luke 13:1-5

In other words, those who are victims of cruel tyranny (the Nazi ovens at Buchenwald) or natural calamities (the Boston Night Club Fire) are not to be regarded as being more sinful than other people just because misfortune has come their way. Since all men equally stand in need of God's forgiveness, such tragedies should be occasions for repentance. The mystery of life can be faced only in personal reliance upon and trust in the omnipotent God who, in ways past our comprehension, holds the destinies of men and nations in his control. This was the faith of the psalmist (Psalm 73) who, trusting when he did not understand, affirmed, "Nevertheless, I am always with thee." It was Job's solace in that moment when his knowledge of God became not mere hearsay, but personal relationship. And above all it was the experience of early Christians for whom the Cross was the sign of God's triumph and who therefore counted it a privilege to go through tribulation (see Romans 8:31-39; I Peter 4:12-19).

Israel and Her Oppressors

In a previous chapter we found that Deuteronomic editors treated the historical traditions of the books of Joshua, Judges, Samuel, and Kings in terms of Israel's covenant with God. The Deuteronomic historians applied the doctrine of rewards and punishments, referred to above in terms of individual cases, to the panorama of Israel's history from the conquest of Canaan on. They believed that "righteousness exalteth a nation; but sin is a reproach to any people" (Proverbs 14:34). Therefore, calamity and distress were visible evidences of God's disfavor, while prosperity and peace were signs of God's blessing. In principle, the great prophets would have agreed with this interpretation of history. But when prophets like Amos, Hosea, Jeremiah, and Ezekiel surveyed the past they found almost a consistent record of defection from the Covenant. Since they saw in the present little evidence of righteousness, they tended to view all of Israel's history as corrupted by sin. In the case of the Deuteronomic historians, there was a greater degree of optimism. In their estimation, there were periods in which "the land enjoyed rest" because the people were faithful to God (see Judges); and there were a few good kings (above all, the good king Josiah who inaugurated the Deuteronomic Reform) who by their zealous devotion to the Law of God turned the hearts of the people back to the covenant loyalty. The Deuteronomic writers were able to concede that peace and success were within the possibility of attainment for one reason: God's demands were explicitly set forth in the book of the Law, and therefore capable of being obeyed by a devout generation. Thus in the introduction to the book of Joshua (a Deuteronomic passage) Joshua is reminded that he must meditate upon "this book of the law" (that is, the book of Deuteronomy) day and night "that you may be careful to comply with all that is written in it; for then you shall make your life prosperous, and you shall succeed" (1:8).

The men of Judaism seem to have claimed that the ideal society—which was realized sporadically and temporarily at certain times in the past—finally had been established by God, who had restored the exiles to their homeland and had sent leaders, like Ezra and Nehemiah, to order the Jewish community according to the divine blueprint. Seemingly the Jews at last had learned the lesson of their past history, namely, that obedience to God brings welfare and disobedience leads to punishment. They turned, therefore, to giving obedience to the legal prescriptions of Deuteronomy and the Priestly Code, confident that they were living in a theocratic community which had achieved the holiness of the ideal period of Moses. The priestly writers of the Pentateuch told how God had revealed the pattern for the holy community to Moses on Mount Sinai. The author of Chronicles–Ezra–Nehemiah revised the history of the past in terms of the priestly interests and institutions of the Jewish community.

Just as the facts of experience failed to confirm the orthodox faith of Judaism for individuals like Job, so also the developments of history failed to validate Judaism's faith that the holy community would continue in peace and prosperity. Evidently the Jewish community was relatively safe and secure during much of the fourth and third centuries B.C., two centuries about which we know very little.[15] But the situation was radically different in the two centuries before Christ. In 333 B.C. Alexander the Great came upon the international scene, bringing the Persian empire to an end, and inaugurating a Greek administration which sought to forge cultural diversities into uniformity by superimposing Hellenistic culture upon the ancient world. Lack of space prevents a discussion of the developments which took place at the death of Alexander in 323 B.C. It is sufficient to say that the Jewish

[15] However, if the book of Esther is dated late in the Persian period, it may contain the reminiscence of a widespread persecution of Jews living in the Dispersion—a persecution which may have been felt also by the Palestinian community.

community, having built around itself "the barrier of the Law" and having intensified its devotion to Jewish traditions and customs, was able to resist this external pressure for a considerable time. Around 200 B.C., however, Greek rulers arose who were determined to subjugate the Jewish community, the one pocket of resistance which had not been brought into the Hellenistic orbit. In 168 B.C. one of these rulers, Antiochus IV Epiphanes, began his program of destroying Judaism by invading Jerusalem and desecrating the altar of the Temple. This was the act that touched off the Maccabean Revolution (see I and II Maccabees in the Apocrypha). After almost a generation of bloody warfare, the Jews, aided by favorable international developments, were able to seize their freedom. This precarious political and religious independence lasted for about a century (142-63 B.C.), but in 63 B.C. the Romans came, imposing a heavy yoke upon them. After a number of feeble attempts at resistance, during which the smoldering fires of nationalism were fanned by messianic expectations, the Jews openly revolted in A.D. 66. This foolishness meant the suicide of the Jewish community in Judah (or Judea). In A.D. 70 the Romans razed the city of Jerusalem, brought an end to the Temple and its priestly worship, and with the utmost cruelty obliterated all vestiges of Jewish statehood. The emergence of Christianity must be viewed against the background of these tumultuous events, and the messianic hopes which they occasioned.

During these centuries devout Jews looked toward the future when God would correct the injustices of history and give the Jewish nation its deserved "place in the sun." We have observed previously that prophets, like Isaiah, looked forward to the coming of a messianic King who would inaugurate a period of universal peace, prosperity, and justice (Isaiah 9:1-7; 11:1-9; cf. 2:2-5). The flame of this hope was rekindled in the post-Exilic Jewish community. Indeed, there seems to have been a messianic movement in the time of Haggai and Zechariah centering around Zerubbabel, a

"Branch" of the Davidic family tree (see Zechariah, chapters 3 and 4). This movement was abortive, but with the passing of the years the hope was intensified that God would yet send a leader from the line of David who would overthrow the foreign domination and restore Jewish independence and peace. This nationalistic hope was strong in Jesus' time.

The messianic hope was also expressed in a highly imaginative type of literature known as apocalyptic, the best example of which in the Old Testament is the book of Daniel. Written to encourage the faithful to remain steadfast during the fierce persecution instigated by Antiochus IV (about 168 B.C.), the book of Daniel envisioned the time when God would intervene miraculously and cataclysmically for the purpose of punishing the "wicked" nations who had mistreated Israel and vindicating the "nation of the righteous." This apocalyptic literature flourished particularly in the last two centuries before Christ. Sometimes the apocalyptic writers envisioned the coming of a supernatural messiah, designated as the "Son of Man," who would inaugurate the final judgment. In his terrible presence the wicked nations would plead for mercy, but the righteous elect would be firmly established.[16]

Just as there are affinities between the prophetic message and the legalism of the priests, so there are affinities between the prophetic message and the passionate messianic hope which focused upon a coming "Son of David" or the dramatic advent of the "Son of Man" on the clouds of heaven. The prophets too believed that the corruptions and injustices of history could never be removed until God himself intervened and established his Kingdom. But generally speaking, apocalyptic writers, unlike the classical prophets, did not preach the imminence of God's judgment upon the chosen people; rather they turned their eyes away from the melancholy present to the dramatic spectacle of the future. The reason for this

---

16 This apocalyptic messianic hope is most clearly developed in the Parables of Enoch (45:2-6; 48:2-3; 62:8-9), intertestamental literature from the last century B.C.

shift of emphasis may probably be traced to the religious assumption of the Jewish community: the restored community was a holy and God-fearing community which had assimilated the teachings of the prophets. As Amos Wilder says, "the eschatological hope was only for those who were righteous." [17] Therefore, just as a "righteous" Job could demand that his moral integrity be recognized by God, so the holy community, or at least the righteous remnant within it, could expect that in the future God would vindicate Israel and reward her faith. Too often apocalyptic degenerated into a kind of sublimated nationalism, as though having the status of a Jew was a guarantee of being on God's side and thus a promise of an opportunity to get even with Jewish foes in the Age to Come. These cruder elements in the apocalyptic tradition, elements which naturally appeared in times of great stress and persecution, should not blind us to the real heart of the apocalyptic faith: a courageous trust in the God who would ultimately resolve all the paradoxes of history and in whose hand were the destinies of Israel and the other nations. Nevertheless, the immediate problem which stirred the apocalyptic writers was the monstrous injustice of a situation in which Israel, who was certainly not *more* wicked than other peoples, was oppressed by tyrants in whom evil and pride were obviously exaggerated. In a world where God rules, why is a weak nation victimized by crucl aggression and ruthless oppression? Why do the righteous suffer and the wicked triumph? Apocalyptic writers gave answer to this baffling question by maintaining the hope that in God's Day of Reckoning the wicked would be cast down and the righteous exalted.

The Decline of Prophecy

In the period of Judaism prophecy slowly declined. Legalism incorporated the prophetic emphasis upon God's demand for obedience in the present, but the will of God was con-

[17] *Eschatology and Ethics in the Teachings of Jesus,* revised ed. (University of Chicago, 1950), p. 32.

ceived as being codified in a book and within the range of attainment by sincere, devout effort. No longer did prophets rise to proclaim God's revelation in events of the present; rather the men of Judaism preserved, studied, and interpreted the recorded revelation of the past. On the other hand, apocalyptic messianism—which stood in uneasy tension with Jewish legalism and eventually was repudiated by official Judaism—preserved the prophetic hope in the triumph of God's purpose in history; but seldom was there an appeal for radical repentance in the present, after the manner of the preaching of John the Baptist or Jesus. For the apocalyptic writer, the imminence of God's action in the future was primarily a summons to the righteous to wait patiently for the vindication that would correct the injustices of history.

Prophets appeared in the period of biblical Judaism but, with the exception of Ezekiel and Second Isaiah, they do not shine as brightly in the firmament of Israel's faith as the constellation of prophets before the Exile. The following diagram will provide a visual summary of the succession of prophets in the Exilic and post-Exilic periods:

Prophet	World Power
Prophets of the Exile:	Babylonia, 610-538 B.C.
Ezekiel, 593-571 B.C.	
Second Isaiah, ca. 540 B.C.	Persia, 538-333 B.C.
Post-Exilic Prophets:	
Haggai, 520 B.C.	
Zechariah, 520 B.C.	
Joel, between 538 and 350 B.C.	
Obadiah, between 538 and 400 B.C.	
"Malachi," ca. 450 B.C. (?)	
	Hellenistic Monarchs, 333-142 B.C.
(Close of Prophetic Canon, ca. 200 B.C.)	(Maccabean period of independence, 142-63 B.C.)
	Rome, 63 B.C. and on.

Of greatest stature among the post-Exilic prophets was Joel, who saw in a terrible locust plague a sign of the impending Day of the Lord and summoned Israel to repentance. Other prophets, like Obadiah, contented themselves with announcing a day of vengeance against Israel's foes, or, like the anonymous author of the book now called "Malachi" (literally, "my messenger"), upbraided the people for their failure to obey the ritual requirements of Judaism. Still other anonymous prophets, whose oracles have been attached to various prophetic books, anticipated the coming glorification of the Jewish people.

Slowly prophecy petered out. In fact, it later became a tradition of Judaism that prophecy ceased in the time of Ezra—probably an inaccurate judgment but, in a sense, profoundly true. The prevailing belief was, as one Old Testament scholar points out, that in the Law Ezra gave the people everything that was required; the revelation of God was complete. In the past, prophets were sent only to warn people of the disaster which results from disobedience to the Law. However, "the generations that had sworn obedience anew to the Law under Ezra . . . had no need for the prophets." Should Israel, as in times past, become disobedient to the Mosaic Law, perhaps God would send prophets again, "but the prevailing feeling was, no doubt, that the time of unfaithfulness, and consequently of the prophetic ministry, was gone for ever." [18]

Although prophecy declined, the prophetic spirit, always latent within a Judaism which had conserved the writings of the great prophets, found other channels of expression. As we have noted, apocalyptic literature like Daniel has a certain prophetic quality, even though it was never included among the prophetic books. One of the finest examples of the prophetic spirit in Judaism is a short story: the book of Jonah.

---

[18] Karl Budde, quoted by A. G. Hebert in *The Authority of the Old Testament* (Faber, 1947), p. 186.

Largely because of a literal treatment of the "whale," the book of Jonah has been the most sadly misunderstood writing in the Old Testament. Actually it is not history but a story. Its purpose is to protest against the narrow, provincial Judaism which had turned inward upon itself and had thought only of saving its own life. The book is a kind of lengthy parable. Jonah was like Judaism—attempting to escape the God-given vocation of carrying the light of God's revelation to the Gentiles, in this case the detested Assyrians of Nineveh.[19] Post-Exilic Judaism, as we have said, tended to be primarily concerned about the preservation of Jewish identity and the avoidance of sins against the Law. The emphasis was upon an exclusive community, walled off from the rest of the world by "the barrier of the Law." The story of Jonah was written sometime between 450 and 350 B.C. as a missionary protest against the narrowing reform of Ezra and as a plea for Israel to remember that, since God's redemptive purpose embraces all peoples, the vocation of the chosen people was to go forth into the world and win Gentiles as members of God's redeemed community. In a similar spirit the short story, Ruth, opposed the narrow exclusiveness of Ezra's reform, one aspect of which was the divorcing of Gentile wives. The story points out that Ruth, a Moabitess and a Gentile, was the ancestress of the great king David.

Judaism failed to heed the message of Second Isaiah and Jonah. Instead of interpreting suffering as the continuing judgment of God upon a sinful people, the Jews—righteous according to the Law—hoped for the day when God would vindicate them before the world. Instead of performing the role of the Servant by suffering vicariously in order that other nations might receive the salvation of God, Jews thought mainly of self-preservation and self-glorification and emphasized those things which drew a sharp division between Jew

---

19 The book of the prophet Nahum, written about the time of the fall of Nineveh in 612 B.C., reflects the bitterness which Assyrian imperialism had engendered in the hearts of Jews (see especially chap. 3).

and Gentile. The book of Esther, a story which Jews later placed on a par with the sacred Law, bears witness to the intense devotion to ties of blood and culture which came to be characteristic of Judaism.

Christianity emerged within Judaism. The deep and vital forces which had been suppressed but not stifled in the six centuries before Christ erupted with volcanic energy and burst upon the Roman world with the irresistible might of God. Jesus came as a Jew, a true son of Israel. He came not to destroy the Law but to fulfill it; nevertheless, his fulfilling of the Law shattered legalism. He came as the long expected Messiah, the Son of David and the Son of Man, but Jews could not recognize his messianic identity without a repentance which altered their entire perspective. Above all, he came to perform the rejected role of Israel: the role of the Suffering Servant. Obedient unto death, even the death of the Cross, he brought to fulfillment the promised salvation of God and created a new community, a New Israel which embraced both Jew and Gentile, and one which joyfully accepted its missionary task to go into all the world and preach the gospel.

7

In the Fullness of Time

IN AN IMPRESSIVE painting, based upon a homily written by a doctor of the Eastern Orthodox Church, a Russian artist depicts Christ's triumphal entry into Jerusalem. In the background is a mountain, from which vantage point watchmen in times past presumably had scanned the horizons for signs of Christ's expected coming. In the center foreground the Messiah rides upon a beast toward the towering and turret-crowned buildings of the City, while tiny children spread branches and garments before him. Jesus is followed by a small company—the Apostles. However, our attention is most attracted by the band which comes out to greet the King, for these are none other than the Prophets of the Old Testament. In the words of the homily: "The Prophets with their trumpets proclaim before Him their mysteries, and as unto the King they pour forth to meet Him praise . . ."[1]

The Bridge Between the Testaments

The painting just described vividly sets forth a conviction which has been basic to Christianity from the very first, namely, that the Old and the New Testaments are as inseparably related as Siamese twins. This becomes evident the moment we open the New Testament and begin reading the first

[1] The painting is reproduced as the frontispiece of *The Throne of David* (Faber, 1941) by A. G. Hebert, and the interpretation and homily are found on pp. 123-126.

book, the Gospel of Matthew. The keynote of this Gospel is the proclamation that the hopes and expectations of the Old Testament have been fulfilled in Jesus, the Messiah or the Christ.[2] The coming of Jesus and the various events of his life were not regarded as isolated happenings, unrelated to the past. On the contrary, "all this was done, that it might be fulfilled which was spoken of the Lord by the prophets." This note of fulfillment is the symphonic theme running throughout the New Testament.

The Old Testament constitutes something of a problem for many Christians today, and in particular the belief in the fulfillment of prophecy does not readily commend itself, because the belief has been grotesquely caricatured by contemporary "gypsies" who tell the fortunes of the future by reading the lines of the Bible. Therefore, in practice many people visit only the oases of the Old Testament, like the twenty-third Psalm, and confine their attention to the New Testament. This approach has been encouraged by liberal Protestants who, applying an evolutionary interpretation to the Bible, often have consigned the Old Testament to the limbo of primitive origins, a study interesting to the antiquarian but largely irrelevant for those who find practically everything necessary for faith and conduct in the New Testament.

In this chapter we shall address ourselves to this issue, and especially to the problem of fulfillment of prophecy. At the moment, however, let us observe that Christians have always regarded the Old Testament as a *Christian* book, and have maintained that it presents the historical preparation for the events described in the New Testament. Just as the conclusion of a novel draws together various motifs stated at the beginning and brings the story to a climax, so the New Testament gathers up the hopes and aspirations of the Old Testament

---

[2] The word Christ (based on a Greek word, *Christos*) means the same thing as the word Messiah (a word which is based on the Hebrew). Both words mean the "Anointed One," in this case the King who is anointed for the task of fulfilling God's purpose.

and brings to fulfillment the spiritual history of Israel. To restrict one's attention only to the outcome of the biblical drama in the New Testament is comparable to the hasty reader who jumps to the end of a novel, rather than following the story step by step toward the resolution of the plot.

At this point it would be well to review the Old Testament phase of the biblical drama, looking backward from the standpoint of the New Testament. The Old Testament begins with a mythological description of the tragedy which engulfs all mankind owing to man's misuse of his God-given freedom. History became the scene of confusion, anxiety, and strife because, as Paul puts it, when men knew God "they glorified him not as God" but rather "worshiped and served the creature more than the Creator" (Romans 1:18-25). Intending to recreate mankind, God took the initiative and elected a people whose history was to be his special proving ground. He entered into a covenant relationship with them, and over a long period of years led them into a deepening understanding of their vocation. But Israel's record, as the prophets testified, was that of a continual breaking of the Covenant. Repeated chastisements proved futile, and finally the judgment fell upon the nation severely, first in the removal of the Northern Kingdom and later in the destruction of Judah and the exile of the people into Babylonia. Israel's failure, however, could not defeat God's redemptive purpose. As Jeremiah proclaimed in a vivid oracle (18:1-6), God, like a potter, would take the marred and imperfect vessel and remake it according to his design. Thus, in God's providence the exiles were restored to Judah with the hope that at last God's purpose was on the verge of fulfillment. Again, however, the chosen people were recalcitrant. Instead of bringing the light of God's salvation to the Gentiles, Judaism walled itself off from the rest of the world, even from the neighboring Samaritans, and attempted to save its life by punctilious obedience of the Law. No longer did prophets rise to speak God's word in historical crises, for Judaism believed that God's revelation, given in the past, was frozen into final form, needing only the legal cleverness of lawyers (scribes) to make clear its implicit meaning. Then came the catastrophe of A.D. 70 when, according to the Christian interpretation, the Romans executed the sentence of judgment upon a barren Judaism. From the Christian standpoint, Judaism's rejection of Jesus was the final repudiation of the task God had given to the chosen people. That is the theme of a parable in which God is described as the Lord of the vineyard, Israel (Mark 12:1-12; cf. Isaiah 5:1-7). Having carefully prepared the vineyard, the master sent his servants (the prophets) to receive the fruit of the vineyard, but one by one they were rejected and mistreated. Finally he sent his only son, his "well-beloved," but him also they rejected.

> God, who to glean the vineyard of his choosing,
> Sent them evangelists till day was done,
> Bore with the churls, their wrath and their refusing,
> Gave at the last the glory of his Son.[3]

As one leaves the Old Testament and crosses the threshold of the New, he enters a world which rings with the gospel or "good news" that God's long awaited salvation has drawn near.[4] According to Mark, Jesus proclaimed a message which was keyed to a pitch of expectancy: "*The time is fulfilled:* repent, for the Kingdom of God is at hand." Men were living in an age when the "unfinished symphony" of the Old Testament was crescendoing toward the Composer's intended finale. From the Christian viewpoint, the tragedy of the time was that so many people were tone-deaf, unable to hear the music of climax and fulfillment.

It is in this biblical setting that we must view the appearance of Jesus and the emergence of the New Israel, the Church.

---

[3] From *Saint Paul,* by Frederic W. H. Myers (Macmillan, 1907).

[4] Our word "gospel" comes from an old English word meaning "God-story" or "good story," and is an apt translation of the Greek *euangelion* which means the "good news" centering in and proclaimed by Jesus. The background of the usage is traceable to such passages as Isaiah 40:9-10; 52:7; 61:1.

"When *the fullness of the time* was come," said Paul, "God sent forth his son" (Galatians 4:4). Before we are in a position to examine the implications of this gospel of fulfillment, we must consider the historical sources at our disposal for the knowledge of the central historical event: the coming of the Messiah. Let us always remember that Christianity is basically a historical religion, that its faith finds expression in the claim that God has acted in history. This being the case, Christians cannot escape employing the method of historical criticism in dealing with the records which witness to God's Event.

Event and Interpretation

Probably it is safe to assume that the sun would continue to rise and set, even though there were not a single person on this planet to experience sunrises and sunsets. Admittedly there are philosophical difficulties involved in this assumption, but common sense nevertheless leads us to say that this would be so. In the case of historical events, however, the situation is different. Events do not occur in a historical vacuum; they occur in the experience of people, and this means that they always occur with an interpretation or meaning of one kind or another. If the event is experienced as a creative, history-making event, it will be remembered and eventually will become part of a historical record. If it is experienced as an insignificant event, it will be forgotten quickly, as is the case with most things that happen during the course of a day.

This consideration helps to account for something which, at first glance, seems startling. Virtually our only sources for a knowledge of Jesus' career come to us from the Christian community of the first century. The New Testament might easily give the impression that what happened in Palestine must have been "headline news" throughout the Roman Empire. But there is no clear and indisputable reference to Christianity in non-Christian sources before the second century. Though Jesus was crucified under the Roman procurator of Judea, Pontius Pilate, the incident evidently was a routine execution which scarcely caused a ripple in Roman affairs of the day.[5]

For Christians, however, the death-and-resurrection of Jesus was the climactic episode in the History of Redemption. The meaning of this mighty event was etched deeply into the memory of the small Christian community. In its light witnesses remembered and more deeply understood the words and works of Jesus during his brief ministry. Just as the redemptive events of the Mosaic period were imprinted indelibly upon the corporate memory of Israel during the long oral period before the writing of J and E, so the traditions of Christianity were passed on orally for at least a generation before there was any sign of literary activity. Every celebration of the "Lord's Supper" was a rehearsal and a reliving of the crucial event which brought God's redemptive action in history to a dramatic climax. This common memory was the basis for the continuing life of the Church.

While the literature of the Old Testament represents the deposit of a succession of crises over a period of centuries, the New Testament deals with one supreme crisis and focuses upon the brief career of one person. These twenty-seven writings were composed, for the most part, during the second half of the first century. Originally the literature was not designed as official, authoritative writing which would supersede the "living tradition," the oral memory of the Church. This is clearly evident in the earliest New Testament literature: Paul's letters. Written during the decade A.D. 50-60, these ten epistles were intended to meet practical situations which arose in the course of Paul's far-flung missionary travels, and in one instance (Philemon) to deal with the case of a runaway slave.[6]

---

[5] Similarly, Egyptians made no mention of the Exodus. See pp. 54 ff.

[6] The genuine Pauline letters, in their approximate order of composition, are as follows: I and II Thessalonians, Galatians, I and II Corinthians (perhaps four letters combined), Romans, Colossians, Philemon, Ephesians, Philippians. Traditionally the "Pastoral Epistles" (I and II Timothy and Titus) and the

Soon after Paul's death the oral tradition of the Church was supplemented with a distinctively Christian literature known as "gospels." The relationship between the Four Gospels—Matthew, Mark, Luke, and John—constitutes a real problem. On close examination we discover that the first three Gospels naturally group themselves together because of a striking interrelationship, while the Fourth Gospel, being remarkably independent, belongs in a category by itself. The first three are called the "Synoptic Gospels" because they present a common view and outline of Jesus' ministry. This close resemblance can be seen easily if one refers to a "Harmony" in which they are arranged in parallel columns. The common subject matter, common phraseology, and common outline of events they display can hardly be accidental. If, for example, three newspapers—the *New York Times*, the *Chicago Tribune*, and the *San Francisco Examiner*—carried a news write-up almost identical in language and organization, we would suspect that all three papers had relied on a common news agency.

Most Protestant New Testament scholars explain the "Synoptic Problem" by a hypothesis which may be outlined briefly as follows:

1) Mark was written first, and later was used as a literary source for the composition of Matthew and Luke.
2) Besides quoting from Mark, the authors of Matthew and Luke also used a hypothetical "lost" source to which is given the symbol "Q" (from the German word *Quelle*—"source"). Q consists of material which is paralleled in Matthew and Luke, but is absent in Mark (for instance, Matthew 6:25-33 and Luke 12:22-31). Since this material seems to consist largely of the sayings of Jesus, scholars think this hypothetical document may have been a manual of instruction for converts.
3) Both Matthew and Luke contain material which is peculiarly their own, to which may be given the symbols "M" and "L" respectively.

Epistle to the Hebrews have been attributed to Paul, but most New Testament scholars exclude them from the genuine Pauline collection.

Like any scientific hypothesis, this one is not set forth with an air of finality. It should be emphasized that no archaeologist has dug up a copy of the "lost" Q source. The very existence of Q is a hypothesis based on literary analysis.[7] Up to the present, however, the above documentary hypothesis in broad outline offers the best explanation of the literary relations of the first three Gospels.

We may sum up the matter briefly in this way. About forty years after Jesus' death a need was felt for a written account of his ministry. In A.D. 64-65 Nero, the callous and careless emperor who had the reputation of "fiddling while Rome burned," began his terrible blood-bath of Christian persecution. As a result, eyewitnesses like Peter were beginning to disappear, and there was a danger that the memory of the events Christians had experienced might grow dim. About the year A.D. 70 John Mark, an associate of Paul and Barnabas (Acts 13:5) and perhaps Peter's interpreter at Rome, wrote a Gospel setting forth the story of God's saving acts in Jesus Christ and emphasizing that all those who "take up the cross and follow" would share in his victory. Later on, about A.D. 85, a Jewish Christian wrote "Matthew," emphasizing that Jesus' career was the fulfillment of the spiritual history of Israel and providing the growing Church with the authoritative teachings of Jesus. This author, unknown to us by name,[8] based his work on Mark and also used the Q manual and material gleaned from special sources. About the same period Luke, also a companion of Paul (Philem. 24; cf. II Tim. 4:11), wrote another Gospel in a similar manner, adding to it a sequel, Acts, in which he described the spread of Christianity into the Gentile world. In these two volumes, which were dedicated to an honored Gentile by the name of Theophilus, Luke sought to commend Christianity to the whole Gentile

---

[7] However, there may be an allusion to the Q "Sayings" in a statement by Papias, a Christian of the early second century.

[8] Despite the early tradition that this Gospel was written by the disciple, Matthew, critics find no evidence to support the claim.

world. Finally, about the turn of the century (ca. A.D. 90-110) the Fourth Gospel was composed. The author of the last Gospel depended upon authentic traditions but worked up the material independently of the Synoptic Gospels as he retold the Story to a new generation which lived and thought within the changed circumstances of the time.

It is important to notice that each one of the four Gospels was not written primarily because of biographical interest in Jesus or historical curiosity about the past. Rather, the main intention of the various writers was to testify that Jesus was the long-expected Messiah. Each Gospel, though representing a fresh slant on the Story, might well have concluded with these words of the Fourth Gospel: "These are written that you may believe that Jesus is the Christ, the Son of God, and that believing you may have life in his name" (John 20:31). This is "history" in the sense that the written records preserve the remembrance of events with a unique meaning experienced in the Christian community.

In recent years New Testament scholars have attempted to push the historical investigation beyond the stage of the earliest *written* Gospel and to penetrate the "silent period" when the stories and sayings of Jesus were imprinted only on the parchment of the human memory. This school of study is known as "Form Criticism" (the English equivalent of German *Formgeschichte*).[9] Form Critics have demonstrated that the writers of the Synoptic Gospels drew from a reservoir of oral traditions that had been preserved and shaped by the mind of the Church as it faced the practical problems of preaching and teaching. According to this view Mark, for instance, was really a compiler or editor who lifted units of material from the common fund of oral tradition—units which already had a "form" as a result of constant oral repetition—and put them together like beads on a string. Form Critics have isolated such independent units of tradition as the following:

[9] See pages 51 f.

1) Pronouncement Stories, that is, brief stories which come to a climax in some utterance which Jesus makes in a situation of conflict (e.g., Mark 12:13-17).
2) Types of teaching material, such as sayings and parables.
3) Miracle Stories.
4) Legends, that is, stories which focus upon the greatness of Jesus, the chief Actor in the biblical drama (e.g., Nativity stories).
5) The Passion Narrative.

Form Criticism has emphasized the important point that the words and works of Jesus were *remembered* in forms suitable to the oral transmission of the gospel and in life situations which impressed the tradition more deeply upon the corporate memory of the Christian community. If it may be said that the Gospels represent the literary deposit of the memory and experience of the Christian community, the same may also be said with respect to "The Gospel behind the Gospels." This is to say that we never arrive at a point in our critical investigation where the "Jesus of history" can be separated absolutely from the "Christ of faith." Even Jesus' disciples who had been with him during his ministry did not remember him as the Man of Galilee; they remembered the words and works of one who after Good Friday was revealed to them as the Resurrected Lord. A critical study of the "forms" of the oral period leads to the conclusion that we see Jesus through the faith-tinted window of the Church.

We can gain some idea of the way Jesus was remembered in the early Christian community by examining some of the sermons recorded in the early chapters of Acts. One of their striking features is the repetition of certain basic themes, as though the early apostles were all speaking from the same sermon notes. New Testament scholars believe that although Luke wrote Acts late in the first century, he faithfully recorded the essential "preaching message" which Christians had proclaimed from the time of Pentecost. The best example is Peter's first address to the Gentiles:

You know the word which he sent to Israel, preaching good news of peace by Jesus Christ (he is Lord of all), the word which was proclaimed throughout all Judea, beginning from Galilee after the baptism which John preached: how God anointed Jesus of Nazareth with the Holy Spirit and with power; how he went about doing good and healing all that were oppressed by the devil, for God was with him. And we are witnesses to all that he did both in the country of the Jews and in Jerusalem. They put him to death by hanging him on a tree; but God raised him on the third day and made him manifest, not to all the people but to us who were chosen by God as witnesses, who ate and drank with him after he rose from the dead. And he commanded us to preach to the people, and to testify that he is the one ordained by God to be judge of the living and the dead. *To him all the prophets bear witness* that every one who believes in him receives forgiveness of sins through his name.

—Acts 10:36-43 (see also 2:14-40; 3:12-26; 4:8-13)

To many of us who are accustomed to hearing something rather different from the pulpit, this does not appear to resemble a sermon, for it is actually a summary of the essential features of the Gospel Story as presented more elaborately in, say, Mark. Probably much of what goes under the name of "preaching" today would have been called "teaching" in the early Christian community. Early Christian preaching was more like the preaching of *Green Pastures*, that is, a rehearsal of the crucial episodes of the biblical drama and especially the recital of the Gospel Story itself. Indeed, the Greek word for "preaching message" (*kerygma*) is based on a verb which means "to announce, to proclaim," and suggests the picture of a herald or town crier proclaiming a message of good news. The early Christian sermon was not a reasoned argument, a beautiful meditation, or a piece of common-sense advice; rather, it was a bold proclamation of "the mighty acts of the Lord," culminating in the raising of Jesus from the dead.

In the next chapter we shall turn our attention to the ministry of Jesus. Here we are concerned with the theme of fulfillment which pervades the early sermons: "to him all the prophets bear witness." This same theme is accented by Paul in an important passage where he gives a quick summary of the gospel which he had received, presumably from early Christian preachers in Jerusalem:

> For I delivered unto you first of all that which I also received, how that Christ died for our sins *according to the Scriptures*: and that he was buried and that he rose again the third day *according to the Scriptures.*
>
> —I Corinthians 15:3-4

Since Paul wrote these words at a time when there were no Christian writings, it is obvious that here he was referring to the Christians' first Bible: the Old Testament. His message, like that of preachers who preceded him, was substantially the proclamation that the Messiah "promised before by his [God's] prophets in the holy Scriptures" (Romans 1:2) had come. Incidentally, Paul's dependence upon the received Proclamation of the Church should warn us against assuming that he was responsible for shifting the center of gravity from the simple religion *of* Jesus to the religion *about* Jesus, from the "Jesus of the Gospels" to "the Christ of faith." Admittedly Christianity was autographed in Paul's unique experience, so that he could rightly speak of "my gospel"; but his message was no radical departure from *the* Gospel (see Romans 1:1, "the gospel of God") which Christians proclaimed from the first. Indeed, he seems to have understood the meaning and implications of Jesus' career better than other disciples, like Peter, who had been nearest to him.[10]

According to the Christian view, then, the whole Old Testament, which in its present form is stamped with prophetic

[10] As an example, consider Paul's understanding of the universal implications of the Christian gospel, and the missionary expansion which seems to have been resisted by the apostolic group in Jerusalem. Commenting on Paul's role in widening the horizons of Christianity, Hans Lietzmann makes the striking observation: "He had never sat at the feet of the Master, but nevertheless was the only one amongst the apostles who really understood him." *The Beginnings of the Christian Church* (Scribner, 1937), pp. 146 f.

influence, bears witness to and is fulfilled in Christ (see John 5:39). This view was inherited as a legacy from Jesus himself who told his followers that he had come not to destroy, but to fulfill the two major parts of the Jewish Scriptures: the Law and the Prophets (Matthew 5:17). Thus there is real precedent for the Russian painting which depicts "the goodly fellowship of the prophets" coming out to greet Christ as he sets his face to enter Jerusalem. The emphasis upon fulfillment of prophecy was native to Christianity from the first.

The Argument from Prophecy

We are now ready to deal with the implications of the Event in which the Christian community experienced the fulfillment of Israel's spiritual history. The claim that Old Testament prophecies were fulfilled *literally* has always been one of Christianity's strong talking points. The human mind, of course, is properly impressed with the alleged evidence that long in advance a prophet was able to peer into God's crystal ball and give an accurate preview of things to come—even to the appearance of "flying saucers," as we are now being told! Thus, from the earliest times to the present the "argument from prophecy" has been used as one of the most persuasive proofs of the inspiration of Scripture and the truth of Christianity.

Early Christians believed that in the career of Jesus prophecy had been fulfilled to the finest details. For instance, crowded into the opening chapters of Matthew are quotations of Old Testament predictions concerning almost every aspect of Jesus' birth and childhood. We are told that Jesus was conceived of a virgin, born in the city of Bethlehem, was carried by the fugitive Holy Family into Egypt to escape Herod's massacre, and finally was brought up in Nazareth—all of this in order that specific prophecies of the Old Testament might be fulfilled. Moreover, Peter's sermon on the day of Pentecost set forth the argument that David, who before the rise of biblical criticism was supposed to have written the Psalms, actually predicted the Resurrection and Ascension in Psalms 16 and 110 (Acts 2:25-28, 34-35). This use of the Old Testament reminds one of modern fundamentalist preachers who, for instance, find in Psalm 22 literal predictions of the exact manner of Jesus' execution and other details such as the parting of his garments among the soldiers.

It would be wrong, however, to classify these early Christians as fundamentalists, as though the heart of the argument from prophecy were a proof-text use of Scripture.[11] It cannot be denied, of course, that Christians used Old Testament passages in this manner. As a matter of fact, there is evidence that a book of "Testimonies"—Scriptural proof-texts—circulated in the early Church. But we must approach this matter by understanding the Jewish matrix out of which Christianity emerged. The first Christians were Jews, and they preached to audiences composed largely of Jews. The proof-text method was a necessary and effective strategy among Jews who were accustomed to accepting no new doctrine unless authority for it could be found in their own Scriptures, all three parts of which (Law, Prophets, Writings) were regarded at that time as being divinely inspired. So, in their early sermons as recorded in Acts, the apostles quoted liberally from the Old Testament to prove to their listeners, many of whom were well versed in Jewish Scripture, that Jesus was the Messiah. Many of the examples of alleged literal fulfillment of prophecy appear to us to be nothing more than clever word plays, resembling the manner in which rabbis of the day used Scripture. One cannot help feeling that this was largely an "ad hominem" argument, a type of argument which the dictionary defines as one directed to another person's prejudices rather than to his intellect. Later on, however, as Christianity moved out upon Gentile soil, the same argument was addressed to the intellect and proved to be cogent to many educated people.

---

[11] For a forceful restatement of the argument from prophecy, see Alan Richardson, *Christian Apologetics*, chap. 8.

We cannot share the prejudice of early Christians and Jews because we have a clearer intellectual understanding of the historic sense of the various Old Testament passages. Therefore, the argument that specific prophecies have been literally fulfilled does not "hold water" because, strange as it may seem, *the argument is not literal enough,* that is, it does not rest upon an accurate interpretation of the original meaning of the passage at the time it was written. Take as an example the passage in Matthew (1:22) which states that the Virgin Birth occurred in order that the prophecy of Isaiah 7:14 might be fulfilled, "Behold a virgin shall be with child, and shall bring forth a son, and they shall call his name Emmanuel," that is, "God is with us." A purely literal exegesis of Isaiah 7:14 yields the following results: (1) The Hebrew word does not mean "virgin" at all (there is a special word in Hebrew for "virgin") but merely a young woman; and (2) Isaiah's specific prediction was that in a very short time—nine months hence—the Immanuel child would be born and so named as an evidence that God would deliver his people from a threatening military coalition (735-34 B.C.). This is the literal, historical meaning of the passage. It is only in a more symbolic sense that the Immanuel prophecy can be applied to Jesus, who embodies God's purposive action in history. The author of Matthew, however, read the Old Testament in its Greek translation (Septuagint) and for some reason the Greek translator chose to render the Hebrew word with the Greek word which means "virgin." Plainly the validity of the doctrine of the Virgin Birth must rest on some other grounds than the literal fulfillment of prophecy.[12]

Still another difficulty arises when we understand this argument to mean the fulfillment of literal details predicted beforehand. According to such a view, history is more or less prearranged; otherwise a detailed preview of the future would be impossible. Just as the scientist's prediction of the date of the return of Haley's comet presupposes that celestial

[12] We shall further discuss the Virgin Birth in the next chapter.

bodies obey natural law, so the prophet's ability to predict the exact date of Jesus' coming [13] and specific historical circumstances in his career would mean that the course of history was fixed long in advance. In this case human beings, though having the illusion of freedom, were actually goose-stepping according to God's prearranged plan and timetable. Such a view does violence to the biblical interpretation of history which takes into account both God's sovereignty over events and man's freedom to make history. We have previously discovered that the role of the prophet was not that of a soothsayer who reads the mysteries of the future. True, prophets made predictions, but their specific forecasts were confined to the immediate future and subject to error and revision owing to the unpredictable element in human action; their major prediction was that in spite of all opposing forces God's Day of Victory was certainly coming. Therefore the language of the New Testament, which seems to imply that things *had to happen* this way in order that prophecy might be fulfilled, should not be strained to mean that men's actions were predetermined.

There is, however, an even greater weakness in the excessive emphasis upon literal fulfillment of prophecy. If, as this type of argument assumes, all the facets of the Christian gospel were announced in advance in the Old Testament period, then the New Testament is robbed of its newness. It is true that the Old Testament, which has a dynamic forward movement, bears witness to and points toward the Messiah. But it is quite another matter to say that the Old Testament bears witness to *Jesus Christ* and the specific events of his career, as some European scholars are doing today on the basis of allegorical interpretation.[14] In this case, the Old and New Testaments

[13] Conservative Christians find a prediction of the date of Jesus' birth in Daniel 9:25.

[14] For a criticism of Wilhelm Vischer's treatment of "The Witness of the Old Testament to Christ," see the present writer's article, "The Place of the Book of Esther in the Christian Bible," *Journal of Religion*, Vol. xxx, No. 1, January, 1950, pp. 32-43.

are made virtually identical. The progressive momentum of history is brought to a standstill in a static situation, the Gospel of Jesus being only a kind of "republication" (to use the Deist word) of truths which had been known previously. If we are to take seriously the idea of historical fulfillment, we must take into account both the messianic continuity of the two Testaments and the movement of the biblical drama toward the new revelation which comes at the climax.

Our knowledge of the way Christian traditions were shaped by the mind of the Church enables us to assume that one of two things happened in these instances of alleged fulfillment of detailed prophecies. In some instances, like the Crucifixion itself, the event took place and afterward devout Christians—eager to find references to Jesus in the earliest Christian Bible, the Old Testament—searched the Scripture for passages which they could claim as "predictions." In other cases, such as Jesus' birth in Bethlehem, certain Old Testament passages indicated that the event *should* have taken place when the Messiah came and, in the popular tradition of Christianity, the Gospel story was embellished accordingly.

For those who take seriously a critical study of the Bible, it is impossible to use the argument from prophecy as it was used by early Christians and by many theological leaders of the past. Today we have a fuller understanding of the original, historic sense of Old Testament prophecies. Thus we are no longer convinced by Matthew, for instance, who finds a prophetic forecast of the Holy Family's flight to Egypt in the words of Hosea (11:1): "Out of Egypt I have called my son." We know that Hosea was referring not to a future event but to the Exodus from Egypt, and that the "son" was not the Messiah but the people, Israel. We must remember that early Christians, who were children of their time, wrote under limitations of knowledge for which they cannot be held responsible. It would be just as much a mistake to follow early Christians all the way in their use of prophecy as it would be to adopt the belief that Moses wrote the Pentateuch just because Jesus and early Christians believed he did. We cannot turn the clock of history backward and live in their day.

It would be equally erroneous, however, to jump to the other extreme and scrap the argument from prophecy completely, just because we cannot follow a literal fulfillment. Actually this early use of the Old Testament is correct *in principle,* and indeed is basic to the Christian faith.

History and Prophecy

What, then, do Christians really mean when they say that the prophets bear witness to Christ? Let us first hear the testimony of one of the greatest Christian theologians and philosophers of all ages: Augustine. It is doubtful whether any of us could better encompass the essence of the Christian faith in a single sentence than Augustine does in these words:

> The fundamental principle, the head of this religion is *history* and *prophecy,* that is, the prediction of the disposition of Divine Providence for the salvation of the human race which needs to be formed anew and restored to eternal life.[15]

In his pre-Christian days, while still a follower of Plato, Augustine accepted the prevailing Greek attitude toward history. According to this view, history constantly repeats itself; there is literally nothing new under the sun. The notion of purpose in history is completely alien to the Greeks, for history, like the revolving shadow on a sundial, moves in circles, without beginning and without end. In Christianity, however, Augustine found a radically new outlook upon history, and it is significant that in his "definition in a nutshell" he links together the two words: history and prophecy. When he spoke of prophetic history he meant that history is a *progression* of unique, creative, unrepeatable events in a purposive drama which has a beginning and an end. Moreover, the dynamic of the forward moving drama of human existence

---

[15] Quoted and discussed by Erich Frank in his article, "The Role of History in Christian Thought," *Bulletin* of the Duke Divinity School, Vol. xiv, No. 3, pp. 66 ff.

is the redemptive activity of God, discerned by prophets and fulfilled in Christ. As Professor Frank points out, "the magic circle of nature was broken and transformed into the straight line of history which was directed toward one ultimate goal." For Augustine, history was no longer measured by the "time of nature," the cyclical movement of the seasons and the planets; time was the measurement of the realization of purpose, and God himself was the "timekeeper." Perhaps the following illustration will help to clarify this important distinction. When we watch the clock, time seems to drag by monotonously and even meaninglessly. However, when we are watching a good movie, completely lost in the story, we forget clock time. Time is measured in terms of the progression of the story from beginning to end.

When the matter is put in this light, the importance of prophecy in the biblical view of history becomes apparent, for this unique time-consciousness pervades the Bible.[16] The Old Testament prophets, as we discovered earlier, had to wage a fierce battle against a Baal nature religion which sought divine reality in the recurring cycles of nature. They spoke in behalf of the God of the Covenant, the God whose word was heard in unique and unrepeatable historical events, and who liberated men from the cycles of nature in order that they might participate in the forward moving drama of history. Indeed, the very concept of the Covenant is the key to the unique biblical perspective upon history. This is indicated in the following words of R. B. Y. Scott:

> Belief in a divine act of choice at a particular moment in history . . . gives to time special significance as the context of divine action and human moral response. *It also gives to history a beginning and a direction.*[17]

For these elected people, history had a beginning in God's purpose and moved toward the realization of his purpose. Each

---

16 See the valuable sixth chapter of Paul Minear's *Eyes of Faith* (Westminster, 1946).

17 *The Relevance of the Prophets* (Macmillan, 1944), p. 119. See also the valuable discussion, pp. 135-140.

event was a *new* act of God in his drama of salvation. Every crisis brought men nearer to the fulfillment of his Promise.

In the Old Testament the argument from prophecy is given magnificent expression in the poems of Second Isaiah. With cutting satire the prophet challenges the idols to show proof that they have been able to announce a purpose in advance and bring it to fulfillment in history. It is Yahweh alone, says the prophet, who manifests his lordship over history by predicting his disposition to save his people and by carrying out his plan throughout the historical career of Israel. He, therefore, is the one who declares "the end from the beginning" and announces things which have not yet come to pass (see 41:21-26; 46:8-10). Since Yahweh is Lord, history is prophecy, and prophecy is the prediction of his triumph in history.

In this manner the prophets of the Old Testament looked toward the future. Their detailed forecasts were confined to the immediate political crises of Israel's history; but they also looked toward the horizons of God's future when the tensions of Israel's history would be resolved and God's purpose would be realized. With renewing hope and imaginative vision they proclaimed that beyond the day of judgment would be God's day of mercy, beyond Israel's doom her Resurrection, beyond the broken covenant the New Covenant. Moreover, as we have seen, prophets and apocalyptic writers increasingly focused their expectations upon the coming of a Messiah who would be God's agent in the fulfilling of the divine purpose. We should notice especially that the messianic hope, whether expressed in the expectation of a coming "Son of David" or a heavenly "Son of Man," was the Hebraic way of saying that *history was moving in the direction of the realization of its God-intended goal.* As Reinhold Niebuhr has put it succinctly: "A Christ is expected wherever history is regarded as potentially meaningful but as still awaiting the full disclosure and fulfillment of its meaning." [18]

[18] *Nature and Destiny of Man* (Scribner, 1947), Vol. II, p. 4. All of chapter 1 is valuable in this connection.

Thus in "the fullness of time" Jesus came among the Jewish people. This phrase is an apt description of the creative character of the event. Time itself was "full." It was heavy and pregnant with the sacred meaning of Israel's past. It was ripe for giving birth to God's "new creation." According to the Gospels, Jesus himself was aware that his appearance on the stage of history had been timed for the moment of climax in the historical drama. He preached that the time had been fulfilled, and told his disciples that they were privileged to see the things which many prophets and kings had desired to see but could only hope for (Matthew 13:17; Luke 10:24). The "New Israel" which he gathered about himself recognized him to be the Messiah, and testified that the whole sacred story of the Old Testament was summed up in him. The election of the people of Israel, their deliverance from Egyptian bondage, their entrance into the Promised Land, the idealized kingship of David, the building of the Temple, the divine judgment of the Exile, Israel's resurrection and restoration in the priestly community of Judaism—all these events were gathered up into the person of the Messiah. The purpose of God, which prophets had discerned dimly and partially in historical crises, was being accomplished. The goal of history, heralded by prophets from a distance, had—in some sense—been reached. The messianic age was dawning.

This enthusiastic conviction led the Church to claim that the various details of Jesus' career had been predicted by the prophets. Rather than accepting all of these claims unreservedly, we must understand the reason early Christians made them. The basic motivation was the conviction that Jesus' ministry was not an isolated event: it was integrally related to the whole sacred drama. The various episodes in his career were not accidental developments; behind them was the prior purpose and activity of God manifested throughout the Old Testament period. Therefore, said Christians, all these things were done in order that prophecy might be fulfilled. The case for the fulfillment of prophecy, however, does not rest upon the accomplishment of precise predictions made centuries in advance. The fundamental "prediction" accomplished was, as Augustine said, God's ancient promise to re-create the human race. In so far as prophets discerned God's redemptive activity in the events of their time, and thereby imaginatively pointed toward the Day when God's purpose would be realized, it is proper to say in the words of the Eastern Orthodox homily: "The Prophets with their trumpets proclaim before Him their mysteries."

Let us not suppose, however, that the New Testament fulfills the Old only by progressing beyond it one stage further, as, say, one reaches higher mathematics by going beyond arithmetic. From Matthew to Revelation we find a constant emphasis upon *newness*: the New Covenant, the New Creation, the New Israel, the New Jerusalem. In one sense Christianity is continuous with the expectations of the Old Testament; but in another and equally important sense it represents a radical break, a sharp discontinuity. This gospel, to use Jesus' figure, was "new wine" that could not be contained in old wineskins; it was a new garment, not just a patch sewed upon the old clothes of Judaism (Mark 2:21-22). Although the prophets foreshadowed the coming of the Christ, men could not recognize *Jesus of Nazareth* as that Christ without a repentance which altered their entire perspective. Their blind eyes had to be opened by the miracle of God's revelation.

The clearest proof of this is that many Jews then (and now) could not accept Jesus as Messiah, nor could they be moved by the claim that their own Scriptures bore witness to him. They had expected a victorious Messiah who would "redeem Israel" by giving the nation its deserved place in the sun, but they had not expected a suffering and crucified Messiah. They had anticipated the fulfillment of God's purpose in history, but they could not conceive of God manifesting his omnipotence in a Cross. According to the tradition, even the disciples were baffled by Jesus' strange role (Mark 8:31-33; 10:35-45) and after the Resurrection entertained the hope that Jesus would soon "restore the kingdom to Israel" (Acts 1:6). This was the stumbling block, that when God's Messiah appeared he was glorified and made perfect through suffering. This was the "divine surprise" which confounded all Jewish nationalistic expectations. As Paul wrote to the Church at Corinth:

> We preach Christ crucified, unto the Jews a stumbling block, and unto the Greeks foolishness, but unto them which are called [that is, grasped by the divine meaning of this Event], both Jews and Greeks, Christ the power of God and the wisdom of God.[19]
>
> —I Corinthians 1:23-24

To the Church, the Cross was the manifestation of God's power in human history, the realization of his redemptive purpose implicit from the first in the deliverance of Israel from Egyptian bondage. And to men of faith the assurance of this was that God raised Jesus from the dead, exalted him to his right hand, and poured out his Spirit upon the Church.

From this new vantage point of faith, the Church read the Old Testament and found in it foreshadowings of the supreme manifestation of God's redemptive action in Christ. Many of the passages to which Christians turned had not been intended originally in a messianic sense. This was the case, for instance, with the "Suffering Servant" passages, Isaiah 53 and Psalm 22. We cannot think of these passages as being fulfilled in the sense that the writers were able to forecast either the coming of one named Jesus or to predict the exact details of his Passion. But in so far as these passages witness to God's redemption through suffering (see I Peter 2:21-25) they do focus upon Him who conceived his messianic role to be that of the Suffering Servant. So Paul could say, quoting the received tradition, "Christ died for our sins according to Scripture" (especially Isaiah 53). Likewise Philip—according to an important story found in Acts 8:30-35—met the perplexity

---

[19] For a discussion of the Christ who came, but not according to men's expectations, see Niebuhr, *op. cit.*, II, chapter 2.

of the Ethiopian eunuch about the meaning of Isaiah 53 by "beginning from this Scripture" and preaching unto him Jesus. Thus the New Testament fulfills the Old, not only by bringing the sacred drama to a denouement, but by altering men's understanding as to the way God accomplishes his triumph and effects his sovereignty over history.

Christianity and the Two Testaments

It is clear, then, that instead of making the Old Testament obsolete for Christians, the event of the Crucifixion-Resurrection opened their eyes so that they could read it rightly. Christ provided the key with which Christians could unlock the Scriptures, bringing forth treasures both new and old. This is the point of a beautiful story found in Luke (24:13-32), according to which the Risen Christ joins two travelers as they walk along the road to Emmaus shortly after the first tidings of the Resurrection. The travelers are puzzled, but the Stranger exclaims:

> O foolish men, and slow of heart to believe all that the prophets have spoken! Was it not necessary that the Christ should suffer these things and enter into his glory? And beginning with Moses [the Law] and all the prophets, he interpreted to them in all the scriptures the things concerning himself.

It is interesting that this story is given to us only by Luke, an educated Gentile who wrote for the purpose of commending Christianity to Gentile readers. However, Gentiles could not easily be persuaded by this appeal to the Old Testament. As long as a Jewish background could be presupposed, it is understandable that Jesus would be seen within the setting of the historical memories of the Jewish tradition and that such Christians in their elation over the rediscovery of the Old Testament would exclaim: "Did not our hearts burn within us . . . while he [the Risen Christ] opened to us the Scriptures?" But as Christianity became increasingly Gentile in complexion, it was not so easy for people, coming out of a different historical and cultural background, to accept the categories of the Old Testament. In time this led to a crisis which threatened the retention of the Old Testament in the Christian Church. To understand the nature of this crisis, we must deal briefly with the development of the New Testament canon.

Throughout the whole of the first century Christians had no Scripture of their own. During this period, however, the Jews had a three-part canon—the Law, Prophets, and Writings—and this was accepted as the Christian's Bible. In fact, whenever early Christians used the word "Scripture" they referred, almost always, not to distinctively Christian writings but to part or all of the Old Testament (Matt. 22:29; Acts 17:2; and so on). Christian writings emerged gradually, evoked by the practical situations in the life of the Church, and increasingly these writings gained prestige in the Christian community. There is reason to believe, for instance, that near the end of the century a collection of Paul's letters circulated among various churches. Moreover, the period of time covered by the Four Gospels (A.D. 70-110) witnessed the appearance of the rest of the literature now found in the New Testament: first, the literature which reflects the persecutions experienced during the succession of Roman emperors from Nero to Domitian (I Peter, the Epistle to the Hebrews, the Revelation of John), and later—after Domitian's death in A.D. 96—literature which reflects the relaxation of persecution and the increasing concern of the Church to consolidate its position by giving attention to questions of faith and conduct (the Pastoral Epistles to Timothy and Titus and the Catholic or General Epistles of John and Jude).[20] But throughout this period, when the Church was expanding and consolidating its position, there was no thought of a sacred canon of uniquely Christian writings. Christianity from the very first had relied primarily

---

20 The clear exception is II Peter, which is usually dated pretty well along in the second century.

upon the oral communications of its message. As late as A.D. 140 Papias declared—at a time when the Four Gospels and other writings were well known—that "what was to be got from books was not so profitable to me as what came from the living and abiding voice."

In the second century, however, the Church faced a new situation. The early eyewitnesses had all disappeared, and the primitive Christian gospel was threatened by the influx of Gentiles who approached Christianity from the standpoint of the predominant categories of Greek culture and philosophy. The issue was brought to a crisis by the teachings of Marcion, to whom we referred in a previous chapter, and whose position rested upon a Greek conception of God—a conception which did not allow any emphasis upon either divine creation of the world or divine action in history. To him it was inconceivable that God could "dirty his hands," as it were, by creating this evil world, and it was equally fantastic that he could be identified with the tragedies and changes of history. On this premise he rejected the Old Testament as Christian Scripture and proposed as a Christian canon a few carefully selected writings now found in the New Testament.

The Church met Marcion's challenge at both points. First, instead of his highly selective method of determining Christian writings, the Church adopted the standard of "apostolic authority," that is, a given writing had to have been composed by a known apostle or associate of an apostle and therefore had to give witness to the apostolic Christianity of the first century. These second century Christians applied this principle to the best of their ability though, of course, not being able to use the methods of "historical criticism." Some of the books now contained in the New Testament were questioned for a time. The authorship of the Epistle to the Hebrews was held to be doubtful by some, and the Revelation of John seemed to be out of line with apostolic writings. Likewise there was some uncertainty whether Second Peter was written by the apostle Peter, and there was question about when the epistles of James and Jude were written. Nevertheless, there was clear consensus that the bulk of our present New Testament was authoritative, not because these writings were selected by ecclesiastical leaders, but because the Church in its common life intuitively recognized that they proclaimed the faith which the Church had received and which was the basis of its ongoing life.[21] In the second place, on this same ground Marcion's rejection of the Old Testament was condemned as a heresy, for it could be demonstrated that his position obviously departed from the apostolic Christianity of the first century.

The ghost of Marcion continues to haunt the Church, especially in our day when some would relegate the Old Testament to a position of "primitive origins" or condemn it to practical disuse. The presence of the Old Testament in the Christian Bible occasions difficulties, some of which we have dealt with in previous chapters, but we can put this down as an axiom: *without the Old Testament the distinctive message of Christianity would evaporate into thin air*. Apart from the New Testament the Old Testament is a mere torso; and apart from the Old Testament the New Testament quickly becomes a non-Christian book. Since Christianity rests upon the faith that God has acted redemptively in history—a conviction which Marcion's Greek mind could not tolerate and which is still "foolishness" to modern "Greeks"—the Christian Church necessarily must embrace both Testaments. It remains true, as Augustine said long ago, that the essence of Christianity is history and prophecy.

---

21 The rest of the twenty-seven writings of our New Testament were gradually accepted as authoritative in the Christian community, and their final acceptance was formally ratified by the Council of Carthage, A.D. 397. For a brief discussion of the growth of the canon, see H. J. Carpenter, *The Interpretation of the Bible*, ed. C. W. Dugmore (London, Society for Promoting Christian Knowledge, 1944), pp. 1-9.

8

God Was in Christ

THE BIOGRAPHER OF Henry David Thoreau relates a characteristic anecdote of the poet-naturalist of New England. When Thoreau was approaching death, his Calvinistic aunt asked the timely question, "Henry, have you made your peace with God?" Unperturbed by the lingering ghost of the Calvinism which had been banished from New England, Thoreau answered pleasantly: "I didn't know we had ever quarreled, Aunt!" [1]

This anecdote illustrates the spirit which has prevailed in America during the nineteenth and twentieth centuries. Jonathan Edwards (1703-58), representing a virile Calvinism, had been the key figure in a "Great Awakening" which spread like wildfire through New England. Through his preaching, people became vividly conscious of the awesome rift which separates sinful man from the holy God. But this Calvinism, even though championed by one of America's greatest theologians and the third president of Princeton University, was not palatable in young America which was just beginning to "feel its oats." The history of America since the time of Edwards has been marked by a steady decline of emphasis upon the reality of sin, and by the ready acceptance of the doctrine that there is no quarrel between God and reasonable, well-intending, and essentially good men. In our own time some

[1] Edward Waldo Emerson, *Henry Thoreau, As Remembered by a Young Friend* (Houghton, 1917), pp. 117 f. I am grateful to my student, John Bridges, for this reference.

psychologists have insisted that the word "sin" should be stricken from the vocabulary. Many ministers hesitate to use the word in the pulpit. And the words of the prayer of General Confession, "There is no health in us," strike most people as being medieval.

It is precisely because men, à la Thoreau, are not troubled by a consciousness of estrangement from God that the New Testament, and indeed the whole Bible, constitutes a problem. From beginning to end, the Bible deals with sin, with man's rebellion against God. From the biblical viewpoint, this is the very stuff of history: man's will in opposition to God's will, man's attempt to live in terms of his own self-defined purpose, man's self-sufficiency in conflict with God's jealous demand that he be the sole center of life. As far as the Bible is concerned there *is* a quarrel between man and God. The New Testament puts it in strong language: men are, before the experience of reconciliation, "enemies" of God (Romans 5:10). But if men are unaware of this quarrel, if "sin" is only a neurosis which educated and mature people outgrow, then the biblical message concerning God's redemption is largely meaningless. In this case, the Bible proclaims the answer to an unasked question. It offers a cure to those who do not need a physician. If such people read the Bible at all, it is only because it is great literature, or because it inspires one to live a good moral life, or because of its lofty conception of God.

The Role of the Messiah

This is not the place to evaluate the modern view, and the various attempts to modernize Jesus so that he might be acceptable in our world. Our primary purpose is to understand the role of Jesus Christ according to the New Testament view. In this chapter we shall be concerned with the *person* of Jesus in the original sense of the Latin *persona,* a word which once referred to the mask worn by actors and therefore to the part played in a drama. We have discovered that the Bible sets forth a sacred drama—a drama which moves forward dynamically from the call of Israel to the establishment of the Church, the New Israel of God. Now we must inquire more deeply into the role which Jesus performs in this drama.

In a real sense all the literature of the New Testament gives variations upon a single theme, stated magnificently by Paul in two sentences which supplement each other: "God was in Christ reconciling the world to himself" (II Corinthians 5:19) and "God shows his love for us in that while we were yet sinners Christ died for us" (Romans 5:8). These words testify that through Christ *God took the initiative* to bridge the gulf which men's sin had brought into being. By the power of his freely offered love (*agape*) [2] he sought to break through the egocentric boundaries of human existence in order that men might acknowledge him whom to serve is perfect freedom. Surely no one can fail to notice the diversities of the New Testament as he reads the Synoptic Gospels, Paul's Letters, First Peter, the Epistle to the Hebrews, the Pastoral and Catholic Epistles, the Johannine writings, or the Revelation. However, just as an organist utilizes the various stops and manuals of his instrument as he elaborates the theme of a Bach chorale, so the New Testament uses the infinite richness of language and experience to proclaim this central message to the world.

As was pointed out in the last chapter, the person and work of Jesus can be understood properly only within the setting which the Old Testament provides. The New Testament claims that God's redemptive purpose, implicit from the first in his deliverance of Israel from Egyptian bondage, was consummated in the greater deliverance accomplished by Christ. It is not surprising, therefore, that the vocation of Jesus is depicted in terms of the categories which in the past had been applied to the people, Israel. He is the "Son" (Hosea 11:1;

---

[2] The New Testament Greek word *agape* takes on the unique meaning of the Christian gospel. It stresses the *outgoing* of God's love to those who do not deserve his favor; that is, as Paul says, it was given "while we were yet sinners" (see also I John 4:10). Thus the word is equivalent to "grace" or "forgiveness."

cf. Mark 9:7), the Elect One in whom God delights (Isaiah 42:1; cf. Mark 1:11), the "Servant" (Isaiah 52:13 ff.; cf. Acts 3:13), and the "Son of Man" (Daniel 7:13; cf. Mark 10:45). Above all, Second Isaiah's description of the Suffering Servant was used, evidently by Jesus himself and certainly by the early Church, to proclaim the meaning of the Cross. God was in Israel reconciling the world unto himself: this had been the testimony of Second Isaiah as he contemplated the tragic and glorious destiny of Israel. God was in Jesus reconciling the world unto himself: this was the unanimous testimony of those who knew him who was glorified through suffering.

This raises questions for many of us. What do Christians mean when they say that "God was in Christ"? In the early centuries serious discussion of the implications of this affirmation led to the formulation of the doctrine of the Trinity, which has been and is still the heart of orthodox Christianity. "God in three Persons [Father, Son, Holy Spirit], blessed Trinity!" These words of the familiar hymn witness to the tremendous claims which Christians make on behalf of Christ. In our more reflective moments, however, some of us wonder about the meaning of what we sing and affirm. Was Jesus divine and human, God and man? What is the relation between the "christology" (doctrine about Christ) of early apostles like Peter and Paul, and the mission and message of Jesus himself as set forth in the Gospels? In other words, what is the relation between the gospel *of* Jesus and the gospel that *is* Jesus, between the message and the man? These are important issues which we should approach with both reverence and honesty.

The Days of His Flesh

We shall approach this subject through the gateway of Form Criticism. At the risk of retreading some of the ground covered in the last chapter, two points must be kept in mind as we discuss the public ministry of Jesus.

First, it is impossible to write a "life of Jesus," if by that phrase is meant a kind of day-by-day diary of his actions and thoughts. It is questionable, for instance, whether we can rely upon the Marcan order of events in Jesus' career, an outline which Matthew and Luke largely adopted from the earliest Gospel. Form Critics emphasize that Mark for the most part merely joined together the various units of the oral tradition by artificial connecting devices (like "as he was on the road," "as he was in the boat," and so forth) and that Mark's selection and arrangement of the material were governed by his own interest and interpretation.[3] If this is true, we cannot trace Jesus' travels, date his utterances, or locate incidents geographically.

In the second place, all the units of the oral tradition were vehicles for expressing the post-Resurrection faith of the Church, as set forth in the early apostolic sermons. The Gospel writers were not biographers but "propagandists" in the best sense of the word. Similarly the preachers and teachers of the oral period remembered the words and works of Jesus in the light of the Resurrection, which cast its rays backward into his earthly career. In other words, in the gospel traditions we do not have a photograph of "the historical Jesus" snapped by a mechanically disinterested camera lens; we have, rather, a portrait of Jesus which artistically registers the impression of the person upon his followers. Any attempt to reach a "historical Jesus"—a kind of hypothetical "x" which lies behind the faith of the Church—soon reaches a point of diminishing returns.

This does not mean that we are driven to skepticism about the historical Jesus, for we would face a similar problem in dealing with, say, Socrates, who left no writings and is known to us only by his impact upon others. As a matter of fact, the fragments of the oral tradition are invaluable to us, for in many cases they give vivid glimpses of Jesus in action, small

[3] Form Critics say that the one exception to this is the Passion Story, which was remembered as a dramatic *sequence* from the very first.

tableaux of various episodes in his ministry. Moreover, within the limitations defined by the nature of the gospel tradition it is possible to reconstruct in outline the broad features of his career and the essential aspects of his message.

At the outset of his career Jesus was associated with John the Baptist. A rugged and dramatic figure who resembled Elijah (compare Mark 1:6 and II Kings 1:8), John preached the coming of the Messiah and baptized those who obeyed his call to repentance.[4] After his baptism, Jesus spent an indefinite time preaching in the province of Galilee. He chose twelve disciples and sent them out on a preaching deputation through Galilee. Here we have evidence that Jesus intended to form a new community which would correspond to the "Remnant" or People of the New Covenant about which prophets had spoken (Isaiah 10:20-22; Jeremiah 31:31-34). Just as Isaiah gathered around him disciples who were to be the embodiment of the Remnant (Isaiah 8:16-18), so Jesus called twelve disciples—one for each of the twelve tribes of Israel—to be the nucleus of the New Israel of God, the Church.[5]

Increasingly Jesus evoked the opposition of the leading elements of Jewish society. Each of the rival parties of Judaism had its own reason for disliking him and joining in a conspiracy against his life: the pious devotees of the Law of Moses (scribes and Pharisees), the priestly aristocracy which represented the vested interests of the Temple (Sadducees), and the left-wing patriots who wanted immediate action against Rome (Zealots). Jesus did not fit into the categories of any of these parties; as a matter of fact, he posed a threat to their

[4] Jews allowed proselytes to join the Jewish community on the condition that they were purified by this water ceremony. John, however, administered baptism to Jews who desired to join the penitent remnant who awaited the Messiah.

[5] Some New Testament scholars dispute the idea that Jesus intended to form a new society, on the ground that the word "church" (*ecclesia*) occurs in only two passages of the Gospels (Matt. 16:18; 18:17), both of which belong allegedly to a late stage of the literary tradition. For a brief defense of the view taken above, see Archibald M. Hunter, *The Message of the New Testament* (Westminster, 1944), pp. 52-65. It will be readily granted, of course, that the small messianic community did not become the Church Militant until the post-Resurrection experience of Pentecost (see Acts 2).

respective interests and party platforms. Not only was Jesus *persona non grata* to Jewish leaders, but his activity aroused the opposition of Roman officials in Palestine. Fearing the political implications of a messianic movement, Herod Antipas, the Roman ruler of Galilee, began to draw his net around Jesus as he had done previously in the case of John. So Jesus, knowing that "a prophet cannot perish out of Jerusalem" (Luke 13:33), left Herod's territory and went into the province of Judea. After a brief ministry in Jerusalem, during which he evoked the hostility of Sadducees who connived with Rome to protect their Temple leadership, he was executed under Pontius Pilate on the charge of pretending to be a messianic King. From the Jewish standpoint this was blasphemy; from the Roman standpoint it was treason. Although Jesus was nailed to death according to the Roman (not the Jewish) form of capital punishment, crucifixion, it must be remembered that both Jews *and* Gentiles co-operated to get rid of him. He was indicted by good, respectable, religious people and crucified under the authority of the most advanced system of law and justice of the time.

This is the skeleton outline of Jesus' public career. What was the meaning of the things he said and did during his brief ministry? Perhaps the best answer to this question is given in a story preserved in Luke's Gospel (4:16-30). Jesus went to the synagogue in his home town, Nazareth. As was the custom in the case of a visiting rabbi, he was given the opportunity to read from the Scripture and to make a brief exposition of its meaning. Turning to Isaiah 61:1-2, he read:

> The Spirit of the Lord is upon me,
> Because he has anointed me to preach good news to the poor.
> He has sent me to proclaim release to the captives,
> And recovering of sight to the blind;
> To set at liberty those that are oppressed,
> To proclaim the acceptable year of the Lord.

The substance of his commentary was: "Today this Scripture has been fulfilled in your hearing." The passage clearly states the purpose of Jesus' ministry and describes his role as that of bringing to fulfillment the expectations of Old Testament prophecy. He was *anointed* (cf. "Messiah") for a unique task, which included preaching, healing, and accomplishing God's promised redemption. Let us look more closely at each of these three aspects of his ministry.

Jesus' Preaching of the Gospel

Jesus' message was set in the context of the belief in the drawing near of "the Kingdom of God." The phrase must not be construed to mean primarily a *realm*, as we would speak of the British kingdom. The underlying Aramaic phrase means basically "Kingly Rule" or "Sovereignty." The Jews of Jesus' day used the phrase in a twofold sense. The rabbis taught that when a man obeyed the Law he took upon himself "the yoke of the Kingdom." Thus God's rule was present wherever faith was found, even though to all outward appearances the world was under the dominion of evil. Also, in the spirit of the prophets and apocalyptic writers, the phrase was used to refer to the time when God would finally manifest his sovereignty by overthrowing the evil forces of history and graciously manifesting his day of favor ("the acceptable year of the Lord"). Thus paradoxically, the Kingdom was conceived as being both present (in faith) and yet to come (in hope).

Jesus' message, belonging fundamentally in the prophetic-apocalyptic tradition of Judaism, stressed the latter part of the paradox, and thus brought the two poles of the magnet—present faith and future hope—close together. According to Mark, he came preaching "the gospel of the Kingdom of God," saying, "The time is fulfilled, and the Kingdom of God is at hand [or, "has come near"]: repent and believe in the gospel" (Mark 1:14-15). Jesus preached with the urgency born of the realization that men were living in the "zero hour" of history when God's "time" was on the verge of being manifested. It was no situation for complacency or quibbling like children at their games (Matthew 11:16-17; Luke 7:31-32). It was a time for action, decision, repentance. Just as night watchers behold the first signs of day in the dawn hours before the sun bursts in full radiance, likewise—even before the Kingdom of God comes in glory—its powers were spreading through the world! In various parables Jesus described the Kingdom as being in the process of arriving. The Kingdom, he said, is like a lump of leaven diffusing its energy through meal, like a hidden treasure which a man stumbles upon in a field, like a tiny seed growing mysteriously and irresistibly, or like a field of wheat and tares ripening for the approaching harvest (see Matthew 13). Already its powers are at work—for those who have eyes to discern "the signs of the times." The near approach of God's Kingdom was the heart of the "good news" proclaimed by Jesus. We must be very careful to distinguish this conception of the Kingdom from modern evolutionary versions of "building the Kingdom on earth," that is, realizing the ideal society.

Closely connected with Jesus' preaching concerning the Kingdom is his teaching on the subject of God. Actually "God" and his "Kingdom" cannot be separated, except in discussion, for the Kingdom is the manifestation of God's sovereign power in history. However, when Jesus spoke about God he proclaimed the good news that God *takes the initiative* to seek and to save. He does not wait for men to approach him; he is like the Good Shepherd who went out into the wilderness to find his lost sheep. He does not wait for his children to ask forgiveness; he is like the father of the prodigal son who was always willing to forgive and who eagerly ran down the road to meet the returning youth and be reconciled with him. The Jewish scholar, Claude Montefiore, insisted that the unique element in Jesus' teaching which could not be paralleled in the Old Testament or rabbinical literature is this picture of God taking the initiative to reconcile his people unto himself. The remark is not quite fair to the prophets, since the belief in divine initiative is at the heart of the doctrine of Israel's election, but at least Montefiore has singled out a central element in Jesus' preaching. The God of Jesus is the God who acts even before men turn unto him. His is the love which goes the whole length in bridging the chasm of self-centeredness (sin) which separates the children of God from the Source of their life.

Jesus' message focused upon the good news of God's forgiveness. Of course, the receiving of forgiveness necessarily presupposes the sense of a *need to be forgiven.* Therefore, Jesus constantly attacked the "good" people of the day whose pride constituted a self-erected barrier separating them from God. With a fine touch of irony, he pointed out that those who are "well" (that is, who suppose that they are) need no physician; the physician can help only those who know they are sick. "I came," he said, "not to call the righteous, but sinners" (Mark 2:17). We miss the point of this remark if we suppose that Jesus accepted Judaism's neat distinction between the sheep and the goats: the righteous being those who fulfilled God's demands in the Law, and the sinners being the religiously outcast who failed to live up to the legal requirements. Jesus' ministry was directed toward those who made no claims for themselves, who knew their poverty-stricken spiritual condition, and who were therefore in a position to receive the forgiveness which God freely offers. Surely one of the main purposes of the sayings now classified under the "Sermon on the Mount" was to oppose the legalism of Judaism which made possible such self-righteousness. "It was said unto you of old [in the Law of Moses] . . . but I say unto you. . ." The things Jesus says to us in the Sermon on the Mount make God's demand so absolute, so inward, so immeasurable, and, in the last analysis, so unattainable that no Christian who is honest can parade his righteousness before God and look down condescendingly upon the other man as a sinner. It is equally out of place for Americans self-righteously to boast, as has been done recently, that United States foreign policy is governed by the Sermon on the Mount, the implication being that our foes are the sinners.[6] The first word of Jesus' preaching is directed to all men alike: Repent!

This explains why Jesus attacked the Pharisees. The Pharisees were the good people of the day. They were religiously devout, morally respectable, and socially minded. Like Job's devout friends, they were representatives of the best of Judaism. But their very goodness and piety excluded them from God's forgiveness, for, as Jesus said in the parable of the Pharisee and Publican (Luke 18:9-14), they "trusted in themselves that they were righteous." The man who went down to his house "justified" [7] was not the self-righteous Pharisee, but the man who in self-despair cried out for divine mercy: "God be merciful to me, a sinner!" The same point is made in the parable of the Prodigal Son and Elder Brother (Luke 15:11-32). Both boys were loved *equally* by the father. However, the elder brother, like the Pharisees, excluded himself from the father's love by his self-righteous attitude ("Lo, these many years do I serve thee, neither transgressed I at any time thy commandment"), while the younger boy, reduced to despair by his knowledge that he had wounded his father ("I am no more worthy to be called thy son"), was in a position to receive the forgiveness freely offered him. "Blessed are the poor in spirit" (those who realize their spiritual poverty), said Jesus in the Beatitudes, "for theirs is the kingdom of Heaven" (Matthew 5:3).

Not only did Jesus preach a message of repentance, but he shocked many people then (and now) by announcing that men could *do* nothing to gain salvation or make themselves worthy of God's forgiveness. If the barrier separating man from God is egocentricity, then, apart from God's grace, man is in a hopeless condition. For try as he will, man cannot extricate himself from *himself*. Effort merely aggravates the

---

[6] See the forceful editorial in *The Christian Century*, "Mr. Truman's Spiritual Blindness," June 28, 1950, p. 782.

[7] "Justified" means accepted or approved by God. We shall encounter this word again in our later discussion of Paul's doctrine of "justification by faith."

problem. As one student wrote in an examination: "When we read the parable of the Pharisee and the Publican, we inevitably thank God that we do not have the pride of the Pharisees, thus showing our pride in being humble!" In this connection one is reminded of a passage in the *Screwtape Letters* where Screwtape, the Devil's Advocate, advises his understudy, Wormwood, on the strategy to be used in undermining the faith of a young Christian:

> I see only one thing to do at the moment. Your patient has become humble; have you drawn his attention to the fact? All virtues are less formidable to us once the man is aware that he has them, but this is especially true of humility. Catch him at the moment when he is really poor in spirit and smuggle into his mind the gratifying reflection, "By jove! I'm being humble," and almost immediately pride —pride at his own humility—will appear. If he awakes to the danger and tries to smother this new form of pride, make him proud of his attempt—and so on, through as many stages as you please.[8]

The best commentary on the human predicament is found in the story of the so-called "Rich Young Ruler" (Mark 10:17-31 and parallels). The story opens with the question: "What shall *I do* to inherit eternal life [the life of the Kingdom]?" Jesus dealt with this young man, who had been nourished on Jewish legalism, by imposing a demand which in his case was impossible of fulfillment. When the astonished disciples asked, "Then who can be saved?" Jesus answered, "The things which are impossible with men are possible with God." Thus Christianity, unlike Judaism and all moralistic faiths, is not a religion of attainment, as though by doing something man could somehow lift himself by his own bootstraps and improve his spiritual condition. The sum and substance of the gospel of the Kingdom is that God's love does for man what man cannot do for himself. God graciously offers the forgiveness which no man can merit by effort, and thus brings men into relationship with him—reconciled, restored, and transformed.

[8] C. S. Lewis, *Screwtape Letters* (Macmillan, 1943), p. 71.

Thus by means of preaching Jesus sought to awaken a sleeping generation to the momentous crisis in which they stood. We are told that his contemporaries remarked that "he taught as one having authority and not as the scribes" (Matt. 7:29). The role of the scribes was to interpret the recorded revelation of the past. Jesus, however, spoke with the authority of the prophetic "thus saith the Lord" as he disclosed the nature of the contemporary crisis in which men were standing. By means of the spoken word he proclaimed that God's sovereign rule was being manifested in a new and dynamic way. He attempted to stir men out of their complacency, and to shatter the self-defensiveness and pride which made it impossible for them to receive the gift of God's grace. Always his message focused upon God's initiative, his action, his coming into human life not only to judge men but to reconcile them to himself. Here we encounter the theme of the Old Testament prophets: the judgment and mercy of God. It will be recalled that in the prophetic message of the Old Testament the present crisis invariably was viewed in terms of God's judgment; God's mercy lay "beyond the judgment." Jesus' message concerning the near approach of the Kingdom and the in-breaking of God's sovereignty, even before its imminent arrival, brought these two themes together. In this case divine judgment and divine mercy were blended together in a gospel that spoke urgently to the present in which men were living.[9]

Jesus' Miracles

Jesus' ministry involved more than proclaiming that already the redemptive rule of God was breaking in upon human life. Not only did he preach this good news; he was its "effective agent." He was the instrument through whom God was accomplishing his purpose to reclaim and to reshape human life.

[9] These two themes are blended together with magnificent counterpoint in the Fourth Gospel. There it is pointed out that the coming of the Son is *both* God's judgment upon the world and the free offer of God's saving mercy (see, for example, John 3:16-21; 12:31-32).

The reality of God's Redemptive Rule was made manifest in what Jesus was *doing*, in the effect of his deeds. This is the central meaning of the miracle stories preserved in the Gospels. To early witnesses, both Jesus' words and deeds were evidences that he had the *authority* of God's Messiah (see Mark 1:27).

For many of us, Jesus' miracles constitute one of the great stumbling blocks in the New Testament. At this point the New Testament does not speak our language. A few of the stories are sometimes explained on the assumption that Jesus was a kind of twentieth-century psychiatrist, but this approach does not carry us very far in dealing with the miracle story tradition as a whole. What can one say, for instance, about the claims that Jesus walked on the sea, raised Lazarus from the dead, or turned water into wine? Such stories seem to violate ordinary human experience and common sense. It is not surprising, then, that some biblical interpreters have treated the miracle stories as curious relics of a prescientific age and have attempted to reduce Christianity to the moral and spiritual teachings of the New Testament.

Many of the things said previously in our discussion of the Exodus would apply, *mutatis mutandis*, to the miracle question in the New Testament. A proper study of this subject would involve a careful consideration of the transmission of the miracle stories in the oral period, with the aid of the method of Form Criticism. Here we can only refer to more adequate treatments of the issue and confine ourselves to a summary of their conclusions.[10]

All the historical evidence we have at our disposal points to the conclusion that the earliest followers of Jesus, as well as his enemies, believed that he performed miracles. Mark, for instance, devotes almost one-third of his Gospel to the subject of miracle. Moreover, Form Criticism has shown that the mir-

---

[10] See especially Alan Richardson, *The Miracle Stories of the Gospels* (Harper, 1942). For a shorter treatment, see William Manson, *Jesus, the Messiah* (Westminster, 1946), chapter 3. I am deeply indebted to both of these scholars.

acle story was one of the "forms" by which the Church gave expression to the messianic faith from the earliest times. The early apostolic sermons of Acts appeal to Jesus' "mighty works and wonders and signs" (Acts 2:22; 10:38) as evidence that God had demonstrated him to be the Messiah. The historical evidence is impressive. As Alan Richardson observes:

> The evidence that Jesus worked miracles is just as strong, and is of precisely the same quality and texture, as that He taught that God is Father and that His disciples should forgive one another. We cannot *on historical grounds alone* accept the evidence for the one and reject that for the other. The evidence that Jesus healed a dropsical man on the Sabbath day is just as good as the evidence that He told the story of the Good Samaritan or the Prodigal Son.[11]

Now, this does not mean that the Christian is under obligation to accept each and every miracle as a literal happening which could have been "taken" with a movie camera. In the New Testament there is less emphasis upon the literal act than upon the meaning which the miracle act conveys. This is clearest in the Fourth Gospel where Jesus' actions, like the symbolic actions of the Old Testament prophets, are regarded as "signs" which have a deeper symbolic significance to those who see in faith. So, for instance, the feeding of the five thousand is less the satisfying of physical hunger than it is the sign of Jesus' power to satisfy men's spiritual hunger with the Bread of Life (John 6:1-59), and the raising of Lazarus is less the reanimation of a corpse than it is the sign of Jesus' power to raise men to new life (11:1-46). But this emphasis upon the *meaning* of Jesus' acts was native to the miracle tradition from the very first, whatever the original nucleus of miracle stories was. Form Criticism emphasizes that the miracle story by its very nature gave free rein to the imagination during the period of the oral transmission of the Christian faith. Nevertheless, the embellishing of the tradition was in itself an expression of the messianic faith of the Church, and this faith, in turn,

---

11 *Christian Apologetics*, p. 170.

rested upon the historical experience that Jesus, as God's Messiah, performed miracles. As Canon Richardson points out, the proper place to begin the discussion of this subject is not with the consideration as to whether such and such a miracle happened, but to inquire into the meaning of Jesus' miracles.

On this point the evidence seems clear and consistent. To the eye of faith, Jesus' miracles were *signs* that the power of the Kingdom of God already was active among men, even before its arrival. Perhaps the key sentence is Jesus' statement as recorded in "Q" (Matthew 12:28; Luke 11:20): "If I by the Spirit of God cast out demons, then is the Kingdom of God come upon you." Commenting on this passage, William Manson says:

> What is indicated . . . is that the Kingdom of God, the most tremendous of all mysteries, has made itself known. It is not only near, it is impinging upon present history: "the kingdom of God has come your length" or "has lighted upon you."[12]

Thus Jesus not only confronted men with the crisis of God's Kingdom through his preaching; the saving purpose and power of God were also revealed in his "mighty works," which were essentially victories over the demonic powers of evil.

According to the tradition, Jesus did not perform miracles to draw crowds or to give indisputable proofs of his divinity. It is a strange fact, often overlooked, that the majority of those who saw Jesus perform miracles did not *see* the real miracle at all, and were not moved to faith merely by the mighty works which took place before them. We cannot appeal to the fact that Jesus performed miracles as a proof which compels belief, any more than could early Christians. The gospel tradition seems to indicate that faith was the prerequisite for perceiving Jesus' messianic identity, just as light is necessary for the vision of the eye. And such faith was not a product of any

---

[12] *Op. cit.*, p. 70.

"flesh and blood" proofs (see Matthew 16:17); it was God's revelation, the miraculous cure of spiritual blindness. When Jesus found this faith, he performed miracles. To those who saw his acts through the glasses of faith, the mighty works were signs of his messiahship and of the Kingdom of God which was impinging upon their lives. To others, his actions were essentially no different than the accomplishments of wonder-workers to be found everywhere among the Jews and Gentiles.

An excellent example of the meaning of Jesus' miraculous acts is found in the story of the healing of the paralytic (Mark 2:1-12). On one occasion when Jesus was preaching in a crowded house, a paralytic was let down through the roof. When Jesus perceived the faith of those who had done this extraordinary thing, he said to the paralytic: "My son, your sins are forgiven." This utterance caused a great commotion among the skeptical Jews, who found therein the blasphemous claim that Jesus himself was wielding the power of God. In answer to their murmurings, Jesus said:

> Which is easier, to say to the paralytic, Your sins are forgiven; or to say, Rise, take up your pallet and walk? But that you may know that the Son of Man has authority on earth to forgive sins. . . I say to you, rise, take up your pallet and go home.

Perhaps it is justifiable to interpret this man's illness as a "functional" paralysis, and to cite the testimony of some modern psychiatrists that in many cases when an individual has received God's forgiveness, his inward conflicts have been removed and, as a consequence, disabling physical symptoms have vanished. So in this instance it was Jesus' announcement of God's forgiveness which released the man from his paralysis. The important point, however, is that the miracle was regarded as a sign of Jesus' messianic authority. Jesus manifested the redemptive power of God which was already at work in human experience, delivering men from the inner frustrations and anxieties resulting from their separation from

God. Today a physician or a psychotherapist can heal a patient and say, "Rise, take up your bed and walk." It is only the power of God's forgiveness which can exorcise the demons which dwell in the unconscious, free men from the paralysis of guilt, and release them from the anxiety of pain and death. Of course, this makes sense only to those whose eyes have been opened to the nature of the human dilemma, as the New Testament discloses it. It assumes that the confusion of human life is the result of man's separation from God (and thus from his *true* self) and it proclaims that God himself has taken the initiative in reaching across the separating chasm with his forgiveness which transforms and makes whole.

It is impossible in this brief space to go into the question of the historicity of each one of the miracles. The miracle story tradition was so expanded in the period of the oral transmission of the Gospel, in terms of the practical interests of the Church, that probably we can never confidently recover the original nucleus. It is important to realize, however, that the real miracle perceived by early followers of Jesus was the power of God's redemptive rule, the renewing and re-creative power of his forgiveness manifested in the deeds of the Messiah. Each story was intended not as a proof compelling unwilling belief, but as a vehicle for communicating the discerned meaning of Jesus' actions. Jesus' exorcism of demons was a sign of God's triumph over the forces of evil. His healings were not so much bodily cures as evidences of God's saving power. The resurrection of Lazarus from the dead was a sign of God's victory over death—not just the death of the body, but the more terrible spiritual death which may beset the living. Jesus' walking on water or his calming of the tempest signified that the Lord of history was also Lord over nature, even as we sing in the words of the Crusaders' Hymn: "Fairest Lord Jesus, Ruler of all nature. . ." Underlying all of these miracle stories—the original nucleus as well as the expanded material—was the faith that "God was in Christ reconciling the world to himself." C. H. Dodd observes that

> ... whatever we may make of particular "miracles," the miracle stories as a whole are saying precisely this: that where Jesus was, there was some incalculable and unaccountable energy at work for the dispersal of evil forces and the total renewal of human life; and that this was nothing less than the creative energy of the living God.[18]

In answer to John's question, "Are you he who is to come, or shall we look for another?" Jesus sent word to him saying, "Go and tell John what you *hear* and *see*: the blind receive their sight, and the lame walk, lepers are cleansed, and the deaf hear, and the dead are raised up, and the poor have good news preached to them" (a Q passage: Matthew 11:4-5; Luke 7:22).

We should ponder Canon Richardson's reminder that Jesus was not put out of the way merely because he discoursed on the forgiving nature of God or gave inspiring ethical teaching. He was destroyed because he claimed to manifest in his words and works the saving power of God, in particular God's power to forgive sin. He claimed to do what only God can do. To Jews this was blasphemy, but to those who saw and heard in faith Jesus' words and works were signs of the near approach of God's Kingdom. Indeed, they gave assurance that already the Kingdom was breaking into history.

Jesus' Passion

Thus far we have seen that Jesus not only preached the gospel of the Kingdom of God; he was the effective agent of that gospel. The message that God does not wait for men to seek him but takes the initiative in seeking them is inseparable from the man who makes the divine action concrete in word and deed. Hence we see that the gospel *of* Jesus and the gospel that *is* Jesus blend together. It is not a far step to the affirmation of the Fourth Gospel: "I am the way, the truth, and the life: no one comes to the Father, but by me" (John 14:6).

---

[18] *The Bible Today*, p. 92.

If the miracles may be described as God's saving power in action, this is even more forcefully the case with Jesus' sacrifice. Form Critics point out that the Passion Story took earliest permanent form during the period of the oral formation of the gospel because the story of the suffering, death, and resurrection of Jesus was the heart of the early Christian witness. Paul insisted that he merely passed on what he had *received* from early preachers, "that Christ died for our sins according to the Scriptures" (I Corinthians 15:3). Mark, the earliest Gospel, devotes a large proportion of space to Christ's Passion. The Cross is the focal point of attention in the literature of the New Testament.

Moreover, the entire New Testament connects the Cross with man's sin. It was the reality of sin which made the Cross "necessary" in the working out of God's purpose in history. For early Christians the Crucifixion-Resurrection was the revelation of God's initiative, his willingness to do for man what he could not do for himself. In this way his forgiveness intersected the self-centered circle of man's existence. The Cross, therefore, was no mere accidental development in history; it was a necessary part of God's redemptive plan (Acts 2:23). Jesus' death was not the death of an ordinary martyr. God himself was identified with the event. He was "in Christ." His forgiveness was "made flesh." He had stepped across the chasm of man's sin and had manifested his sovereign power.

A critical study of the gospel materials makes plausible the conclusion that this interpretation of the Passion was no after-thought of the Church. There is evidence that Jesus himself conceived his role to be that of the Suffering Servant of God, who through his vicarious death was to institute a New Covenant between God and Man.[14] Scattered throughout the Gospels are references to the effect that "The Son of Man [that is, the Christ] must suffer." In some cases these statements are filled with details of the Passion week itself, for instance, the rejection by the priests and elders, or the manner of exe-

[14] This position is vigorously defended by William Manson, *op. cit.*, chap. 7.

cution (cf. Mark 8:31). Unless we are to assume that Jesus was omniscient, and therefore could predict the exact details of a predetermined future, we must conclude that the Gospel writer has introduced these details by projecting backward his knowledge of the precise outcome of the story. But there is no *a priori* reason why Jesus could not have seen, well in advance of his last week, that his vocation involved suffering. This would have been the case, no doubt, if Jesus not only preached about God's love, but also regarded himself as called to translate the gospel into concrete deed.[15]

One of the most striking passages in the Gospels relates an incident which in the Marcan outline follows immediately after Peter's confession of faith that Jesus is the Messiah (8:31-33). We are told that Jesus "began to teach them that the Son of Man must suffer many things." Peter immediately rebuked his Master, for Jewish traditions gave no place to the role of a suffering messiah. Whether coming as the "Son of David" or the apocalyptic "Son of Man," the Messiah, it was believed, would accomplish God's triumph in history in a way which all men would recognize as a triumph. It was inconceivable that God could actually manifest his omnipotence in suffering and seeming defeat. But Jesus, we are told, turned upon Peter with the stinging reply: "Get thee behind me, you Satan! For you understand not the things of God, but the things of men!"

We may pause to recognize that even yet it is difficult for us to grasp the truth that God manifests his sovereign power by suffering and enduring the evil which men commit. Normally, human beings exercise power in order to overwhelm the opposition, either by forcing it to a compromise or driving

---

[15] Some scholars believe that Mark 10:45 is an authentic saying of Jesus, in which he pointed out to his disciples that the role of the Messiah was not to be served, but to serve and "to give his life a ransom for many." The language is reminiscent of Second Isaiah's description of the Servant of the Lord who serves God's redemptive purpose by pouring out his lifeblood, and offering himself as a "trespass-offering" for the guilt of others (see Isaiah 53:10-12).

it to its knees in unwilling surrender. This is the pattern of action in power politics, and too often this tyranny of one will over another is displayed in our personal relationships. With this attitude, many people often wonder why God "allows evil." Why does he not intervene with a tremendous display of power which would conquer the forces of evil in a single stroke, as Jews hoped that God's Messiah would do in the last days? The answer is that God, having endowed man with the gift of freedom, wants something more from his people than forced subjection and unwilling submission. He desires from each person a love that is genuine and spontaneous; he wants men to realize their freedom in voluntary dependence upon him; he wants, not the capitulation of fear, but the trustful acknowledgment of him as the one true center of man's life.[16] So he manifests his love, indeed his omnipotence, by bearing and taking unto himself the sinful expression of man's freedom. The Cross is the supreme evidence that the "things of God" are vastly different from the "things of men." As Paul said, this is the "weakness of God which is stronger than men" and "the foolishness of God which is wiser than men" (see I Corinthians 1:18-31). It is the confession of faith made by those who are grasped by the truth of the Cross.

It is difficult to see how the Church would have preached the "foolishness" of the Cross unless Jesus himself taught his followers that his mission involved suffering and death. Through the traditions which the Church has preserved, and even modified according to its own practical interests, we see the historical figure who voluntarily assumed the role of the Suffering Servant, and taught his followers that suffering was the necessary prelude to his final exaltation as the "Son of Man." This interpretation of Jesus' sacrificial act is enshrined in the rite of the Last Supper or Holy Communion. In the

---

16 Contrast the classical religion of Islam. The "submission" (a "Moslem" is "one who submits" to Allah's sovereignty) emphasized in the Koran is based upon the awareness of the terrors of the Final Judgment, and the delights which are held in store for the faithful.

earliest account of the Lord's Supper (I Corinthians 11:23-26) Paul points out that he had "received from the Lord"—that is, from a tradition going back to Jesus himself—the interpretation of the bread and the cup. These two elements, the unleavened bread and the cup of wine, were elements of the Jewish Passover Feast which Jesus had shared with his disciples on the last evening of his life, and whose symbolism was modified in terms of his imminent sacrifice (see Mark 14:22-25). By transforming the traditional symbolism, Jesus made vivid the meaning of his sacrificial act. "This [bread] is my body, which is broken for you"; "this cup is the new covenant in my blood." Undoubtedly this rite and its interpretation were handed down from Jesus.

Two things are especially noteworthy about the received interpretation of the Lord's Supper. First, Jesus regarded his sacrifice as being vicarious; it was made *for* others.[17] Rightly do Christians say, quoting Isaiah 53:

> He was wounded for *our* transgressions,
> He was bruised for *our* iniquities.
> The chastisement of *our* peace was upon him;
> And with his stripes we are healed.

Secondly, his sacrifice effected a *new covenant,* a new relationship between God and man. Just as Moses had solemnized Israel's covenant on the basis of a blood ceremony,[18] so in a deeper and more lasting sense Jesus' *healing* sacrifice had the effect of reconciling men to God in the New Covenant. God's freely offered forgiveness was the basis of this new and closer relationship, even as Jeremiah had anticipated:

> This shall be the covenant that I will make with the house of Israel: After those days, saith the Lord, I will put my law in their inward parts, and write it in their hearts; and will be their God, and

---

[17] The Greek word translated "for" means "on behalf of" and appears in such statements as "for our sins" (I Cor. 15:3), "for many" (Mark 10:45; 14:24), "for me" (Gal. 2:20), and so on.

[18] See Exodus 24:3-8, especially the phrase "the blood of the covenant."

they shall be my people.... *For I will forgive their iniquity, and I will remember their sin no more.*

—Jeremiah 31:33-34

Thus to Christians the love of God was made known in the marvelous truth that "even while we were yet sinners, Christ died for us." This was the strange omnipotence of God's love which released men from the bondage of sin and death.

The God-Man

We have seen that the Passion of Jesus proved to be the very essence of Jesus' role or *persona*. Not only did he preach that the Kingdom of God was at hand; not only was he the effective agent of that gospel as he performed the "mighty works" which broke the strangle hold of evil in men's lives; he also *embodied* God's intention to reconcile men to their Creator by going to the Cross of Calvary.

Since men could not escape the conviction that "God was in Christ," the role of Jesus could not be contained within ordinary categories. His followers unhesitantly attributed to him a medley of titles: Teacher, Prophet, Son of David, Son of Man, Son of God, Servant of the Lord, High Priest. He could be described by any and all of these titles, and yet none of them adequately described the meaning which men had experienced. After the Resurrection, the central affirmation of Christians was that Jesus is "Lord." The title Lord (*kyrios*) had been used in the Greek translation of the Old Testament for God. Early Christians applied the title to Jesus, not out of theological reflection but because of the inescapable conviction that God had spoken to them in Jesus, had acted for their salvation through him, and had exalted him to glory. There was no thought, at least in this early period, of denying the full humanity of Jesus. As a matter of fact, the early gospel tradition preserved the historical details which make his full manhood indisputable. Nevertheless, the Church ascribed to him the highest claims in order to do justice to his unique dignity. He was named Emmanuel, in token of the conviction that "God is with us" (Matthew 1:23). It was maintained that "in him dwells the whole fullness of deity bodily" (Colossians 2:9). Another writer affirmed that the Son "reflects the glory of God and bears the stamp of his nature, upholding the universe by his word of power" (Hebrews 1:3). The author of the Fourth Gospel identified him with the pre-existent Logos (Word), co-eternal with God and truly divine, who was incarnated (made flesh) as the "only-begotten of the Father" (John 1:1-18).[19] It is particularly important to note that Christians made these tremendous claims on behalf of Jesus without forsaking monotheism.

Even though the word "Trinity" does not appear in the New Testament, it is plain that the way is prepared for the formulation of the doctrine (see Acts 2:33; II Corinthians 13:14; Ephesians 4:4-6). Later creedal discussion was carried on largely in the language of Greek philosophy. Using non-biblical language, theologians attempted to guard the biblical witness that, on the one hand, Jesus was completely human and, on the other, that the power of God dwelt in him fully for man's salvation. To say that Jesus was only a man would have denied the claim that "God was in Christ reconciling the world to himself." Conversely, to say that Jesus was only God would have denied that God's revelation had any true anchorage in the stream of human history. Attempting to steer a narrow course between Scylla and Charybdis, the Church finally formulated the doctrine of the Trinity.[20]

Christians should not regard the doctrine of the Trinity as a meaningless mystery, a kind of mathematical formula of

---

[19] Taken by itself, the prologue to the Fourth Gospel has a superficial similarity to certain strains of Hellenistic philosophy, in which *logos* was the divine reason, immanent in man and nature. However, when viewed in the total context and Jewish setting of the Fourth Gospel, the Prologue stands in the Hebraic tradition, recalling the creative Word (Genesis 1; Psalm 33:6,9), the prophetic "Word of the Lord," hymns to Wisdom, etc. See W. F. Howard, *Christianity According to St. John* (Westminster, 1946), chap. 2.

[20] For a clear and stimulating discussion of this, see D. M. Baillie, *God Was in Christ* (Scribner, 1948).

three-in-one and one-in-three. Undoubtedly, sound theological discussion which rests upon the witness of the New Testament will lead to the doctrine of the Trinity. But the Trinity is not the proper place to begin. To use an apt phrase coined by Harry Emerson Fosdick, we must in this case "beat the crust back into the batter," that is, we must seek to discover the "batter" of the religious faith which eventually took form in the "crust" of the doctrine. In other words, instead of starting with the "person" of Christ, as that can be analyzed metaphysically in terms of two "natures" (human and divine), we should begin with the *persona* or role of Jesus as it is described in the New Testament.

The message of the New Testament is reducible to these two claims: (1) Jesus was a real historical individual whose appearance and career came at the climax of a series of historical events of which the Old Testament is the witness; and (2) Jesus confronted men with the eternal power and truth of God, not just in his message but in his life, his actions, and his person. Man was in Christ—man as God intended him to be at the creation; and God was in Christ, reconciling his lost creation unto himself. Both of these things must be said equally confidently if we are to do justice to the faith of those who were apprehended by God's revelation in Jesus.

The paradoxical emphasis upon both Jesus' humanity and deity in the gospel tradition may be illustrated by a brief consideration of the Virgin Birth. Too often we ignore the fact that both Matthew and Luke testify to Jesus' full humanity by tracing his "family tree" back *through Joseph* (not Mary!) to Abraham in one case (Matthew 1:1-16) and to Adam in the other (Luke 3:23-38). Yet the same Gospels find no difficulty in affirming that Jesus' birth was a miracle of the Holy Spirit, and that in Jesus God came to dwell among men. The historian will point out that the doctrine of the Virgin Birth was not a feature of the earliest Gospel tradition. It is not mentioned in John, I Peter, Mark, or Paul's epistles; moreover, the doctrine is conspicuously absent in the early apostolic sermon-summaries as given in Acts. Thus even though we could prove scientifically that such a biological miracle could have taken place, the historical evidence seems to be against it. But this does not warrant jumping to the conclusion that the doctrine is meaningless. Actually the Christian faith rests upon *both* claims, namely, that Jesus was a true son of Israel who came in the normal successions of the generations of Judaism, and that Jesus was the Son of God whose coming was a divine miracle wrought in human history. At the level of logic, these two affirmations seem contradictory, and the prosaic literalist will insist on either the son of Joseph or the Son of the Virgin Mary. However, the doctrine of the Virgin Birth must be interpreted not in the light of biology but in the light of the central Christian message that God's redemptive action was "made history" in a man whose parentage was well known by his contemporaries (see John 7:27), but a man whose unique significance in the divine scheme could be understood only by tracing his line to Abraham, the man of faith, or to Adam, the creation of God. Thus Christian faith dares to embrace the paradox that Jesus is the God-Man.

Christians do not subscribe to the divinity of Christ as a result of a rational investigation in which they explore and explain the mystery of the Trinity. Moreover, one will never see the decisive significance of Jesus in the historical drama merely by examining the historical evidence concerning his career and the cultural situation of the first century. The starting point is decision, commitment. When men see meaning in history or discern values in their social experience, they do so from a *standpoint* which is taken by faith. The "christological question"—"Who do you say that I am?" (Mark 8:29)—must not be understood as a question about the metaphysical nature of Jesus; rather, it is the question as to whether he is truly the one who embodies God's redemptive action, and is therefore the absolutely unique, absolutely decisive figure in human history. The answer lies beyond the scope of science and historical investigation; for when dealing with the question of the ultimate meaning of history, we are in a realm where faith precedes reason, where decision underlies any understanding of the whole. So in faith the Christian affirms that the appearance of Jesus Christ is *the* revealing event. Like the lightning flash which enabled Browning's Guido to see Naples, this Event illumines the whole landscape of history in the light of God's purpose. But the Christian makes this claim with respect to the whole human scene because, first of all, Christ reveals the meaning of his own life as it is a part of the historical drama. In the light of this revelation, he sees himself as he is: a creature, a child of God, a prodigal son, a sinner. His pride is exposed; his self-sufficiency is condemned; his sin laid bare. But more than this he hears the good news of God's forgiveness, and receives a new life which in itself is the assurance that God was in Christ effecting a new creation. As Browning writes in his *Saul:*

'Tis the weakness in strength, that I cry for! my flesh, that I seek
In the Godhead! I seek and I find it. O Saul, it shall be
A Face like my face that receives thee; a Man like to me,
Thou shalt love and be loved by, for ever: a Hand like this hand
Shall throw open the gates of new life to thee! See the Christ stand!

Christians who experience the impact of Jesus upon their lives, and who find in him the embodiment of the good news he proclaimed, boldly exclaim, as did "doubting Thomas," "My Lord, and My God" (John 20:28).

9

The Power of His Resurrection

IN THE ACTS OF THE APOSTLES (17:18-32), Luke records an instance when one of Paul's most polished sermons "fell flat." During his second missionary journey Paul had arrived in Athens, the cultural capital of ancient Greece. Certain philosophers, whose love of wisdom made them avid to hear and discuss any new doctrine, invited him to speak in their forum that they might know at first hand what his strange "babbling" was about. Taking his stand on Mars Hill, not far from the famous Acropolis, Paul moved swiftly to the climax of his sermon: the call to repentance on the basis of the near approach of the Day of Judgment. The assurance of the imminent consummation of history, he said, was contained in the good news that God had raised Jesus from the dead. The effect of the sermon on the philosophers is indicated in these laconic words: "And when they heard of the resurrection of the dead, some mocked: and others said, We will hear thee again on this matter."

The Centrality of Christ's Resurrection

Now it is important to recognize that the Athenian philosophers had no quarrel with Paul over the belief in a future life. Actually Greek thought, resting as it did upon a sharp dualism of *body* and *soul*, logically culminated in the doctrine of the immortality (deathlessness) of the "soul," the eternal element supposedly imprisoned within the body. What offended the Greeks was the notion of the resurrection of the *body*, and, in particular, the claim that already this had been witnessed in the case of Jesus.

Diogenes would not have to walk very far in the streets of a modern city before encountering a man whose honesty would compel him to admit that he finds difficulty in accepting the doctrine of the resurrection of the body. Many modern people mock; others, bewildered, say that they would like to hear more about the strange doctrine. In this realm, if no other, there is conclusive proof that we find it much easier to accept the categories of Greek philosophy than the thought framework of the Bible. The consequence is that, at least in liberal Protestant churches, Jesus' resurrection is often treated merely as an example of the survival of personality after death. The "resurrection of the body," it is thought, is just an unsophisticated way of talking about the immortality of the soul, of which the triumphant life of Jesus is an example. So, the Christian festival of Easter has lost much of its ancient meaning and has come to be a time when well-dressed people make their annual parade to churches to "enjoy" innocuous sermons on the "intimations of immortality."

This chapter is addressed primarily to those who, in fairness to the traditional Christian witness, say, "We will hear thee again on this matter." Though we may find the New Testament to be difficult at this point, it can scarcely be disputed that from the very first the center of gravity in the Christian message was the Resurrection, or, more exactly, the Crucifixion-Resurrection. Early Christians did not go out into the world preaching an ethical code, or a system of philosophy, or a utopian gospel of social improvement. Those who think that the essence of Christianity in the New Testament period was the Sermon on the Mount, or the doctrine of the "Fatherhood of God and the brotherhood of man," have the evidence of critical, historical scholarship against them. The Church was established on the Resurrection faith, summed up in the creedal affirmation: Jesus is Lord.

This is not to deny the importance of the Fatherhood of God or the Sermon on the Mount. We are merely demanding that these matters be placed within their proper context of faith if one is to do justice to the New Testament. Christianity is not just the belief in one God; Christians worship the God who raised Christ from the dead (see Romans 4:24; I Peter 1:21; and so on). Christianity is not just a noble ethic; ethical motivation arises from the fact that men are "raised together with Christ" in order that they may "walk in newness of life" (Col. 3:1; Rom. 6:4). Christianity is the religion of the Resurrection. Herein lies its distinctiveness and power.

Since all of us have been influenced by the scientific attitude with its concern for *fact,* we would like to begin our discussion of the Resurrection with the question: What really happened? However, this is the wrong starting point. Historical events do not just "occur"; they occur with a meaning in the experience of individuals or a community. Thus we must begin by attempting to project ourselves into the thought framework of early Christians and to view the event from their perspective. In brief, we must consider the place of the Resurrection in the biblical drama, to which it is integrally related.

God's Triumph in History

Early Christians who "turned the world upside down" with their fearless preaching were confident of one thing: in the words and works of Jesus of Nazareth they had encountered God and had witnessed his decisive triumph in history. From the perspective of their faith, the Resurrection was the crowning climax of a long series of God's "mighty acts" in history. This event gave them the assurance that "God was in Christ," transfiguring his suffering with glory, crowning his seeming defeat with victory, and declaring him to be "the Son of God with power" (Romans 1:4).

It is extremely difficult for us of the West to understand the Hebraic claim that God manifested his triumph *in history* by raising Christ from the dead. We betray our inability to "think Hebraically" about the Resurrection whenever we detach the event from the biblical drama and treat it as referring primarily to an after-life, far removed from the struggles of history. In many circles today the Christian faith is caricatured as an egocentric, otherworldly affair, a promise of "pie in the sky, pie by and by." Frequently the gospel which is preached is one of salvation *from* the evils and troubles of life; the world is regarded as a scene of preparation for blessedness in eternity; and faith is the springboard from which one leaps out of history. In all of this there is a striking resemblance to the Greek "salvation" cults of the first century, which offered men release from time into eternity.

Surely no one would deny that God's Word in Christ is addressed to the individual, or that the gospel releases men from frustrations and fears, or that the Christian faith points confidently beyond the horizons of death. But early Christians meant much more than this when they gave witness to the Resurrection. To them this event was not a mere signpost pointing the way toward eternity; rather, this was the transfiguration of history itself. It was the lightning-thrust of God's Truth in the light of which the whole landscape of human existence was brilliantly illumined. It was the assurance of God's triumph in history.

Therefore, in order that we may understand the meaning of the Christian claim that God raised Christ from the dead, we must project ourselves into the Hebraic framework of thinking. In particular, we must consider the Resurrection in the light of the messianic interpretation of history and the Hebraic view of human nature. In what follows we shall not argue for the literal accuracy of the details of the biblical framework of thinking; our concern is to understand the Semitic idiom in terms of which early Christians proclaimed God's triumph.

Too often we ignore the fact that during the first century the belief in the resurrection of the dead was inseparably related to the messianic hope for the future. Jewish messianic expectations, particularly the apocalyptic type, pointed to the consummation of history when God would establish his rule over his whole creation. At the time of the "fulfillment of all things," it was believed, God would raise up the dead in order that preceding generations, as well as those living at the time, might witness God's final triumph in the historical drama. The resurrection of the dead is taught clearly in only two passages in the Old Testament, both of them belonging in the apocalyptic tradition (Isaiah 26:19; Daniel 12:2-3). In the book of Daniel we read:

> And many of those who sleep in the land of dust shall awake, some to everlasting life, and others to everlasting reproach and contempt. Then those who are wise shall shine like the brightness of the firmament, and those who have led the multitude to righteousness like the stars forever and ever.

This belief was elaborated during the "intertestamental period," was championed by the Pharisees during Jesus' day,[1] and formed the framework of early Christian thinking (I Thessalonians 4:14; Acts 24:15; John 5:29; and so on).

Not only does the doctrine of the resurrection of the dead presuppose a messianic interpretation of history, but it also rests upon the Hebraic view of human nature. In Hebraic thought, man is a body (dust) animated by the Spirit or breath of God (see Genesis 2:7). Contrary to the Greek way of thinking, there is no eternal element (or "soul") imprisoned in the physical body. Man's life is a unity, the unified existence of a creature responsible to his Creator. When he dies, his personal existence ceases. His body returns to the dust and his "shade"—a vague double of his former self—goes down to Sheol, the land of darkness and death. Con-

[1] Sadducees, the other main party-group within Judaism, did not accept this doctrine. They found no authority for it in the Pentateuch, and could not accept the Pharisees' oral interpretations of the Pentateuch, eventually codified in the Talmud, which made it possible to claim Mosaic authority for the belief. Like the Pharisees, Jesus accepted the belief (see Mark 12:18-27).

sistent with this view of human nature, if man is to have a future *life* there must be a new miracle, a *re*-creation. God must raise up the body from death, reanimate it with his life-giving Spirit, and restore man to the God-relationship which is the source of his life.

It is important to notice, then, that the belief in the resurrection of the dead—unlike the Greek belief in the immortality of the soul—does not imply an escape from history into eternity. Actually the belief is profoundly this-worldly. It is associated with the faith that God's Kingdom would come, at which time his will would be done on earth as it is done in heaven. According to this way of thinking, the resurrection occurs at the end or the goal of history, that is, (symbolically) at the Final Judgment.[2] Just as the individual before death finds meaning in a covenanted community, so likewise he cannot reach the goal of his historical life unless he is permitted to be a member of the redeemed community, the Kingdom of God. Hence after a period of waiting, faithful individuals are, by an act of God's grace, *raised up* in order that they may take part in the messianic community. In this view the emphasis is not on man's self-centered longing for eternal life, but, rather, upon the fulfillment and completion of history.

The Resurrection of Jesus is a part of this view of history. It is the emphatic witness of the New Testament that God's raising of Jesus was the assurance—as Paul said in his sermon on Mars Hill—that the final consummation was near. To early Christians it gave evidence that already the powers of God's kingdom were manifest, already God's victory was being won, already men were citizens of that new Age of the fulfillment of God's purpose for mankind. The in-breaking of the powers of the Kingdom, which had been experienced in the words and works of Jesus, had reached a tremendous intensity in the Crucifixion-Resurrection of the Messiah. As

---

[2] We shall return to the myth of the "end of history" in the next chapter.

Paul wrote, "now is Christ risen from the dead, and become the firstfruits of them that slept"—that is, he is the first in the "harvest" of those who await the final messianic resurrection; indeed, his victory over death is a foretaste of God's final Kingdom and his ultimate subjection of the entire creation to his rule (see I Corinthians 15:20-28). To put it metaphorically, early Christians believed that they had one foot in the Kingdom and the other foot in the present age. They were citizens of two epochs: the new order, present but not realized; and the old order, judged but not yet ended. As the author of the Epistle to the Hebrews said, Christians had already "tasted . . . the powers of the Age to Come" (6:5).

The doctrine of the immortality of the soul, regardless of the question of its validity on other grounds, would have been a wholly inadequate vehicle for expressing the Christian conviction that God's triumph in Christ was truly a historical miracle, a "mighty act" of God himself. As Canon Michael Ramsey reminds us, Jesus did not automatically survive death because his soul was deathless, but—to use New Testament language—"Christ was *raised*," "God *raised* him from the dead." [3] The accent is upon God's action. It was not the event of the Resurrection itself that mattered, for, after all, other "resurrections" were believed in that period, and Pharisees would have had no *a priori* difficulty with its possibility. What made this resurrection unique—and to the Pharisees unacceptable—was the Christian emphasis upon God's redemptive action in the event, his vindication of one who was hailed as the Messiah.

Christians viewed Christ's Resurrection as of one piece with the drama of Israel's past in which they discerned the redemptive activity of God. Just as the Exodus was regarded as a divine miracle which liberated Israel from bondage, so Jesus' death was the "New Exodus" in which God liberated men

[3] At many points in this discussion I am indebted to Canon A. Michael Ramsey's little book, *The Resurrection of Christ* (Westminster, 1946), in which he presents a stimulating critical and theological treatment of the subject.

from the greater bondage of sin and death. Just as the return from the Babylonian Exile was a miracle in which God raised Israel from the grave and gave her new life, so likewise God raised Christ and, with him, the New Israel—the Church (Ephesians 2:4-10). The Exodus, the Exile-and-Return, and the Crucifixion-Resurrection were the crucial events in biblical history, and in each of them men of faith discerned the action of God. Here we are dealing with a view which recognizes that human history is controlled by something more than natural or human factors. Though the modern mind may have difficulty with the notion of God's intervention in human affairs, let us recognize honestly that we cannot exclude this dimension from the Bible without completely revising it and falsifying its witness.

Early Christians soon came to realize the indispensability of the category of the Resurrection as an expression of God's triumph in history. As Christianity moved out onto Gentile soil it was involved in a life-and-death battle with a type of Greek thinking known as Gnosticism. Even in the first century this philosophy challenged Christianity, and the issue came to a crisis in the second century, about the time of Marcion. Gnostic Christians, starting from the premise of a sharp cleavage between soul and body (the eternal and the temporal), argued that Christ was a celestial being whose career in the flesh was only an *appearance*. Obviously, they argued, the spiritual Christ could not have been truly incarnated in a physical body, any more than all eternity could be crowded into a single moment of time. Therefore, it was thought, his *bodily* suffering, death, and resurrection were only an illusion. Jesus *seemed* to die and arise from the dead, but actually his immortal soul was untouched by death. Of course, this all follows logically once the premise is granted; for if the soul by nature is deathless it is obviously a contradiction in terms to speak of it being raised again to life. Christians came to realize that the distinction between Jesus' immortality and Jesus' resurrection was freighted with serious implications.

They had the wisdom to see that the Gnostic view would have destroyed the very essence of Christianity as a historical religion, that is, a religion which rests upon the revelation of God in historical events. If the birth, suffering, death, and resurrection of Christ were not real, then God did not really reveal himself in history! The "Apostles' Creed" was the answer of the early Church to this dangerous type of thinking. The Creed put sharp emphasis on the affirmations that Jesus was *born* of the Virgin Mary, *suffered* under Pontius Pilate, was *dead* and *buried*, and on the third day *rose from the dead*. This was the Church's way of safeguarding the apostolic witness that Christ's victory was an *event in history*, not merely an escape into eternity.

The Resurrection, then, is the dominant category of a religion which rests upon a conviction intolerable to Greek thought: God's action, his coming into history, his self-revelation in historical events. The question as to what happened on Easter morning lies out on the fringe. We are dealing here with an issue of historical interpretation which cannot be put aside easily. Is history what the men of the Bible declared it to be: a meeting place between God and man? Is the Crucifixion-Resurrection, as Christians claim, the historical event in which men encounter the Lord of history and witness his triumph? On this issue Christianity cannot surrender without ceasing to be Christian. As Paul reminded Christians at the Greek city of Corinth, "If Christ be not risen, then is our preaching vain, and your faith is vain" (I Corinthians 15:14). Surely it is no exaggeration to say that if Christianity were severed from its rootage in the soil of the resurrection faith, it would soon lose its vitality and wither away.

The Historical Evidence

Up to this point we have attempted to project ourselves into the thought framework of early Christians and, in so far as possible, to think Hebraically about the Resurrection. Since the Bible is written in an idiom more or less strange to us, we must learn the new language, lest we completely misunderstand the faith early Christians attempted to communicate. Now we must raise the question as to the historical evidence for Christ's resurrection. The point bears repetition that since Christianity is a historical religion, it cannot escape the problems of historical investigation and must employ the most critical methodology in dealing with the evidence. It seems fair to point out, however, that the presuppositions of historical criticism should be derived from the Bible itself—that is, commitment to the Lordship of Christ rather than some other standpoint of historical interpretation; otherwise the historian, perhaps unconsciously, will dismiss or distort some evidence in order that the past may be understood according to his own categories or the categories of his time.

It will come as a shock to the newcomer in biblical studies to learn that the New Testament does not give a clear-cut and harmonious picture as to what happened at the Resurrection. This will become evident as we review briefly the New Testament story, considering first the witness of the Gospels, then the account given by Paul, and finally the preaching message of the early apostles during the oral period. In this manner we shall work backward toward the earliest testimony concerning the event.

In its earliest known form, the Gospel of Mark contained no story of the appearance of the resurrected Christ. The event of the Resurrection is implied, indeed is predicted several times earlier in the Gospel; but in the earliest extant Marcan narrative the reader is left with the picture of the women running in terror from the empty tomb, unable to understand the words of the white-robed young man, "Behold he goes before you into Galilee." Of course, we are familiar with the passage at the end of the Gospel in our modern Bibles (16:9-20). But this passage, which is written in a different style than the remainder of Mark, was evidently the work of early editors who sought to make the story complete. As a matter of fact, in the two best codices of the New Testament (Vaticanus and Sinaiticus) the Gospel ends with the words of 16:8: "For they were afraid." It is a moot question among New Testament scholars as to whether Mark originally ended in this abrupt manner, or whether the original ending has been lost.

Matthew seemingly builds his story on the Marcan words: "Behold, he goes before you into Galilee." Accordingly, this Gospel describes Jesus' appearance to his disciples in Galilee. *No appearances in Jerusalem are mentioned.* Moreover, Matthew embellishes the story according to his own interests. For instance, instead of Mark's restrained description of the scene at the tomb, Matthew speaks of an earthquake, the angel rolling away the stone, and Jesus' appearance being like lightning. Practically all scholars agree that the story of the sealing of the tomb and the placing of the Roman guard (27:62-66; 28:11-15) developed in the gospel tradition to refute the criticisms of non-Christians who maintained that Jesus' body had been stolen.

Luke likewise follows the story of the empty tomb, but reports that Jesus appeared to his disciples in Jerusalem and its vicinity. *No appearances in Galilee are recorded.* Luke alone gives the beautiful story about the Stranger explaining the Scriptures to the two disciples on the road to Emmaus, and tells how later the Risen Christ was made known to them as they broke bread. In other ways too, Luke handles the Resurrection narratives in an independent manner.

Finally, the Gospel of John also follows the tradition of the empty tomb, but adds other details, such as the visit of Mary Magdalene to the tomb alone, and the visit of Peter and John to confirm Mary's report. Interestingly, John harmonizes the Galilee (Mark, Matthew) and Jerusalem (Luke) traditions by stating that the main resurrection appearance was in Jerusalem, and pointing out in an epilogue which may be from another editor that later Jesus appeared to the disciples while they were fishing in Galilee (chapter 21).

Summarizing this evidence, we may conclude that it is impossible to harmonize the details of the Gospels into a completely consistent story. All the Gospel writers depend upon a common tradition which emphasized the evidence of the empty tomb and the subsequent appearances of the risen Jesus to his disciples. There are important divergences such as the issue over "Galilee" or "Jerusalem." Moreover, each Gospel writer embellishes the tradition according to his own interests and literary motives. Various situations in the Church—for example, Jewish criticisms—contributed to the development and expansion of the tradition. However, the lack of consistency and the fact that the account was embellished need not call into question either the historicity of the event or its religious meaning. Actually, we would be more suspicious of the tradition if it were completely harmonious and if every detail fitted perfectly into a carefully, artificially worked-out scheme. Let us always remember that the Gospel writers were not so much "historians" as they were religious artists who attempted to portray to their contemporaries the victory of Christ. We miss the religious meaning of these stories if we expect from them literal accuracy, just as we miss the beauty of a Monet painting if we examine the details from a close-up perspective.

The earliest literary witness of the Resurrection is given to us by Paul, especially in I Corinthians 15. The historical value of this chapter is great, for though I Corinthians was written around A.D. 56-57, Paul claims to hark back to the time of his conversion, perhaps within ten years after the Crucifixion. Moreover, Paul insists that he passed on to the Corinthians the gospel he had *received* from early preachers and witnesses,

> ...that Christ died for our sins in accordance with the scriptures, that he was buried, that he was raised on the third day in accordance with the scriptures, and that he appeared to Cephas [that is, Peter], then to the twelve. Then he appeared to more than five hundred brethren at one time, most of whom are still alive, though some have fallen

asleep. Then he appeared to James, then to the apostles. Last of all, as to one untimely born, he appeared also to me (verses 3-8).

Paul's list of the Resurrection appearances deviates considerably from the Gospel tradition; for instance, there is no record elsewhere of an appearance to James. Strikingly, in his summary of the received tradition he does not allude to the story of the women at the tomb. Paul attaches the greatest importance to the "appearance" of the risen Christ to a number of individuals, beginning with Peter and ending with himself. At this point Paul's witness is somewhat astonishing. He maintains that his vision of the Risen Lord (see Acts 9:17) was precisely the same type of experience, and therefore gave him the same apostolic authority, as that of the early apostles (I Corinthians 9:1; Galatians 1:11 ff.). Moreover, he goes on to argue in the remainder of the chapter that the resurrected body of the Christian is not a body of flesh ("flesh and blood cannot inherit the Kingdom of God") but a spiritual body, miraculously transformed into the likeness of Christ's "glorious body" (see also Philippians 3:21). Just as a seed, planted in the ground, alters its form as it rises into the sunlight (for "God gives it a new form"), so likewise in the case of the resurrection, "It is sown [that is, it is born] a physical body, it is raised a spiritual body" (I Corinthians 15:44). If this was true in Christ's case, he argues, it will be true of all men at the consummation of history.

It is highly interesting that the earliest literary witness of the Resurrection assumes that the mode of Christ's resurrection was not crassly physical. To be sure, the body was "buried" in the grave, but, says Paul, the physical body was miraculously transformed—in a way past our comprehension—into a new and glorified body. It was in this form that God raised Christ and revealed his Son to various followers. On the basis of this earliest documentary evidence, many scholars believe that as the story of the Resurrection was passed on in the Christian community it was modified so as to place greater stress upon the physical aspects of the body of the Risen Christ. Thus Luke, while at times suggesting a spiritual body which could mysteriously appear and disappear (24:31, 36), also describes the body as having "flesh and bones" (24:39) and reports that Jesus ate a piece of broiled fish (24:42). This tendency was accentuated evidently by two factors: first, the practical need to convey in concrete, pictorial language the reality of an event which could not be described objectively; and second, the attempt to defend Christianity against Gnostics who insisted that Jesus was no real human being, but a "celestial phantom" who could have no contact with matter.

It must be admitted that if we are to think literally of a physical body, the Ascension presents something of a problem, at least in terms of the modern view of the universe which astronomy presents. The idea of Jesus being carried "up" to heaven on a cloud is hardly tenable today, except in the symbolic sense that Jesus was exalted "to the right hand of God" as Lord. The Ascension, like the second coming of Jesus on the clouds, belongs in another dimension than our physical senses can describe. It is interesting to observe that only Luke describes a physical ascension (Luke 24:50-52 and Acts 1:9). The other Gospels make no mention of it.

When we move back beyond the written records into the period of the oral transmission of the gospel, we discover again that the main emphasis is placed upon the appearance to the disciples. The apostolic sermons preserved in Acts do not mention the testimony of the women at the sepulchre, and in this respect accord with Paul's summary of the "received" tradition. The apostles stressed their conviction that God had raised Jesus from the dead "after three days," and that the risen Lord appeared to them (see Acts 3:15; 10:40; 13:30-31). Though mention is made of Jesus' burial, their main witness was not that they had failed to find Jesus' corpse in the tomb, but they had "seen" the risen Christ.

This, in brief, is the historical evidence with which we must deal as we start from the comparatively late gospel literature and move backward toward the earliest testimony concerning Christ's resurrection. In the nature of the case it is impossible to be dogmatic. There seem to be two main traditions: one which affirms that Christ appeared first to Peter, probably in Galilee; and one which starts from the women's testimony at the tomb in Jerusalem. Most Protestant critics today believe that the former is the oldest tradition, and that the gospel evidence of the empty tomb is secondary. Others, like Canon Ramsey, argue vigorously that the empty tomb formed a part of the earliest testimony, along with the witness that Christ had appeared to the apostles.[4]

Regardless of where one takes his stand in this debate, this point is clear: according to the traditions, both early and late, *Jesus appeared only to his followers*. Unbelievers could not see the Risen Lord. This should warn us against supposing that the Resurrection was an objective event capable of being seen by any one, in the sense that an eclipse of the sun is visible to the naked eye. Even those (like Ramsey) who take a more conservative attitude toward the testimony concerning the empty tomb recognize that the Resurrection belonged in a dimension of spiritual existence for which "corresponding powers of spiritual discernment" were necessary. Only in faith could men behold the miracle of the Resurrection.

By way of concluding this phase of our discussion, two things should be said. First, there is no reason to question the reality of the event in the experience of the early Christian community. Without the Resurrection, there would have been no Christian Church. Some mighty event took place in the experience of the disciples to convince them that Jesus was not a mere martyr and that Good Friday was not the end. Every line of the New Testament gives witness to the reality of this

---

[4] *Op. cit.*, pp. 59-74. C. H. Dodd, though defending the other position, admits that the historical evidence concerning the empty tomb is "more serious and impressive than is sometimes allowed for in modern discussions" (*The Bible Today*, p. 104).

event which was the foundation upon which Christ's Church was established. Moreover, we have impressive evidence of this tremendous reality in the early custom of Christian worship on "the Lord's Day" (I Corinthians 16:2; Acts 20:7; cf. Revelation 1:10). We must remember that early Christians were Jews who had been nurtured in a Judaism which emphasized the sanctity of the Sabbath, the seventh day of the week. Only the most revolutionary event could have enabled them to forsake the deeply established practice of worshiping on what we call Saturday, and to worship on what we call Sunday. The earliest tradition emphasizes that at least as early as A.D. 50 Christians worshiped on the first day of the Jewish week because this was the day of the Lord's resurrection ("on the third day he was raised"). Cumulative evidence of this kind makes reasonable the statement of one New Testament scholar: "Surely it is no exaggeration to say that belief in the resurrection of Jesus is the best-attested fact of ancient history." [5]

Secondly, the event was experienced with a meaning on which there is unanimous agreement in the New Testament: God had visited and redeemed his people. The sifting of the historical evidence does not necessarily lead us any closer to the meaning or the truth of the Resurrection. Even though we could demonstrate scientifically that the tomb was empty on Easter morning, we would not arrive at the biblical meaning of the miracle. The skeptic, admitting that some freakish event may have occurred two thousand years ago, would say in good collegiate style: "So what?" Conversely, even though the gospel evidence concerning the empty tomb falls like a house of cards when examined critically, the reality of Christ's resurrection would not be affected in the slightest. In the final analysis, the truth of the Resurrection lies not in the field of factual inquiry, but in the field of historical interpretation. Was Jesus truly God's Messiah? Did he manifest God's sover-

[5] C. T. Craig, *The Beginning of Christianity* (Abingdon-Cokesbury, 1943), p. 133.

eignty over history? Was he the one who actualized God's power and grace? These questions are answerable not by examination of the evidence, but by a faith which either affirms or denies. The Christian interpretation of history, like any view of history, rests finally upon decision.

The Conquest of Sin and Death

We have said that the Resurrection, when viewed Hebraically, was the climactic moment in the biblical drama. It was the act by which God demonstrated the Crucified Messiah to be Lord, and at the same time brought to fulfillment the promise made to the fathers of old. What "happened" was viewed from the perspective on history which defined the mental outlook of early Christians. To the Church the Resurrection was the sign and assurance that God had won a decisive victory, the final victory in the historical drama. And, paradoxically, this victory had been experienced even before the consummation of history which is symbolized by the words "the Last Judgment." At this point two planes, as it were, intersected: the horizontal plane of man's history (the Man of Galilee was crucified under Pontius Pilate) and the vertical plane of God's action (God *sent* his Son and *raised* him from the dead).

The nature of the divine victory is indicated by Paul in these words: "If Christ has not been raised, your faith is futile and you are still in your sins" (I Corinthians 15:17). Such a statement indicates that the Resurrection is inseparable from the work and Passion of Christ discussed in the preceding chapter. The apostolic affirmation, "Christ died for our sins according to the Scriptures," is incomplete apart from the event which gives assurance of that truth, "He rose again on the third day according to the Scriptures." Good Friday and Easter morning may be separated on the calendar, but they merge together in the Christian faith. Indeed, the Church became a dynamic power when on the day of Pentecost the

Crucifixion and Resurrection were fused together into *one* divine Event by the power of the Holy Spirit.

Most people fail to realize that early Christians discerned in the Resurrection not primarily the evidence for an after-life, but the assurance that God had conquered sin and therefore had liberated men from a more terrible death than the death of the body. In the Bible, sin and death are associated closely.[6] Death is regarded as the punishment of sin. As Paul put it, "the sting of death is sin" (I Corinthians 15:56) or "death entered the world by sin" (Romans 5:12). In other words, when man rebels against God he invites upon himself the judgment of death—"death" in this sense being separation from God. If man is created in the image of God and made to find the fullness of life in dependence upon his Creator, then his repudiation of the manifest design of God is really the destruction of his own life. It is a kind of suicide which, viewed from two angles, may be regarded as either his own self-wrought punishment, or God's sentence of judgment upon him. In this sense, "the wages of sin is death" (Romans 6:23). Though one's pulse may still be vigorous, he is actually in a state of "living death" when estranged from God's purpose (see Romans 8:6; Ephesians 2:1-5; I John 3:14-15); when bodily death occurs the futility of his existence becomes apparent.[7] On the other hand, "life" is conceived in terms of man's relationship to God, his acceptance of the will of the Creator. Such life has an infinite qualitative difference from the kind of existence which may be described organically. It is life-in-relationship-to-God; it is the fulfillment of man's being as a dependent creature, made in the image of God. The unique biblical meaning of the words "life" and "death" is illustrated

[6] See Paul Minear's treatment of this matter, *Eyes of Faith*, pp. 122-128; also A. Michael Ramsey, *op. cit.*, pp. 22-24.

[7] One Shakespearian critic sees dramatized in Macbeth and Lady Macbeth: "the ebbing of life within these two, their death while they still live, for here is the essential tragedy . . . in the sleep-walking scene we see her already spiritually dead . . . the man's living spirit does seem at last to shrivel to a cipher . . . he too is dead before he dies." Quoted by H. Wheeler Robinson, *Two Hebrew Prophets* (Lutterworth, 1948), p. 28.

in such a passage as Deuteronomy 30:19: "I have set before thee *this day* life and death . . . therefore choose ye life!"

Early Christians found in the Resurrection assurance that God had won a victory over "the law of sin and death" (Roman 8:2) and had made available "newness of life." The gift was offered for *this day;* already men could participate in the life of the Kingdom; in the *now* they could drink from the fountains of eternal life. As God raised Christ from the dead, so had he raised them from death in order that they might share, both now and hereafter, in the "new creation." Thus, for instance, the Fourth Gospel proclaims that men do not have to wait to receive the gift of eternal life. Even now it is available, for death and darkness have been overcome by the life and light made available in Christ.[8]

Justification by Faith

The implications of God's victory over sin and death were given distinctive formulation by Paul in his well-known words "justification by faith" and not by "the works of the law." This doctrine, which later became the keynote of the Protestant Reformation, was developed incidentally by Paul in his Epistle to the Galatians, and was worked out with masterful beauty in his Epistle to the Romans (see especially chapters 1-8).

Paul did not formulate this doctrine while sitting in an easy chair one sunny afternoon. It came out of his personal experience, and bears the impress of his own intense struggles as a devout, God-fearing Jew. Essentially his problem was how he could find peace or acceptance before God, how he could have the right inward relation to God. The rabbis of that day supposed that man's nature is made up of two tendencies, the "good impulse" and the "evil impulse." Moreover,

[8] The Christian belief in life beyond the grave is expressed in the category of the resurrection of the (spiritual) body, as in the Apostles' Creed. For an exposition of this, see Reinhold Niebuhr, *Beyond Tragedy* (Scribner, 1938), chap. 15.

they believed that these tendencies were in such balanced equilibrium that by the study of the law and devout spiritual effort one could be righteous. Paul did not find it so. As he wrote in the classical seventh chapter of Romans: "I do not do the good I want, but the evil I do not want is what I do. . . . Wretched man that I am! Who will deliver me from this body of death?"

In this situation, Paul found that the Law—that is, the commandments of God in the Pentateuch—only aggravated the problem. The Law, being the expression of God's holy will (Romans 7:7-14), told him what he should be, and therefore told him in the same instant what he was not. For instance, the very fact that God must command men to love him, so that love takes the form of law, implies that men as a matter of fact do not love God spontaneously and with their whole hearts. God's "ought-to-be" presupposes man's "refusal-to-be." Thus the Law not only represents the perfect will of God; it also teaches men the meaning of sin (Romans 3:20; 7:7) and the impossibility of lifting one's self by his own bootstraps up to the level of God's righteousness. This is no less true, says Paul, if one approaches the matter, not from the standpoint of Jewish law, but from the moral law ("conscience") of the Gentiles (Romans 2:14-16).

The transition from the seventh to the eighth chapter of Romans is one of the most remarkable in Scripture. As though moving from the narrow walls of a prison cell into the open sunlight, Paul exclaims:

> There is therefore now no condemnation to them which are in Christ Jesus [that is, in his "Body"—the Church]. For the law of the Spirit of life in Christ Jesus has set me free from the law of sin and death.

The good news which Paul proclaims is that of God's grace, the free offer of his love to men despite their persistent sinfulness. The word "justification" is almost equivalent to the word "forgiveness." Paul's teaching is that men can do absolutely nothing to win God's approval or to merit his love;

therefore they have no grounds for *boasting* of their attainments (Philippians 3:4-11). Yet, miraculously, what is impossible with man has been accomplished by God himself in the Cross and declared unto all men in the Resurrection. Thus Paul, like Luther later, discovered that the "righteousness" of God is not just a legal standard demanding perfection. God's righteousness is the outgoing of his mercy and salvation.

It is worth noticing, in passing, that Paul's emphasis upon God's freely given grace is paralleled in many of Jesus' parables, just as "the bondage of the Law" is paralleled in Jesus' condemnation of the legalism of the Pharisees. As an example, we may cite the parable of the Workers in the Vineyard (Matthew 20:1-16) which ends on the strange note that all the laborers received the same compensation whether they had worked all day or had started just before quitting time. The teaching is this: from the legalistic standpoint it seems highly arbitrary for all men to receive the same wages; some men surely *deserve* more consideration! Yet God is no bookkeeper. His forgiveness is bestowed upon all men alike, because all men—despite their legalistic pretensions—stand in need of God's mercy. Such parables should warn us against drawing a sharp cleavage between Jesus and Paul.

We come now to the question of the place of "good works"—that is, ethical obligation—in the Christian life. In all of his letters, Paul makes it clear that freedom from the Law does not mean license to do what one pleases. Actually, sharing in the victory of Christ's resurrection provides the strongest motivation for performing the things which are pleasing in God's sight. "If then you have been raised with Christ, seek the things that are above. . . ." (see Colossians 3:1-17). The connection between the "doctrinal" and "ethical" sections of Paul's epistles is not a disjointed one; on the contrary, the proclamation of what God has done in Christ provides the dynamic for social obligation, as, for instance, in the Epistle to the Romans where the elaboration of the theme of the Gospel in chapters 1-11 sweeps to a climax in 12:1 with the pivotal word "therefore"—the word which introduces the ethical discussion of the following chapters (see also Ephesians 4:1). God's victory over sin does not free men from the requirements of the Law of the Kingdom; it merely frees them from the anxious belief that their status before God is dependent upon the perfect keeping of his law. God's forgiveness does not mean that we should "continue in sin that grace abound" (see Romans 6:1-14), any more than at the human level the receiving of a friend's forgiveness gives one an excuse to be meaner than ever. Rather, God's gift of forgiveness awakens gratitude in the human heart, and this gratitude makes obedience of God's will a privilege, not a duty. In a word, God's forgiveness does not relieve the Christian from ethical obligation; it merely changes his perspective upon Christian conduct. Calvin sums up the matter beautifully in these words:

> Those who are bound by the yoke of the Law are like servants who have certain tasks assigned to them daily by their masters. Such servants think that nought has been done and they dare not come into the presence of their masters until the exact amount of labour has been performed. But sons who are treated in a more candid and liberal manner by their parents hesitate not to offer their works that are only begun or half finished, or even with something faulty in them, trusting that their obedience and readiness of mind will be accepted, although the performance be less exact than was wished.[9]

The peace which the Christian knows is the peace of God's forgiveness, and the liberty which he enjoys is freedom from the bondage of moralism and self-will.

The Sermon on the Mount

In this connection we may properly discuss the place of the Sermon on the Mount in the Christian life. Those who say that their religion is the Sermon on the Mount not only fail to understand the character of Jesus' teachings, but unknowingly

[9] *Institutes of the Christian Religion*, III, xix, 5.

transform Christianity into the very legalism which it once opposed. In the previous chapter it was pointed out that one of Jesus' reasons for making such pronouncements as are now classified in Matthew 5-7 was to shatter the Pharisaical confidence that one could be "righteous" before God. To be sure, Jesus came not to destroy the Law, but to fulfill it. He fulfilled the Law, however, not by presenting men with a new law code or a blueprint for social action, but by declaring the pure and perfect will of God, unattained and; humanly speaking, unattainable. The Sermon on the Mount stands witness to the fact that no man can merit God's approval by moral effort.

We must always remember that the context of Jesus' sayings was the message that God's Kingdom was near at hand and that, by repentance and faith, men stood on the very borderline between the old age and the New Age which God would introduce. Perhaps this could be illustrated by visualizing two circles—one representing the "present age" with its magnetic attractions and the other representing "the age to come" with its divine power and glory. These circles come so close together that they touch and begin to overlap. The Christian stands at the point where they meet. Therefore he is under the obligation of an absolute righteousness. Jesus did not legislate for the old order which was judged but not yet ended; nor did he attempt to clarify the Christian's dual obligation to Caesar and to God (Mark 12:13-17). Above all, Jesus' demands were not based upon a consideration of the practical possibilities of the human situation. In the Gospels we are presented with the "absolute ethics" of the Kingdom.[10]

The New Law of the Kingdom has several important characteristics. In the first place, it is searchingly inward in its demand. Men are condemned for anger even though they refrain from the outward act of murder, for lust even though adultery is not committed, for the insincerity which makes it impossible for a man's word to be his bond (thus making an

---

[10] See C. H. Dodd's discussion of New Testament ethics, *op. cit.*, pp. 79-86.

oath necessary). God looks upon the heart. Therefore, the Christian's heart must be pure, sincere, trustful, selfless. Secondly, the New Law demands everything for God without any reservations or qualifications. Judaism had measured out God's will by carefully defining the laws to be obeyed and had even found it possible for one to go beyond his statutory duty. The Law of the Kingdom, however, is as immeasurable as the sovereignty of God. The obligation to forgive one another, for instance, cannot be limited legally (Matthew 18:21-22). No man can have the occasion for boasting before God or claiming merit; at best he can only acknowledge himself to be an unworthy and dutiful servant (see Luke 17:7-10). Finally, Jesus made love central. This love is no natural sentiment or prudential consideration; it is love patterned after the love of God. As God's outgoing love is bestowed unconditionally upon those who do not deserve to be loved, so likewise the Christian must love even those who seem to be most loveless—for instance, social outcasts or despised enemies. To use the phrase from John Knox, Jesus demands nothing less than "the ruthless repudiation of self as the center of one's world." This is the "righteousness" which must "exceed the righteousness of the scribes and the Pharisees."

Therefore, if one says that his religion is *only* the Sermon on the Mount, he is in a situation far more desperate than that described by Paul in Romans 7. For Paul's discussion presupposes the Jewish Law, not the more radical requirements of the Sermon on the Mount! It is quite true that Jesus seriously meant that men should be "perfect" and that the New Law should be the pattern of life within the New Covenant. However, is it possible or proper for any one of us to claim that his inward life measures up to Jesus' radical demands? De we really love our neighbors, to say nothing of our enemies, with a love which is completely selfless? Are our motives for serving our fellow men, and even for worshiping God, absolutely pure and sincere? Can we honestly say that we face tomorrow without anxiety, trusting God's providence as naturally as the birds of the air accept the bounties of nature? Surely if our relationship with God is contingent upon our fulfilling these inward, immeasurable, radical, and absolute demands, our inevitable question will be that of the disciples after the sorrowful Rich Young Ruler had turned away: Who then can be saved?

The Sermon on the Mount discloses the truth that man's relationship with God is not on the basis of ethical or religious attainment. The Sermon on the Mount fulfills the Law by destroying legalism. Christ is the "end of the Law" (Romans 10:4). As William Manson writes:

> Jesus was speaking to men who thought they knew the Will of God, for had they not the Law, and did not the Law say, or was it not at least understood to say that "Thou shalt love thy neighbor, and hate thine enemy"? Over against this obscuration of the truth, Jesus sets the Will of God in all its radiance and white-winged purity. And though the revelation of it humbles us to the dust, exposing the hollowness of our moralism, reducing our complacency to shreds and patches, and bringing us under a boundless sense of sin, this is only what we must expect if we are ever to know God. Only in the searching light of this exposure can we know the radical nature of any truly religious experience—penitence, grace, the forgiveness of sins, hope, blessedness, life.[11]

The Christian, however, reads the Sermon on the Mount, not from the perspective of Romans 7, but from the perspective of Romans 8. As Paul Minear says, he reads it "as if he were hearing the Messiah speak from his cross." That is to say, he reads it not only in the knowledge of God's judgment which calls to repentance, but in the knowledge of God's freely offered forgiveness. No longer is the Christian oppressed by the burden of commands which are beyond the reach of attainment; instead, the gift of God's love evokes a gratitude which becomes the new motivation for obeying God's will. Since Christians are privileged to stand before God as sons rather

---

[11] *Jesus, the Messiah*, pp. 130 f.

than slaves, as Calvin said, they do not hesitate to offer to him half-finished tasks or actions which have some fault in them. Therefore, the Sermon on the Mount is not a standard of perfection which drives the Christian to despair (for "there is now no condemnation to them that are in Christ"), but is a compass which gives direction to his action as, impelled by the stimulus of Christ, he seeks to improve and transform society.[12]

Christian ethics, then, are essentially "resurrection ethics," since they derive their motive and pattern from the love of God manifested in Christ. Christian action is not motivated by mere humanitarian concern or social idealism; rather, it is impelled by the grateful awareness of what God has done for men in Christ. This is stated magnificently in a passage of I John:

> In this is love, not that we loved God but that he loved us and sent his Son to be the expiation for our sins. Beloved, *if God so loved us, we also ought to love one another.*[13]

Thus the "power of his Resurrection" supplies the dynamic for aggressively facing the tribulations and problems of this world (see Philippians 3:10-12).

Strangers in This World

According to the New Testament, the Christian is a kind of "amphibious" creature: he lives in two orders. He is a citizen of the present age, and at the same time is brought under the dominion of Christ's Kingdom. As Paul put it somewhat paradoxically, he lives "in the flesh" (human nature) and also "in the Spirit" (the new dimension introduced by Christ). Awareness of this dual citizenship led early

---

12 For further treatment of the point that "the Sermon on the Mount and the Epistle to the Romans belong together" see A. M. Hunter, *The Message of the New Testament*, chap. 8.

13 See I John 4:7-21; John 13:34-35; Ephesians 4:32; Luke 6:36; etc.

Christians to say that they were "strangers" in the present historical era (I Peter 1:1).

Ever since the New Testament period Christianity has had to steer between two dangers. On the one hand, Christians have been tempted to detach themselves from the evils and problems of this world on the assumption that Christ's Kingdom is not of this world. On the other hand, they have been tempted to make a too easy identification of the Kingdom with something in this world—either the Church, as in Roman Catholicism, or the ideal human society, as in liberal Protestantism of the past. However, the message of the New Testament basically is this: the Kingdom is not *of* this world, yet it has been made manifest *in* this world through the life, death, and resurrection of Christ. Although God's Kingdom is a higher order than any political reality or human ideal of the present age, it has touched and penetrated the kingdoms of this world—not as a tangent touches a circle but as a vertical line intersects a horizontal plane. The task of the Church is to bear witness to this "vertical dimension" of history and, in so doing, to seek to leaven and redeem society in the name of Christ. This point has been made forcefully by Gilbert Baker in an article in which he deals with the problem of making the Christian witness under the Chinese Communist regime. Pointing out that Christianity is not to be identified with any political system, though its witness is made easier under some than others, he says:

> The Christian is perhaps like a sea bird following a ship in its plodding way, resting on the ship too. But the bird lives in another dimension, it makes rings around the ship, it can see better than the captain which way the ship is going, and yet it is the captain that has to steer the ship, not the bird. Yet there is something hopeful about the bird, for when he sees it, the captain knows that he is going in the right direction, and it may give him hope.[14]

---

[14] "The Christian Church under non-Christian Rulers," *Theology Today*, April, 1950, pp. 93 f.

The Christian, then, in his actions and thinking bears witness to the heavenly order, Christ's Kingdom. He lives in the world yet is not of the world, for the compass of the Kingdom gives him his sense of direction. His citizenship is in heaven, though at the same time he seeks to transform the kingdoms of this world. Toynbee has pointed out with Christian discernment that this attitude toward society is not one of "detachment" but one of "transfiguration," involving a rhythm of "withdrawal and return," worship and action, faith and works. Having such a perspective, the Christian will not be resigned fatalistically to the collapse of Western Civilization; if, however, the "City of Destruction" does fall, he knows himself to be a member of the ecumenical or "catholic" fellowship of Christ's Invisible Body in which, as at the time of the fall of the Roman Empire, the values of civilization providentially may be preserved. As Augustine wrote in his *City of God*—a work which was composed three years after the fall of Rome, the "Eternal City"—history is the scene in which two "cities" are mixed together: the City of God and the City of Man, the heavenly order and the secular order. In the power of Christ's resurrection the Christian stands at the borderline of these two orders, straddling both. He is a "stranger" in this world because his action, his conscience, and his outlook toward the future are governed by the fact that, so to speak, he has "one foot in heaven."[15]

---

[15] See further John Bennett, *Christianity and Communism* (Association Press, 1945), especially chap. 4.

10

The Beginning and the End

In the previous chapters we have followed the movement of the biblical drama from the Exodus to the appearance of Christ and the emergence of the Christian Church. In review we may observe that this is actually a three-act drama, the cast of which is God and Israel, and the plot of which is the divine Actor's entrance into history for the purpose of reshaping human life. Act I carries us back to the Mosaic period when God called Israel and began to lead her into a deepening understanding of the Covenant. During most of this Act the covenanted people understands itself as a *nation.* As the curtain falls we see the Babylonian army executing the judgment of God upon the rebellious house of Israel. Act II opens in the gloom of the Babylonian exile where the prophets, Ezekiel and Second Isaiah, give assurance that God has not forgotten Israel. The scene then shifts to Palestine. During the remainder of this Act the covenanted people understands itself as a *holy Jewish community.* The curtain falls on a scene in which these people—forgetful of the Servant's world mission—are barricading themselves within the walls of legalistic Judaism. Act III begins with the appearance of John the Baptist, who summons complacent and self-righteous Jews to repentance and announces the coming of God's long awaited Messiah. The denouement of the drama comes in that moment when God asserts his sovereignty over history by raising Jesus from the dead. Empowered by this "mighty act" of God, disciples explode the gospel message which eventually was to be heard around the world. In this Act the covenanted people understands itself as a *community of faith* which has no other boundaries than commitment to the Lordship of Jesus Christ (Colossians 3:11).

It lies beyond the scope of this book to trace the history of the ongoing Christian Church: the initial problems it faced as it burst the framework of Judaism, the expansion of the movement in ever widening circles through the missionary travels of men like Paul, the attempt to consolidate its position during the later years of the first century, and the ever renewing vitality which sustained it through the long persecutions which ceased only when Christianity was finally declared the official religion of the Roman Empire. In this final chapter we shall consider the fact that the three-act drama, which Christians call The History of God's Redemptive Acts, has a prologue and an epilogue. The prologue begins with an account of the creation of the world and the "fall" of man; the epilogue gives an imaginative description of the Last Judgment and the New Creation. Thus the whole drama is set within a vast and baffling time-span. The biblical pageant moves from the beginning of history to the end of history, from Creation to Consummation, from the book of Genesis to the Revelation of St. John.

Unaccustomed as we are to thinking in these terms, the biblical stories of the beginning and the end present many difficulties, and in particular raise the question as to the relation between science and the Christian faith. Generally speaking, Christians have taken one of two attitudes toward these stories. Literalists have insisted that the accounts—supposedly dictated by God—are as factually accurate as the most reliable modern journal of science. This prevalent attitude toward Scripture is illustrated by the case of the North Carolina fundamentalist who recently caused an international stir by venturing beyond the Iron Curtain to look for the remains of Noah's Ark. On the other hand, modernists have argued that Christianity is in no way bound up with the prescientific "mud-pie" theory of creation or with the early Christian illusion that Jesus would come again on the clouds of heaven. These stories, they argue, must be surrendered by the Christian who is willing to take seriously the conclusions of modern science.

It is rather striking that in this argument both sides have displayed the scientific mentality of our age. This is true not only of liberal Christians who, by means of science, have presented an intellectually "purified" Christianity; it is also true of fundamentalists who have maneuvered themselves into the position of trying to defend the authority of Scripture by harmonizing it with modern science.[1] Many people have the idea that if science can prove Christianity to be true, it must be true—which of course shows where modern man's faith really lies! Undoubtedly this is the explanation of the phenomenal popularity of the book by Immanuel Velikovsky, *Worlds in Collision,* a book which, in the estimate of competent reviewers, should be catalogued with the fantasies of H. G. Wells.

Both sides bear witness to the modern climate of scientific thinking in their common assumption that the biblical stories were intended to be factually accurate descriptions of the universe, thus presenting us with either reliable science or naive pre-science. For instance, fundamentalists believe that the miraculous creation of Adam out of the dust was a fact, as unassailable as the fact that water is wet. The opposition has maintained, however, that what was once thought to be a fact is no longer tenable as good science. In the following pages we shall attempt to shift the discussion to more biblical ground, and to do justice to the idiom of the Bible. If we suppose that the stories of Genesis pretend to give accurate information about nature, we read into the Bible a scientific concern which is alien to it. The truth of the stories of the beginning and the end lies not in their scientific or factual accuracy, but in the realm of the biblical framework of historical interpretation to which they are integrally related.

---

[1] See Harry F. Rimmer, *The Harmony of Science and Scripture* (Eerdmans Publishing Co., Grand Rapids, 1945).

Myth and History

Let us pave the way for a consideration of these stories by giving attention to three general observations. In the first place, the Bible is concerned with beginning and end because of its unique interpretation of history. We have said repeatedly that the biblical view of history is *purposive.* The very idea of purpose, however, implies both the initiation of purpose (a beginning) and the attainment of purpose (an end). Purposive history moves forward in the direction of the realization of a goal. Instead of the endless circles of nature, there is the straight line of history, bracketed by a beginning and an end. Therefore, the Bible deals with the "first things," that is, God's initiation of the drama of human history; likewise it deals with the "last things," that is, the conclusion of the historical drama in the purpose of God. Beginning and end are the terminal points of an interpretation of history which measures time according to the realization of God's purpose.[2]

In view of this, it is wrong to suppose that the biblical writers were primitive scientists who speculated on the origin and dissolution of nature. When the Bible speaks of the beginning, it is not presenting an account of the evolution of nature which competes with the conclusions of modern astrophysics, geology, or biology. Likewise, when the Bible speaks of the end it is not presenting a description of the dissolution of the universe as we might speak of this in terms of the second law of thermodynamics. These scientific questions are outside the Bible's range of primary concern. The very fact that Genesis dovetails *two* accounts of creation which differ strikingly on the details concerning nature suggests that the priestly editors of the Pentateuch were interested in the religious meaning of the stories, not in a scientific and consistent account of the way nature evolved.[3]

---

[2] See pages 170-174.

[3] Observe also that in Genesis 1 the P writer articulates his story into six creative days, not for a scientific reason, but for a religious one, namely, to

The Bible, then, affirms that the historical drama has meaning because it is embraced within the time-span of God's redemptive purpose. To say that God is Creator is to assert, first of all, that history has its source in him who gives it a beginning and a direction; and to assert that God is the Final Judge is to declare that history points forward to a goal which is assigned by him who is "the beginning and the end." In other words, the historical drama, both at the beginning and the end, is bounded by and a part of the incomprehensible mystery of God's eternity, God's Time.[4] Clearly we are dealing here with an interpretation of history which lies beyond the scope of science. It must be admitted, of course, that this has implications with respect to the assumptions that the scientist makes about nature. The idea of the world existing in infinite time, a view which is often presupposed by scientists, is alien to the Bible. According to the Bible, nature is finite, God is infinite; the world is created, God is Lord over his creation.[5]

Secondly, these stories not only place history within God's time-span, but they emphasize that the whole creation is included within God's redemptive purpose. It is noteworthy that the stories of the beginning and the end have a universal range of interest; they concern all mankind and not Israel narrowly. Of course, this is dependent upon another biblical truth which we discussed in a previous chapter, that is, "the scandal of particularity," God's special revelation to a chosen People and finally in a single Person (see chapter 2). Therefore, in the strict sense the Bible "puts the cart before the horse" by starting with the creation story, for Genesis would not have been written had it not been for the prophetic interpretation

---

show the sanctity of the Jewish sabbath. On the seventh day God "rested"; the Hebrew verb *shabath* is the basis of the word "Sabbath," the day of rest. Thus at the very beginning, says the writer, God ordained this institution of Israel's historical life.

[4] See the important book by Oscar Cullmann, *Christ and Time* (Westminster, 1950), where this point is developed.

[5] It is interesting to observe that modern scientists are beginning to question the notion of the universe existing in infinite time. See *The History of Nature* (University of Chicago, 1949) by C. F. von Weizsacker—especially chap. 6.

of Israel's history. That is why, incidentally, in this book we began not with Adam but with the stories concerning the Call of Israel; and that is why, furthermore, we have postponed our consideration of the beginning and the end until after the treatment of the New Testament revelation. For it was in that unique series of events, beginning with the Exodus and culminating in the coming of Christ, that men of faith discerned the redemptive activity of God. Nevertheless, there was throughout the biblical period an increasing realization that God's special revelation to Israel not only illumined the meaning of Israel's history in particular but also exposed the meaning of all human history in general, and that God's election of Israel was for the universal blessing and redemption of all mankind. So the stories of Genesis 1-11 indicate that the God of Abraham, Isaac, and Jacob is the God of all nations; the whole human drama had its beginning in the creative Word of God. And likewise the book of the Revelation indicates that Christ is actually King over all peoples; the whole historical drama ultimately will be summed up in the divine purpose. Thus God's special revelation to Israel and in Christ discloses the fundamental unity of "world history." [6]

Finally, the Bible speaks of the eternal boundaries of the human drama in the language of myth. To many people, unfortunately, the word "myth" stands for what is purely fictitious and unreal—a kind of religious fairy tale. This dismissal of myth and other types of religious symbolism usually rests upon the belief that the meaning of life can be defined by reason and that truth can be measured by the scientific method. Yet most of us realize that there are areas in which the most important truths have an immeasurable quality, as in the case of falling in love, and that we must turn to poetry, song, and art for the expression of life's deepest experiences.

---

[6] Cullmann (*op. cit.*, p. 178) diagrams the biblical drama as beginning with a universal range, narrowing increasingly to a small focus, and then broadening out again to a universal scope: "Creation—mankind—Israel—the Remnant—the One—the apostles—the Church—mankind—the new creation."

Life has a "fourth dimension" which cannot be flattened out upon the canvas of the sense-bound world with which reason deals. Wordsworth's "Peter Bell" typifies the pathetic blindness of the prosaic mind:

> A primrose by a river's brim
> A yellow primrose was to him,
> And it was nothing more.

To the poetic eye, however, a "flower in the crannied wall" is "something more" than a flower. Thus the poet communicates life's deeper dimension by transforming the things of the everyday world into the language of symbol and imagination. So also the biblical writers use myth and symbol to communicate the faith that human history, which is the theater of God's purposive activity, reaches backward and forward into the endless Time of God. A myth may be defined as a kind of parable or word-picture which uses the language of time and space pictorially to give expression to history's "fourth dimension." Just as the truth of a poem is in no way identified with the literal accuracy of its figures of speech, so the truth of myth lies not in the correctness of the details but in the historical truth which is expressed.[7]

The dictionary defines a myth as a story dealing with the actions of the gods, in contrast to a legend which deals with the actions of men. This is a helpful distinction, if for no other reason that it puts the accent upon divine action. We know that many myths circulated in the ancient world and that this mythology profoundly influenced the biblical tradition. The biblical writers borrowed freely from the common fund of mythology, though purging the myths of their polytheism and other crude features.[8] It is important to notice, how-

---

[7] Discussions of biblical myths are given by Alan Richardson, *A Preface to Bible Study*, chap. 7; C. H. Dodd, *The Bible Today*, pp. 112-119; Reinhold Niebuhr, *Beyond Tragedy*, pp. 3-24.

[8] According to Babylonian mythology, Marduk slew the watery monster of chaos, Tiamat, and made the earth and firmament by splitting the goddess' body in half. Reminiscences of this myth are scattered throughout the Bible;

ever, that in biblical usage the stories of divine action became unique for the reason that they were incorporated into, and received their meaning from, the biblical interpretation of history. In other words, biblical myths are, without exception, myths of history.[9] To be sure, the details of the myths reflect the archaic views of the ancient world; indeed, they are absurd if we literalize them. But when read in the framework of the biblical view of history, these myths set forth a conviction which is basic to the Christian faith: God's action inaugurates the historical drama, and God's action brings it to completion.

Those who want to purge the Bible of myth and other "anthropomorphic" features usually offer a conception of God which is nonhistorical and impersonal. So today in some circles we hear that God is "the ideal realizing capacity of the universe," "the principle of concretion," and so on. These intellectual abstractions are completely alien to the Bible. The God of the Bible is not an immanent force in nature; nor is he "the best in human nature." He is the holy and transcendent God who enters into personal relationship with men in history. It is obviously deceptive to speak of God walking in a garden in the cool of the day and looking for Adam, for God himself is invisible and men are permitted to know him only through his actions. But how could the truth be symbolized more vividly that man is addressed by God, that he is responsible to his Word, and that he is lonely and lost outside a personal relationship with his Creator? The meaning of this word picture will be appreciated, not by the carping critic or the prosaic literalist, but by the man of faith for

---

for instance, in Genesis 1 the Hebrew word "deep" (*Tehom*) is cognate with Tiamat; and, moreover, God is described as separating "the waters which were under the firmament from the waters which were above the firmament." In Genesis, however, the crudity and polytheism of the Babylonian myth are no longer evident, even though the same general cosmology is presupposed. Notice that, in contrast to the Babylonian version, nature is not regarded as being divine; God stands over against nature in holiness.

[9] Thus we must distinguish between biblical myth and the myths of Plato in which timeless, that is, nonhistorical truth, is symbolized.

whom such a personal encounter with God is the deepest meaning of his life.

The Myths of the Beginning

In a real sense analysis destroys a myth, just as the beauty of a poem or a symphony vanishes when it is dissected into its component parts. A myth must be viewed in its totality, every detail of language and every development of the story blending into a poetic whole. This is true, for instance, in the Priestly story of creation (Genesis 1:1—2:4a), which should really be read aloud in order that its majestic cadences of speech and dramatic climax may be appreciated fully. It is also true in the more picturesque J narrative which constitutes such a closely knit unity that, both on literary and theological grounds, it is wrong to separate the Creation (2:4b-25) from the Fall (3:1-24). Nevertheless, in the following pages we shall focus attention on certain facets of each myth, though recognizing the inadequacy of any attempt to state the meaning of the story in propositional form.

Scholars often speak of the period covered by Genesis 1-11 as "prehistory," a term which may be misleading if it suggests that the stories deal with something that happened before the "dawn of history." Actually these stories are prehistorical in the sense that they describe in mythical terms the character of all history. Just as we could not think without certain basic presuppositions, so there could be no history without the basic realities symbolized in myth. The Adam story, for instance, is an artistic portrait of man in any and every historical situation when his life is seen in relation to God. Indeed, the word "Adam" is really not a proper name in Hebrew, but merely a word meaning "mankind" or "man" in a generic sense. Likewise, the word "Eve" is the Hebrew word for "life" or "living." This in itself should warn us against treating these stories as a factual account of something that happened once upon a time.

The Creation of Man

Rather than lingering over the question of the relation between the P and J accounts of the Creation, let us confine our attention to one point of paramount concern: the relation of man to nature. Genesis 1 reaches a climax in these words:

> And God said, Let us make man in our image, after our likeness: and let them have dominion over the fish of the sea, and over the fowl of the air, and over the cattle, and over all the earth, and over every creeping thing that creepeth upon the earth. So God created man in his own image, in the image of God created he him; male and female created he them.

What does it mean to say that man is made in the "image" of God? Plainly this is no physical likeness, for the priestly writer takes pains to stress the holiness and transcendence of God. The image of God is man's God-given freedom, that is, his ability to impose his will upon nature and to face the historical question as to the meaning of his life on this earth. As God transcends his creation, so man in a lesser, though comparable, sense transcends the order of nature. Though man's life is *in nature,* he himself stands *above* nature, for he has the freedom to acknowledge the claim of the Creator upon him and, within that relationship, to exercise dominion over the earth. Man is a person because he stands in a personal relation with God. This is man's uniqueness and dignity. This is the crowning glory of God's creation (see Psalm 8).

The J story states the same truth in more naive language. We are told that man, like the animals, is made out of dust and returns to dust. The evolutionary hypothesis could not give more forceful expression to the indisputable fact that man stands within the animal kingdom. Man's life is a part of the decay and death, the flux and impermanence which is the law of nature. But the J story discloses that man is more than a natural creature, for—unlike the animals—into him is infused the life-giving spirit (breath) of God (Genesis 2:7). He is a creature who is responsible. He has the capacity to hear the Word which God addresses to him, and to respond to the divine demand with either Yes or No.

Thus these stories give a profound description of man in relation to nature. Though man lives in nature he is, by virtue of his divine origin, a stranger to the natural world. In one place in his *Song of Myself* Walt Whitman sings wistfully about the placid animals which, being completely "at home" in nature, do not worry about God, sin, or death. Such, however, is not man's lot. He knows the natural limitations of his life and in the act of knowing stands above nature. He knows that death comes to him as to the animal and, like the melancholy author of Ecclesiastes, can stare into nothingness and face the question of the meaning of his life. Any scientific hypothesis which man devises—whether a nebular theory, a doctrine of evolution, or a behavioristic psychology—is possible because of the freedom which enables him to transcend nature. And from the biblical point of view, this freedom enables him to hear the Word which God addresses to him in history and to decide whether he will serve God or an idol of his own making. Man is a creature of decision. Therefore he is an actor in the arena of history.

Perhaps we are now in a position to clarify the relation between science and the Christian faith. Let us keep in mind a figure of speech drawn from drama. Nature is the stage, the finite setting, on which is enacted the drama of man's history. Science is concerned with studying the stage and the various stage properties. The scientist may alter our understanding of the setting. He may lift a curtain which allows the scenery to include the vast vistas of modern astronomy; he may trace the evolution of nature within finite time; or he may throw new light upon the biological limitations of human life. But as a scientist he is not qualified to interpret the meaning of the drama enacted upon nature's stage. This question is the chief concern of the Bible, or, for that matter, of any interpretation of history. If we literalize the creation myth we arrive at a description of nature which is plainly a scientific error—an error which cannot be removed by allegorizing the first chapter of Genesis so that each "day" represents a stage in the evolutionary process. The men of the Bible had a very limited understanding of history's natural setting. They accepted the prevailing view that the earth was a flat surface with four corners, that it rested upon a subterranean ocean and was overarched by a blue dome which supported the celestial waters, and that it was the center of the universe. These inaccuracies, however, are no more essential to the truth of the biblical myth than belief in ghosts or witches is essential to the truth of Shakespearian drama.

There need be no conflict between science and religion provided the scientist confines his attention to the objective study of nature (the stage) and the man of religious faith to the question of historical interpretation (the drama). The warfare between science and the Christian faith has resulted from a confusing of issues: either Christians have transgressed the field of historical interpretation and have set forth the Bible as a rival book of science; or scientists have overstepped the boundary of the objective study of nature and have become philosophers who make categories drawn from physics or biology ruling principles for the interpretation of the meaning of life. By literalizing the myths of Genesis the fundamentalist Christian has attempted to dictate the conclusions of scientific research, and thereby has made the issue a struggle between bad science and good science. Likewise the scientist, when moving out of the field in which *as a scientist* he has a right to make a judgment, has converted the struggle into a rivalry of opposing faiths. In so far as man's life is in nature, science can aid our understanding through the contributions of biology, psychosomatic medicine, and naturalistic psychology. But in so far as man transcends nature by virtue of his divine origin and endowment these disciplines are incapable of defining the ultimate meaning of human life. The alternative is not science or Christianity, but the Christian faith or some other view of human history. Christianity, however, stands upon the unyielding faith that man is a creature made in the image of God, that he is responsible inescapably to the Will of God, and that the deepest meaning of his life lies in a personal relation with the Lord of history.

The Fall of Man

The stories of Adam's Fall, Cain's murder of Abel, the Flood, and the Tower of Babel are linked together closely by the fact that they give expression to the J interpretation of history. Of course, we must recognize that the J stories also include naive answers to such questions as why people wear clothes, why the serpent is hated, and why there are many languages in the earth. These "etiological" questions, however, are secondary to J's primary concern. We must distinguish between the individual units of the tradition, each of which had a history of its own, and the way J has joined together the individual stories by breathing into them a unique interpretation of history. Since this interpretation is similar to that of the classical prophets of ancient Israel, J is called a prophetic writing. Remember that J is usually dated around 850 B.C., about the time of Elijah.

In view of the prophetic character of the J narrative, it would be well to say a word in review of the prophetic message. According to the prophets, Israel's history was corrupted by man's proud refusal to acknowledge the sovereignty of Yahweh. Economic, social, and political disturbances were traced to the will of man which turned from God to pursue ends of human choosing. This is what made the stark contrast between the "innocence" of nature and the "maturity" of Israel's sin. Animals instinctively went to their owner's stall; God's "sons," however, rebelled against him and plunged the land into sickness (Isaiah 1:2-9). Birds followed their migratory instincts naturally; but Israel had no "homing instinct" which led her to the God of the Covenant (Jeremiah 8:7). The prophets knew that God had created Israel in order that she might spontaneously acknowledge the sovereignty of his will; but Israel in history was a rather sorry figure: a rebellious son, an adulterous wife, a traitor to the King. Israel was a "fallen" creature—the object of God's judgment, though also the recipient of his mercy.

From this understanding of Israel's history the J narrative looks backward to the very beginning of things, in such a way as to suggest that this is actually the inner character of all human history. With a kind of literary counterpoint, J blends together two familiar prophetic themes: the first is the corruption of human history owing to man's rebellion against his Creator; the second is God's intervention into men's affairs in acts of judgment and mercy. After the exile from the Garden of Eden, we are told, things went from bad to worse. Family life was torn apart by jealousy (4:1-15); the first city was built by a murderer (4:17); the lust for vengeance found its bitterest expression in Lamech's fierce song of blood-revenge (4:23-24); and the depth of sin was reached in the strange incident described in Genesis 6:1-4. Since "every imagination of the thoughts of man's heart was only evil continually," God determined to bring judgment upon mankind. The judgment took the form of a mythological flood.[10] But even amid the terrors of God's wrath his mercy was evident. In Noah's Ark a "remnant" was preserved—the nucleus of the new mankind. Moreover, the Flood was followed by God's Covenant with Noah and the promise of his mercy upon all mankind and all created life—a promise which P beautifully symbolizes by the sign of the rainbow. No prophet could have given more eloquent expression to the faith that beyond God's judgment lies his mercy. But despite God's acts of judgment and

---

[10] The Flood story, found in both J and P, is strikingly paralleled in the Babylonian Gilgamesh Epic; for a translation see G. A. Barton, *Archaeology and the Bible*, 7th ed. (International Sunday School Union, 1937), pp. 327-331. Floods of local proportions were common in Mesopotamia, and gave rise to a number of flood stories. The biblical writers drew upon the oral reservoir of flood mythology and, after purging the myth of its cruder elements, used it as a vehicle for symbolizing the universal scope of God's judgment upon mankind.

mercy, sin persisted. Noah, we are told, became "civilized": he planted a vineyard (9:20) and this led to an incident which was (and is) the attendant of civilization—his shameful drunkenness. Finally, in the story of the Tower of Babel (Genesis 11) J describes the political ambition which motivated builders to "make a name for themselves" and to try to storm the very citadels of heaven. In this instance J symbolizes the futility of the attempt to achieve order and security on the basis of the pursuit of human ends. The "City of Man" was left unfinished for the same reason that all empires ultimately fall: men "could not understand one another." From J's standpoint, the frustration of the enterprise was evidence of the judgment of God upon man's bold defiance of his Creator. But even this did not spell failure in the accomplishment of God's purpose. Determined to win back his lost creation, God, in a new act of grace, chose one of the descendents of this rebellious stock (Abraham) to be the ancestor of the people through whom all the nations of the world would be blessed.

It will be apparent from this brief survey that the stories which deal with the period before Abraham are not "historical" in the sense that the events described actually happened long ago. Only with the appearance of Abraham do we leave the realm of mythology and walk upon the more solid ground of history, or, at least, semi-history. To be sure, the story of Abraham is overlaid with legendry. Nevertheless, a good case can be made that Abraham was a historical individual, and that the stories of Genesis 12-50 reflect the conditions of the patriarchal period. On the other hand, the historicity of Noah, Cain, or Adam cannot be defended.

Having placed the myth of the Fall in the framework of J's interpretation of history, let us briefly consider some of the insights of the story itself. Notice that in the mythological scheme the Fall comes after the Creation. Though this time-sequence must not be taken literally, it does symbolize an important truth, namely, the source of sin is not to be traced to the world of nature, to the body, or to man's finiteness. The creation story of the first chapter of Genesis contains the recurring refrain, "God saw that it was good." Jewish-Christian thought, when it has been true to its biblical heritage, has consistently emphasized the goodness of God's creation and has opposed religions or philosophies which regard the material world or the body as evil. By speaking of a time of perfection before the Fall, the J writer stresses that God intended man to live in security and peace amid the blessings and bounties of nature.

Why, then, is history as it is? Why does man's urge to live convert the world into a scene of struggle for power, the consequence of which is never ending suffering? Why are man's natural instincts transformed into unnatural appetites, as in the case of the perversion of the sex drive into an American cult of Aphrodite or the perversion of the need for food into forms of economic exploitation? Why are the bounties of nature a source of anxiety to men who live in the atomic age? This is a modernized version of the questions with which the Adam myth deals. The Bible unerringly goes to the heart of the matter: the source of all historical difficulties lies in man's freedom. Adam's sin was possible because, though he was like the animals in constitution, he was not an animal. Endowed with the precarious power of freedom, he could not live peacefully in nature. Spontaneous obedience to God's Word was too tame a thing for such a man. To quote from St. Augustine, he was motivated by "the desire of making trial, of making the full experience of his own power through the lust after knowledge." "Ye shall be as the gods, knowing good and evil." The words of the subtle serpent expressed man's inner awareness of the possibilities of making himself the center of life, thereby usurping God's throne.[11] Adam's freedom was his greatness; it was also his downfall.

---

[11] In antiquity the serpent was thought to possess an uncanny wisdom (see Matt. 10:16). It is wrong to identify the serpent with Satan. The figure of Satan, the fallen angel and archenemy of God, belongs to a later stage of biblical mythology.

We may observe a contemporary ring in the Adam myth in modern man's conviction that he is the architect and controller of his destiny. He is lord of nature, not because God has given him the vocation to serve him by subduing the earth, but because of his own knowledge. He seeks knowledge not primarily because it is virtue, as Socrates taught, but because it is power. Science makes it possible for man to harness the tremendous forces of nature and thereby achieve the ends that he sets for himself. "History is simply the activity of man pursuing his own ends." Those words are from Karl Marx, but they could also appear in the context of American "democratic" faith. The average American believes in "building a better world," fashioned according to the blueprint of modern ideals. Often this goal, worthy in itself, is justified by an appeal to traditional Christianity so that the real motivation is disguised. Contemporary "atheists," like Marxists and some American philosophers, are bold enough to tear away the theological disguise and honestly reveal the true character of the political motivation. From the viewpoint of biblical prophets, history is the scene of man's Promethean defiance of God in order that he may follow his own reason and will. Our own times have merely exposed in stark realism what prophets of old saw hidden beneath the forms of popular religion.

There is a pathetic grandeur in the picture of Adam reaching out to taste the fruit of the tree of knowledge of good and evil. Knowledge is man's capacity. His freedom to leave the innocence of nature is precisely what elevates him above the animal. But when man's capacity for knowledge becomes the occasion for power and self-exaltation, inevitably it results in a fall from the life of perfect trust and spontaneous goodness which God intended. Obviously we cannot recover the mythological innocence of Adam "before the Fall." Indeed, the Garden of Eden is purely a figment of the religious imagination. Nevertheless in imagination the religious man knows this is the way life *should* be, even though he cannot attain it. We may not be able to trust in God's sovereignty as naturally and spontaneously as the birds of the air or the flowers of the field accept the bounties of nature (Matthew 6:25-34); but when Jesus exclaims, "O ye of little faith," the word of judgment strikes home for we know that our faith and goodness should be that "natural."

It is unnecessary to resort to theological dogma to sense the realism of the Adam myth. Novelists, poets, dramatists, and psychiatrists are giving us an extended commentary upon the essential problem involved. In our most honest moments we know that there is a wide chasm between the person that should be and the person that is. We are overwhelmed by the glaring contrast between the ideal world in which knowledge would be used for the common welfare, and this insecure world in which science and technology make possible the destruction of mankind. As James Hilton pointed out in his novel, *Lost Horizon*, every man has within himself a longing for a valley of Shangri-la, far away from so-called civilization, where men could realize their yearnings for a better world. Somehow, somewhere man has fallen from his true nature. The leaders of the Enlightenment traced the problem to man's intellectual environment, and advocated throwing off the medieval chains of ignorance and superstition. Marxists trace the problem to man's economic environment, and advocate revolutionary change. The Bible, however, traces the problem to man himself. It insists that when man is alienated from God he is at odds with himself and his neighbors. But even in his lost state, he is driven on by a hunger of which he is unaware, a restlessness at the very center of his being. As Augustine said in his well-known prayer, "O Lord, thou hast made us for Thyself, and our hearts are restless till they find rest in thee."

The Fall describes man in any moment of history; but it is also the "beginning of history." If we could conceive of man living in the perfection of the Garden of Eden, we could visualize the impossible: man having the full powers of manhood, yet not "making history." Such a "man" would be living in nature but would not be living in history, and therefore he would be less than a man. The driving force of human history is the freedom which enables man to pursue his own ends; or, stated theologically, it is man's self-assertive disobedience of his Creator. The very stuff of history is the precarious and dynamic power of freedom. "Civilization" is the scene of the struggle, suffering, and anxiety which corresponds to the situation after the banishment from the Garden. It is the witness of the Bible, however, that the divine Actor enters into the historical drama to transform tragedy into triumph and to recreate the human race. Thus the myths of Genesis 1-11 form the appropriate prologue to the call of Abraham, the initiation of God's redemptive purpose through the chosen people, and the accomplishment of his design in Jesus Christ.

The Myths of the End

We have said that the Bible views history as a purposive drama, and that the drama sweeps forward from beginning to end, from the initiation of God's plan to the realization of his design for the whole creation. Just as the men of the Bible projected their faith backward into the mythological past, so they projected their view ahead into the mythological future. The Bible, therefore, has an *eschatology*, that is, a doctrine of the end (*eschaton*) or "last things" (*eschata*) of history. This is the most important, though for the modern mind the most difficult, aspect of the biblical message. We can readily understand that history advances toward a goal which will be realized *in* history; indeed, this is the gist of the secular doctrine of progress and the Marxist ideal. But we find it hard to understand how the goal of history lies at the end of history or beyond history itself. Christians affirm this, however, out of the faith that the whole human drama is enfolded within the redemptive purpose of the God who stands above history, yet is active within it. So the horizons of history—looking in either direction, past or future—recede beyond understanding into the endless time of God's eternity.

The Bible resorts to myth in speaking of "the end of the world." The latter phrase, which appears in the King James translation of the New Testament (for instance, Matthew 28:20), is an unfortunate translation, for it may easily suggest the cessation of life on this planet and the coming of a time when, as science tells us, the world will become "a whiff of smoke drifting in desolate skies." The phrase, however, could be rendered more accurately "the end of the age," that is, the end of history as it is and as it always has been—the kind of history in which man presumes that he can define and pursue his own ends. Here we have left the domain of scientific and historical investigation. Amos Wilder writes:

> Eschatology is myth. But whereas most myth represents the unknown past and gives a symbolic picture of unknown origins, eschatology is that form of myth which represents the unknown future.[12]

We cannot conceive of man standing at the end of history any more than we can conceive of him at the beginning of history. Just as the poet uses language imaginatively to communicate life's deepest experiences, so we must use the language of history symbolically to speak of that which, in faith, lies at the end. As Amos Wilder says, biblical eschatology "carries a weight of spiritual truth such as only the greatest art can convey."

The Day of Judgment

To consider properly the myths of the end or *eschaton* of history we must turn again to the prophets, for eschatology was basic to their message. They consistently looked beyond the present, in which God's purpose seemed to be temporarily opposed by man's rebellion, to a time when God would mani-

---

[12] *Eschatology and Ethics in the Teachings of Jesus*, p. 21. This illuminating chapter on "The Nature of Jewish Eschatology" deserves attention.

fest his victory. Prophetic predictions of the triumph of God's purpose were expressed in phrases like "the Day of the Lord," "the last days," "that Day," "the Age to Come," and "the Kingdom of God." In their vision the consummation of history was to be a time of reckoning when all rebellious powers would be judged and destroyed. It was also to be the beginning of a New Creation in which nature and human nature would be transformed. No longer would there be war, and even wild animals would be tame. The pictures of the messianic age remind us of the idyllic peace and harmony of the Garden of Eden "before the Fall." The prophets believed that man's rebellious will had corrupted history and had even destroyed the harmony of nature. But with the removal of sin, men would live together in unity and peace, enjoying the blessings of a marvelously transformed earth. In that Day history would be ended, that is, the kind of history which is the expression of man's disobedience and will-to-power.

The prophets preached that the Day was near. Indeed, they described it as the very next moment of history. Amos and Hosea discerned the imminence of God's judgment in the tense political crises of their day; Isaiah connected the impending downfall of man's pride with the aggression of Assyria; Jeremiah envisioned God's action in the coming of the Babylonian foe; and Second Isaiah interpreted the conquests of Cyrus of Persia as the approaching salvation of God. Always the prophets spoke of the impending End in terms of the concrete political circumstances in which men were living. But they did not cease preaching the nearness of the divine Event when a certain crisis had passed by. They merely revised their eschatological message in terms of the new circumstances. Though the prophets used the language of history to describe the eschatological event, they did not identify God's Day of Victory with any political development. It was sufficient to announce that every crisis brought men nearer to the victory which only God could achieve.[13]

[13] See pages 110-121.

The prophetic message was further elaborated in a type of literature which we have called apocalyptic. The theme of apocalyptic, as in the case of prophecy, is the near approach of the time when God will assert his sovereignty over history and nature. It is characteristic of apocalyptic, however, that specific historical events recede into the background, and the contest between God and rebellious forces assumes a cosmic scale. The Kingdom of God stands opposed to the well-organized Kingdom of Evil which is under the mighty leadership of Satan, the archenemy. The End will be heralded by persecutions, unusual "signs," and cataclysms which disrupt the order of nature. On the Day of Judgment God, or his messianic agent, will destroy all powers opposed to his reign and will create a new heaven and a new earth. The dead will be raised up in order that they may take part in the dramatic inauguration of the New Age. As we noted in a previous chapter, the purpose of apocalyptic writers was to encourage the faithful to remain steadfast in a dark hour when the meaningfulness of history was temporarily eclipsed by foreign tyranny or the victory of evil.

Modern "students of prophecy" who base their predictions of the end of the world on biblical apocalypses plainly fail to understand the character of the biblical idiom. As Amos Wilder points out, the use of fantastic imagery in books like Ezekiel and Daniel clearly indicates that the language was intended to be imaginative; moreover the inconsistency of detail in the apocalyptic program shows that the writers never intended their words to be forced into the narrow categories of the literal and prosaic mind. Probably it would be going too far, observes Dr. Wilder, to say that the apocalyptic pictures were meant only as poetry; but, on the other hand, we would be equally mistaken in attributing to them the crass literalism of modern prophecy schools. Here we are dealing with an oriental way of thinking in which "the distinction between historical and imaginative events was not clear cut." The heart of the apocalyptic message was the intense certainty that God's purpose could not be frustrated—a certainty which found expression in the nearness of the End.[14]

We shall conclude this brief discussion of Old Testament eschatology by drawing attention to an interesting secular parallel. Marxism is a secularized version of biblical eschatology—a fact which is not too surprising when one considers that Marx himself was a Jew whose thinking had been influenced by his religious heritage. Marx believed that he was living at the end of the times. In the distant past, he said, man had lost the primitive peace of the *gens* community in consequence of the introduction of private property (the Fall). Subsequent history was a long struggle between the "haves" and the "have-nots," and finally the accumulated evil of the ages had concentrated itself in a bourgeois class which was gradually strangling itself to death. Men were living in the last hour. The "end of history"—the millennium of the classless society or the restored *gens* community—was at hand. The workers of the world needed only to unite in order to give the coup de grâce to capitalism and to usher in a paradise of universal peace and happiness.

From the Christian standpoint the insidious danger of this view is that it rests upon the illusion—so flattering to modern man—that it is possible to establish a sinless society in history, a society which does not stand under divine judgment. According to the Marxist view, the end or goal of history lies *in* history. The Bible, however, is written in the name of the God whose Kingdom, by transcending every historical achievement, puts all forms of social organization under divine judgment, and places an ultimate restraint upon the exercise of power. Thus Canon Alan Richardson observes:

> The biblical standpoint condemns as illusion every attempt to find salvation in history, or permanent well-being on earth, whether it be the *Pax Romana* of the ancient world, the theocratic imperialism of the Middle Ages, the nation-state of modern times, the humanist's

---

[14] *Op. cit.*, pp. 24-30.

vision of a League of Nations, the classless state of communist theory, or the "planned society" of the scientific sociologists.[15]

These words should not be construed to mean that all social action is useless and that, for instance, the Church should have no dealings with the United Nations. On the contrary, the divine imperative makes the Christian more sensitive about his social responsibility and more determined to bring about a better social order in which there will be freedom and justice for all. But man as a "fallen creature" has no right to presume that he can build a sinless society on earth. To say that the goal of history lies beyond history or at the end of history means, in practical terms, that all forms of social organization, regardless of how advanced or how just they are, stand under divine criticism. In every age men must act and live with the prophetic awareness that the Final Judgment is near. The first word they must hear is "repent."

The Second Coming of Christ

Christians inherited the Hebraic view that history is the interval between the beginning and the end. This eschatology, however, was radically transformed by the Christian gospel which affirmed that already the powers of God's Kingdom had broken into history in the person of Jesus of Nazareth, above all in the death and resurrection of the Messiah. As Peter proclaimed on the day of Pentecost, quoting an eschatological passage from the prophecy of Joel, already men were living in "the last days" (Acts 2:16ff.).

It is a moot question among New Testament scholars as to where the line should be drawn between the eschatology of Jesus and the eschatology of the Church. It seems likely, however, that Jesus thought in the framework of Jewish apocalyptic, though purging it of Jewish nationalism, lust for revenge on enemies, desire for a sensuous paradise, and other crude

[15] *A Preface to Bible Study*, p. 106.

features. Moreover, while he conceived his messianic role to be that of the Suffering Servant, it seems that he also related himself to the figure of the coming Son of Man, the heavenly figure who would appear on the clouds at the final consummation of history (See Mark 14:62). In any case, early Christians clearly believed that the appearance of the Messiah in the role of the Suffering Servant was an eschatological event. It was their conviction that already the *eschaton* had entered history, giving assurance of the near approach of the Day of Judgment and the final "restoration of all things" (Acts 3:20-21). The Cross was the divine sentence of judgment upon man's sin and all the powers of darkness; but God's victory in the Resurrection had already made possible a "new creation" for those who were in Christ (II Corinthians 5:17). For early Christians, Jesus Christ had an absolute and final significance in the time-scheme which we call history.

We have had occasion to observe that the later Church attempted to state the finality of Christ in the language of Greek philosophy—an attempt which led to the paradox of the God-Man, the second Person of the Trinity. Early Christians, however, expressed the decisive significance of Jesus in history by using the language of mythology. They projected the faith of the present into the mythological past, affirming that Jesus was the incarnation of the Creative Word by which God made the heavens and the earth (John 1:1-14). They also projected the faith of the present into the mythological future, declaring that at the End Christ would descend on the clouds of heaven "to judge the quick and the dead." Thus both the beginning and the end of history were "made flesh" in him who was the central figure of a vast eschatological drama.

The vision of the Second Coming of Christ is a myth which employs the language of time ("he comes again") and space ("on the clouds of heaven") to communicate the Christian faith that God's redemptive purpose, revealed in history in the Suffering Servant, points forward to the ultimate victory over history which only God can achieve. We can never know exactly what the figure of the heavenly Son of Man meant to early Christians, from whom we are separated not only by many centuries but also by those subtle differences which distinguish the Orient from the Occident. Probably the myth originally possessed a primarily imaginative meaning, as in Daniel 7:13-14 where the heavenly figure represents the everlasting Kingdom which descends from above, in contrast to the transitory earthly kingdoms which rose like monsters from the depth of the sea.[16] We find it difficult to understand an oriental idiom in which there was no sharp distinction between a historical event (as the historian today knows events) and the certain divine Event which evoked the language of religious imagination.

It is important to recognize that in the early Christian message the center of gravity lay not in the anticipation of the Second Coming but in the proclamation that Christ's "first coming" was itself an eschatological event. To be sure, there was a tendency, at least in some circles, to shift this center of gravity from the past to the future and to engage in speculation as to when Christ would reappear. Paul, for instance, had to counsel Christians at Thessalonica to cease speculating about the future Advent and to stay at their work (II Thessalonians). Likewise the author of II Peter—the latest writing of the New Testament—addressed himself to current disillusionment arising from the delay in Christ's Second Coming (chapter 3). But the New Testament in general places the emphasis upon the victory which has already been won in the Crucifixion-Resurrection, and shuns any attempt to pry into the mystery of the future which lies in the sole authority of God (see Matthew 24:36; Acts 1:7). Oscar Cullman expresses this matter in an apt figure of speech:

> The decisive battle in a war may already have occurred in a relatively early stage of the war, and yet the war still continues. Although

[16] In ancient mythology, the sea was represented as the locus of the rebellious powers which threaten the divine rule. See Revelation 21:1, "and the sea was no more."

the decisive effect of that battle is perhaps not recognized by all, it nevertheless already means victory. But the war must still be carried on for an undefined time, until "Victory Day." [17]

Thus, as he continues to point out, the awareness that the decisive battle had been won intensified the early Christian faith that the end was near, but since the Christian faith was centered upon that one decisive battle, Christians did not concern themselves with counting the days until the End. Christians expected to stand before "the judgment seat of Christ" because already they knew the reality of God's judgment in Christ (II Corinthians 5:10; Matthew 25:31-46). They expected that the goal of history would be the victory of Christ, the "Son of Man," because already they knew the power of Christ's Resurrection (I Corinthians 15:20-28). The end would merely vindicate the faith of the present, just as the faith of the present foreshortened the arrival of the end.

It is still true that the Christian faith is oriented, not toward an unrealized future, but toward the victory which God has won in Christ. Faith turns toward him who is the embodiment of God's redemptive purpose, the One in whom the beginning and end of history are represented. Yet from this faith springs hope, the hope that lays hold imaginatively upon that which is not yet seen: the summing up of history in Christ. In the language of the Christian myth, he will come again on the clouds of heaven as the Final Judge and the King of kings.

The New Testament concludes with a book called the "Revelation" or the Apocalypse of John.[18] This book begins and ends with the note that the second coming of Christ is imminent. Students of Bible prophecy have found here a happy hunting ground in their search for predictions of the exact date of the end of the world couched in cryptic symbolism. The

---

[17] *Op. cit.*, p. 84. All of this chapter is important in this connection.

[18] Although tradition ascribes the Apocalypse to John, "the beloved disciple," modern scholars insist that the real author is unknown. It seems impossible that the author was the same writer as the author of the Fourth Gospel, for the style of the two books is so different.

number of the "Beast" (13:18), for instance, has given rise to wide speculation. A humorous example is the identification of the Beast with Führer Adolph (actually spelled "Adolf") Hitler, for each word of the name allegedly has six letters and thus corresponds to 666. Actually, however, the number was intended as a veiled reference to a Roman Caesar.[19] This calls attention to the fact that the Apocalypse was written as a "tract for the times," probably during the persecution of the Church which occurred at the latter part of the reign of the Roman emperor, Domitian (A.D. 81-96). The author used a kind of spiritual code which the Christian "underground" would understand, since he could assume familiarity with other apocalyptic literature, especially the book of Daniel. Clearly the Apocalypse was not written to chart out events in the twentieth century. The writer's purpose was to encourage Christians to remain faithful in persecution.

The book of Revelation brings to a magnificent climax the biblical drama which opens with the myths of Genesis. In highly imaginative language the writer expresses the biblical faith that the ultimate source and goal of history lie "beyond history," and that the whole historical drama is embraced within the redemptive time-span of Him who is "the Alpha and the Omega, the beginning and the end" (21:6). True to the Christian faith, he affirms that the Kingdom of Christ has already broken into history, even while Satan holds temporary and limited power in "the present age." The divine victory, which in the present evil age can be discerned only by faith, ultimately will be openly manifest, for "all flesh" will behold the triumph of God's redemptive love. Thus the Lamb (Christ) that was slain is pictured imaginatively as the final Conqueror who at the End will overthrow all the demonic forces which had corrupted history. The Final Judgment will

---

[19] In the Hebrew, each letter of the alphabet had a numerical equivalent. When we add up the numerical equivalents of "Nero Caesar" the sum is 666. It seems probable that the writer intended to allude to this despised Caesar who first began the terrible persecution of the Church.

usher in the "new heaven and the new earth" and the reign of peace and blessedness in which sin and death will be destroyed. Thus man will be created anew and restored to the life which God originally intended for him in the first Creation.

It is characteristic of biblical eschatology that the myths of the End draw elements from the myths of the beginning. So, for instance, the symbol of the "tree of life" reappears in the Apocalypse (22:2), and the idyllic peace of the Garden of Eden before the Fall is matched by the New Creation in which there will no longer be suffering, anxiety, or death. It would be wrong, however, to view this as a return to a primitive Golden Age, as though the biblical drama moves in a vast circle which returns to the starting point. The book of Revelation does not envision a return to the innocence of nature; rather, it visualizes man, like a returning prodigal son, receiving the forgiving and redemptive Love which conquers sin and brings his manhood to true maturity. It is significant, then, that the mythological End is described not under the figure of the Garden of Eden, but in the symbolism of the New Jerusalem descending from the skies. Though the City of God descends in heavenly splendor, and is clearly posthistorical, it nevertheless brings to completion the redemptive drama which had centered in Palestine, and, in so doing, brings to fulfillment the separate histories of all peoples.

Christ the Turning Point of History

In A.D. 525 a certain Roman Abbot, Dionysius Exiguus, reckoned backward to what he thought was the year of Jesus' birth and so established the custom of dating Western Christian history from "the year of the Lord."[20] Eventually this led to the establishment of our calendar system, with its time-

[20] It is well known that he made a slight error in his reckoning, for if Jesus was born during the reign of Herod the Great, as the New Testament attests, the date must have been ca. 8-6 B.C. Using the same calendar reckoning, Herod's death occurred in 4 B.C.

division B.C. and A.D. Today we accept this calendar as a matter of convenience and seldom, if ever, consider the implications of finding a fixed point which gives unity to world history. What event in all the stream of history is so momentous that it can be used as a point from which to look backward and forward over the whole course of history? Moslems find such a fixed point in Mohammed's flight or hegira from Mecca (A.D. 622) and date events from "the year of the hegira." Jews find the fixed point in God's revelation to Moses and, in deference to the ancient tradition that the Pentateuch was dictated to Moses, date all events from the year of the Creation (supposedly 3760 B.C.). Christians, however, find the fixed point in the historical figure, Jesus of Nazareth. It is their conviction that his appearance on the stage of history was not only a creative event, as any historian will recognize, but that it was an eschatological event. In him the *eschaton* or goal of history was revealed, thereby giving the historian a vantage point from which to survey the entire sweep of the human drama from beginning to end. Christ's coming was the turning point or the "center" of history.[21]

The New Testament closes where it does because the ancient Church bore witness to the faith that God had spoken and acted "once for all" (Romans 6:10; I Peter 3:18; Hebrews 7:27) in the life, death, and resurrection of Jesus Christ—viewed as a single Event. Hence the New Testament includes only those books which, in the judgment of the early Church, came from the apostolic period when men's minds and hearts received the direct impress of this momentous, eschatological event. But let us not suppose that the closing of the New Testament canon means that God has ceased speaking. Actually it is basic to the Christian faith that God is always acting in history, that he lays his claim upon men in the crises of the present just as surely as he did in the past, and that he continues

---

21 Cullmann's book, to which we have alluded, is a commentary on the implications of the Christian calendar. See also Erich Frank, "The Role of History in Christian Thought," *loc. cit.*

to lead men into new truth. So we read in the Fourth Gospel that shortly before Jesus' departure he said to his disciples:

> I have yet many things to say to you, but you cannot bear them now. When the Spirit of truth comes, he will guide you into all the truth (16:12-13).

Thus the Holy Spirit, which is the Spirit of Christ, is still present in the Church, leading men into the Truth. However, all Christian experience and insight since the New Testament period is not an advance beyond Christ, but a deepening understanding and expanding proclamation of the meaning of God's decisive victory in Christ.

To the Christian, therefore, Christ is "the center of history," the figure who so profoundly reveals the meaning of the whole historical drama that he breaks history in two, dividing everything into "before" and "after," B.C. and A.D. But this is not just an interpretation of history which applies only to mankind in general. Indeed, the Christian recognizes that Christ occupies the center of the stage of world history because, concretely and confessionally, he is the center of the believer's private history, the turning point of his own life. Thus the decision of the meaning of history in general cannot be separated from the decision as to the meaning of the individual's life in particular.

The Christian does not read the Bible with the academic curiosity of a student of antiquities; nor does he survey the unfolding drama from beginning to end with the detachment of a spectator. What makes the Bible sacred scripture in the Christian Church is its power to make the reader know that he is an actor in the historical pageant of God's redemption. In this book we have repeatedly referred to the biblical "drama." We know, of course, that the test of truly great drama is the dramatist's ability to make his audience feel that they are involved in the story. As an example, we may cite Margaret Webster's striking production of *Julius Caesar* in modern style. The audience can hardly view the play with the detachment of spectators, especially when the actors are garbed in the dress of modern tyrannies and the play is enacted against a background of banners and insignia dreadfully familiar to all of us. Miss Webster's cast has brought home to many audiences that Shakespeare's story of Julius Caesar is our story too. The abuse of power, on the one hand, and the chaos and revenge loosed by the assassin's breach of law and order, on the other, are living issues in our tumultuous period, just as they were forcefully relevant to the practical affairs of Shakespeare's England. This analogy need not be pressed too far, for *Julius Caesar* is great literature and the Bible is sacred Scripture. But in a somewhat analogous sense the Christian reads the Bible with the realization that he is part of the drama. He is involved personally. To allude to the words of the well-known Negro spiritual, he knows that he *was* there at the Crucifixion, that he *was* there at the Resurrection. This is really his past, his present.

To be sure, the biblical drama is staged in an ancient setting and describes events which happened long ago. But these pages bear witness to the victory which God wrought in history once for all, to the revelation which casts its light across the centuries. The Bible deals with the question of the ultimate meaning of human life—the question which is of inescapable concern to every person as he must decide the meaning of his existence and the whole fabric of historical relationships in which he is involved. If in the decision of faith the Christ of the Bible reveals the true meaning of history, then one unhesitantly will join the generations of the Christian Church in affirming that this Book is the Word of God.

Index of Subjects and Authors